ACT LIKE IT'S YOUR BUSINESS

Branding and Marketing Strategies for Actors

Jonathan Flom

THE SCARECROW PRESS, INC.
Lanham • Toronto • Plymouth, UK
2013

Published by Scarecrow Press, Inc.
A wholly owned subsidiary of The Rowman & Littlefield Publishing Group, Inc.
4501 Forbes Boulevard, Suite 200, Lanham, Maryland 20706
www.rowman.com

10 Thornbury Road, Plymouth PL6 7PP, United Kingdom

British Library Cataloguing in Publication Information Available

Library of Congress Cataloging-in-Publication Data

Flom, Jonathan, 1977–
  Act like it's your business : branding and marketing strategies for actors /
Jonathan Flom.
      pages cm
  Includes bibliographical references and index.
  ISBN 978-0-8108-9158-6 (cloth : alk. paper) — ISBN 978-0-8108-9159-3
(pbk. : alk. paper) — ISBN 978-0-8108-9160-9 (ebook) 1. Acting—Vocational
guidance. I. Title.
  PN2055.F58 2013
  792.02'8'023—dc23   2013009275

∞™ The paper used in this publication meets the minimum requirements of
American National Standard for Information Sciences—Permanence of Paper
for Printed Library Materials, ANSI/NISO Z39.48-1992. Printed in the United
States of America.

Contents

Preshow Announcement

How many people get to wake up every day excited about getting out of bed and going to work? Ask around—your parents, your friends, your coworkers—and I'll bet you'll find that the statistics are staggeringly low. On the whole, my guess is that most people are split down the middle between tolerating their jobs and loathing them.

You are reading this book, I assume, because you have made the choice to pursue a career in theatre, acting, or the arts. Some would say this is a noble profession; others would call it a pipe dream. I say you are to be commended if you have in fact decided to commit yourself to this path. I can honestly tell you that I wake up every single morning and tell myself how lucky I am to be able to make my living doing what I love to do. I run a tremendously exciting musical theatre training program; I get to direct plays and musicals regularly, both on the university campus and in professional venues; I get to travel around the world lecturing and coaching on audition technique and the business of theatre; and I get to write about the subject I love! What more could I ask for?

I know a lot of actors—it's a hazard of the trade. Many of the actors I know are absolutely miserable, scared, stressed, and utterly baffled on a daily basis by the rigors of this business. They feel as though their unhappiness comes with the territory: they've chosen to be artists, ergo, they must suffer. But I also know a handful of actors who wake every morning with optimism, joy, and determination. No, it's not because those happy few all have steady work or because they got lucky and got their big breaks. It's because they have a sense of confidence, motivation, and self-direction. Those qualities come as the result of a combination of three factors that I can identify:

1. Having a plan by which to guide their careers (that's right—I assert that even a lowly actor can choose to guide his own career!)
2. Being financially free and solvent
3. Recognizing that each audition, just like each paid or nonpaid gig, is a chance to spend a little bit of time doing what they *love* to do

Furthermore, the actors I know who are living happy, fulfilled lives know who they are and what they can do. They are not desperately pounding the pavement trying to sport their versatility and willingness to do absolutely *anything* to be noticed. They have the quiet confidence to know what makes them tick and to know how to showcase their particular gifts as only they can.

This book is about helping you achieve that fulfillment in your life as you pursue your acting career. It's about helping you create a plan by which you can gain a great deal of control over your destiny. It's about reminding you to feed your soul with your art, rather than letting it starve you as you struggle day to day. Believe me, it is entirely possible. But it will take a great deal of willpower, determination, hard work, focus, and commitment.

I truly believe that if you don't just skim this book for ideas, but rather utilize it as a step-by-step guide to crafting your career, you can find success, happiness, and inner peace. The information in the pages ahead is laid out in a deliberate, step-by-step process for you. Take the time to really read each chapter and absorb it before moving on to the next. I offer you specific exercises throughout the book, some of which can be done quickly in your head, others that will be longer-term, more involved projects. But whatever the case, I suggest you really give each of the exercises a thorough go before moving on. This way you'll know you've taken every step possible to ensure you have control over your career.

I cannot take credit for all of the ideas put forth in this book. Over the years I have been teaching, I have developed an approach to training my students that comes from a solid combination of my own observations and personal aesthetic along with many great lessons and influences of other very wise people. This book is simply my way of combining the ideas that I have found most serviceable all in one compact manual. It is essentially the distillation of a course I teach called "Preparation for the Theatre Profession." As we go along, I will certainly give credit where credit is due, and I will offer you recommended reading and Internet research where apropos.

Overture

Before we can begin our work on launching your career, there are two items we must address: the first has to do with finances and the second has to do with self-awareness. I know it's only the first day of "class," but I already have a couple of homework assignments for you.

Let's begin with the financial discussion.

I am going to assume that you are a college student, a recent graduate, or perhaps a person who is making the transition to becoming a professional actor. In any of these cases, I'm also going to surmise that you might likely not be in a state of utter financial solvency. Most young artists I meet are stressed about student loans, the high rent and cost of living in major cities, and perhaps racked-up credit card debt from their college years—that was certainly my story coming out of college. The first major stumbling block you'll encounter in trying to kick-start a performing career is the exorbitant cost of it all. It's mesmerizing! Just think: you'll need great headshots, nice resume paper, audition attire, a constant influx of new audition material, money to take classes, not to mention time away from work to facilitate your availability to audition. Any way you cut it, it's not an inexpensive venture.

I know many young actors who get quickly discouraged by the vicious circle that financial constraints place upon them. They need to pay rent so they get a day job that requires too many hours. They set a timeline for making money, after which they plan to "have enough" to be able to start auditioning. Then they feel out of the loop and out of practice and they find it hard to motivate themselves to get back on the proverbial horse and get into the audition room. Once they finally do get in the room, their confidence is not what it was directly out of school, and they suddenly find themselves rusty, cynical, and frustrated. I hate to be negative, but I see some variation of this cycle all the time, and I truly believe that with a little foresight and planning, it can be avoided.

But you must start taking steps now! You can't wait until you're over your head and trying just to stay afloat, because any city—be it New York, DC, Chicago, LA—will eat you alive and make you feel buried if you let your finances get out of control. I tell you this to scare you a little bit, if I'm being honest, but I speak from personal experience. I went to an out-of-state school and graduated with student debt. Additionally, I got a credit card to help make life easier and more fun in college, and I let it get out of control, so that once I arrived in New York after graduation, I was already in a financial quagmire. I had to eventually go through a credit-counseling agency just to get things reined in and manageable, and of course, that damaged my credit for a long time afterward.

Eventually, though, I discussed my money management issues with my dear friends Joe Abraham and Christine Negherbon at The Thriving Artists (www.TheThrivingArtists.com), and they helped steer me in the direction of regaining control. Joe and Christine are both actors, but they are also entrepreneurs with their financial fingers in many different pies. They are truly two of the happiest artists I know, and I realize that their happiness stems largely from being unburdened by debt. Joe began by encouraging me to read *Rich Dad, Poor Dad* by Robert Kiyosaki as well as *The Money Book for the Young, Fabulous, and Broke* by Suze Orman. Both of these books, along with countless other pieces of sage advice from this "power couple," really helped me to put things in perspective. I gave myself some feasible steps to follow, and I'm happy to report that a few short years later, I bought my first home and got my credit completely back on track!

So let's get you working on a couple of those steps now, so that you don't end up swamped like I was back then. I want you to do two things—one of them is immensely simple and you may already be ahead of the game on it; the other is a bit more challenging and time consuming and will take a great deal of discipline and willpower.

The first action I want you to take is to open up a savings account if you don't already have one. I don't care if you put $5 or $500 in it right now, but the most important thing is just to have one. It would be really smart to attach it to your checking account so that you can move money directly into savings online (and also so that you have an emergency backup fund should you overdraw your checking). But your discipline has to come in (a) not moving money from savings to checking every time you overspend, and (b) making sure that you find a bit of money each pay period, each birthday, and each time you come into extra cash to move over into savings. Realistically assess your income and what you can afford to live on, and whatever money you find is over and above the minimum required cost of living, put into savings. This will be the start of your own personal "nest egg." You will find it comes in handy when those theatre business expenditures start to pile up. I'm not suggesting you never touch your savings, but I'm saying that you limit its use to furthering your career.

The second action is the really difficult one: I want you to start and maintain a month-long budget log for yourself. For the next thirty days, I want you to literally write down *every single penny* that you spend in a journal or a computer spreadsheet; just the amount and a description of what you spent it on. This sounds easy, but it can be quite challenging. For starters, make sure you keep your log either in your phone or in a very small, portable notepad that can be taken with you everywhere. This way, you won't have the excuse of forgetting to notate something. The other option is to collect receipts and log everything at the end of each day, but it's easy to let that slip through the cracks, especially since we don't actually get receipts for everything we purchase.

Now, many of my students ask me questions like: "Should I log unusual/emergency things that don't normally come up in an average month (such as schoolbooks for the start of term, a flat tire or speeding ticket, or headshots that you only buy once every few years)?" The answer is *yes*. Log everything! I don't care if you spend $0.25 on a piece of candy, $1.63 on a cup of coffee, $20 to loan a friend, or $600 for a new transmission for your car; you must enter every cent. The other question they ask is: "Can I just use my checkbook (real or online) and balance it to fulfill the assignment?" The answer to that question is no. The problem with looking at a balanced bank account log is that it includes both withdrawals and deposits. For our purposes, I don't want you concerning yourself with what's coming in; I only want us to track what's going out.

Be disciplined about this so that you don't fall behind on it, and don't balk at facing your monthly number, no matter how scary it might prove to be. You may find that in the midst of having to log everything, you suddenly second-guess yourself about a daily trip to Starbucks because you're personally shamed out of spending that money and having to write it down. Although this is not the intent of the exercise, it has certainly been known to happen, and I can't tell you that it's a bad by-product of the assignment. But either way, know that this journal is deeply personal, and you don't have to share it with anyone but yourself, so don't cut corners. Just take my word for it, and for the next thirty days write down every single expenditure of money, cash or credit.

In the middle of this book—the chapter I call "Entr'acte"—we will come back to our discussion on finances and I'll check in with you on your budget log. But for the time being, just get it started and keep it going as we move on to other things.

The second item I told you I wanted us to look into before we move forward has to do with self-awareness. I want you to indulge me in a simple but crucial exercise here, which will prove helpful to you in dozens of circumstances along your journey to becoming a successful artist. The exercise is simply to craft an introduction of yourself—a sixty-second pitch, if you will—that encapsulates who you are so that when the question "Why don't you tell me about yourself?" comes up on a job or an agent interview or in a social situation, you're not left stammering and fumbling for words.

To get started, I am going to offer you some prompts below, which you may choose to think about and incorporate into your introduction. These are just some suggested items to consider, and you can take any, all, or none of them. Just be sure to avoid making your sixty-second intro all about theatre and your life in theatre. Trust me, nothing can be duller for an industry person to listen to than how your whole life is that industry. Instead, I want you to think outside the box a little.

SELF-KNOWLEDGE QUESTIONNAIRE

1. Where are you from? Did you grow up in a small town or a city? Is there anything particularly quirky or interesting about your hometown? (For instance, I have a student who tells people she comes from Round Rock, Texas—so named because of the big round rock in the heart of town.)
2. What is/was your family like? Were your parents working class? Were they military? Did someone other than your parents raise you? Do you have siblings? If so, are you like them at all or are you different?
3. What kind of child/teenager were you? Were you a bookworm? An athlete? An ugly duckling? A social butterfly? A wallflower?
4. What hobbies or interests do you have besides acting? Do you enjoy watching/playing sports? Are you an avid reader? Do you do outdoor nature activities? Do you perhaps draw or paint?
5. Are you passionate about any causes? (Be careful not to get too political or religious so that you don't risk offending someone. Use your best judgment as to what should or should not be fodder for an interview.)
6. If you had to choose a profession other than theatre, what would it be?
7. Do you have any serious lifelong goals or desires, such as major traveling, high-risk adventures, or other quirky little conversation starters?
8. Is there anything else particularly interesting about you that makes for a great icebreaker?

Once you've taken the time to answer these questions for yourself (or at least to use them as a springboard for generating other interesting facts about you), begin crafting a personal statement that will ultimately run about forty-five to sixty seconds, based on the information you have compiled. You do not need to write a formal monologue to be memorized and recited each time you meet someone new; however, you should have a pretty good idea of how you want to make a first impression on someone and what, if anything, can be told humorously or memorably. Let me give you an example of what one of these "pitches" might sound like.

> My name is Jonathan Flom. Flom rhymes with home. My students tend to call me J-Flo. I am currently the head of the Musical Theatre Program at Shenandoah Conservatory in Winchester, Virginia. But I'm also a published author, a professional director, and an occasional playwright. I really grew up in south Florida, but I have always identified myself as a New Yorker. I love my grandparents, but I remember feeling utterly betrayed when they sold their condo in Bayside and moved permanently to Delray Beach, like all Jewish grandparents seem to do, so I had no one in the city to go visit. And so ever since my teenage years, I was always determined to live in New York. I did in fact move there after finishing my BFA at Penn State, where I became a die-hard Nittany Lion fanatic, but I left New York to pursue a master's degree and I haven't moved back since. I dabbled in Chicago a bit, and "the sticks" of northeastern Vermont before settling in Winchester six years ago. When I'm not immersed in teaching or directing—and in fact, even sometimes when I *am*—I am an obsessive baseball fan. I unfortunately love the New York Mets because in 1986 when my dad decided to teach me about baseball, he said, "Son, this is baseball and this is our team," and they won the World Series. So I've been stuck with them ever since.

Reading this statement out loud runs about a minute. You'd be amazed at how much I had to cut out to keep it at a minute. Sixty seconds is not a whole lot of time in which to pack introductory information, so you have to choose carefully what you wish to share. But I think it is important to distill your intro down to a minute or less, as people tend to lose interest and fade away after the sixty-second mark. You want to make it easy for people to listen to you without checking out, and you also want to leave some facts out and open the door for questions and further conversation. So go ahead and pick some highlights and try to craft an interesting, if somewhat entertaining self-introduction.

Once you've written your statement, try it out on people. See if your humorous bits land as you hoped they would. See if people who know you feel like you've been genuine and covered the most interesting and important parts of your life. Most of all, see if you can speak coherently about yourself without "um"ing or "like"ing all the way through. A good introduction can be the difference between an agent wanting to learn more about you and signing you or thanking you for your time and taking a pass. It can also serve you in the exercises ahead when we start talking about branding. Suffice it to say, filling out the questionnaire, giving some thought to who you are and what makes you tick, and being able to articulate your personal values will go a long way toward making you a self-aware person, and self-awareness is very sexy in this business.

Act I

---○---

PREPARING FOR YOUR CAREER: WHAT IS IN YOUR CONTROL?

Scene 1

———○———

Begin with Goals

IT MAY SOUND CLICHÉ, but I cannot emphasize to you enough the power of setting goals. My friends at The Thriving Artists always begin by stating, "A goal is a dream with a deadline." What a perfectly apt description! Some people may think setting concrete goals and writing them down is hokey or just downright frightening (they don't want to be faced with what they have to accomplish in order not to be considered a "failure"), but the achievement of a goal can be the most uplifting and fulfilling exploit and can give you the confidence to dare and risk even more.

A few years ago I attended a workshop in Manhattan led by choreographer Tara Young. She had us do an exercise that I'd like to offer to you right now. On a sheet of paper (or on your computer, phone, or favorite technological writing gizmo), write down the following numbers, leaving a lot of space between each one:

1
2
5
10

Now, beside each number, I want you to ask yourself what you envision for your life that many years from now and write it down. Really take some time and brainstorm this. It may be that you can come up with a good solid list of goals in one sitting; it may be that you're a little fuzzy on the long term right now, but you have some clear-cut short-term aspirations. Whatever the case may be, I want you to spend some time with this and I want you to push yourself to be very specific. Do not second-guess yourself or shortchange what you really want. And don't allow yourself to think that anything is off the table. You may want to be in a Broadway show more than anything else, but you may think that it is unrealistic. Well, perhaps where you are now it's unrealistic in the next year or two, but who's to say that if you make it a five- or a ten-year goal, you can't take steps to achieve it? I want you to shoot for the moon on this (I also want you to be honest with yourself about your actual capabilities). I'm going to hold you to whatever you write down!

Let me give you some examples of weaker goals, which are unspecific and difficult to quantify and achieve in a tangible, measurable way:

- I want to be happy
- I want to be successful
- I want to be wealthy
- I want to be working
- I want to be physically fit

Do you understand why these are a little vague for our purposes? Realize that there's nothing wrong with wanting any of those things, but when people set goals that are as general as those listed above, it's very easy to lose track of them. You need to set goals that are both specific and finite. Just as you must establish objectives as an actor playing a character—objectives that are clear, specific, measurable, and testable—you need to do the same for your own real life. Here are some examples of clearer, more specific goals that may very well apply to you as an actor:

ONE YEAR

- I want to graduate from college with $2,500 saved in my bank account.
- I want to have an internship or apprenticeship set up for when I graduate.

- I want to book professional summer theatre work this year.
- I want to move to Chicago and start to find my way around.
- I want to be on a regular exercise routine where I'm working out four or five days a week.

TWO YEARS

- I want to book a ten- to twelve-month gig at a regional theatre.
- I want to be living in New York and taking classes at least twice a week to keep my skills sharpened and to increase my contacts.
- I want to get certified as a Pilates or yoga instructor so I can have my own business.
- I want to book a national tour or cruise ship gig so I can live rent-free for a year and see the world.
- I want to move to Seattle and start my own not-for-profit children's theatre company.

FIVE YEARS

- I want to have at least six New York performance credits on my resume.
- I want to be signed with an agent in Los Angeles and working on commercials and television.
- I want to originate a role in a musical at the Off-Broadway or major regional (LORT)[1] level.
- I want to be making at least 75 percent of my income as a performing artist.
- I want to have conquered my fear of heights and gone skydiving.

TEN YEARS

- I want to own a home and have a family of my own.
- I want to have performed in at least three Broadway shows.

---

1. LORT stands for League of Resident Theatres. It is basically the organization of major Equity regional performance venues.

- I want to have moved from New York to Los Angeles and begun booking feature films and/or television.
- I want to be a well-known commodity in the commercial and industrial arena and I want my living to be made from regular appearances on camera.
- I want to be enrolled in a graduate program, so I can work my way to teaching theatre.
- I want to open a gourmet pizza restaurant called Brick Oven Jonny's.

What I've given you above is a pretty broad array of possibilities, some of which may even apply to you. I want you to get a sense of just how specific and articulate you must be about your personal goals. For each goal you write down, ask yourself if it is: (a) achievable, and (b) measureable. You have to know that it is physically conceivable to attain an objective you set for yourself, and you have to know how you will measure your success so that you can enjoy crossing something off your list when you've crushed it!

Before you continue reading further, take some time and see what goals you can come up with for yourself for each of the four years you listed.

I hope that you were able to come up with some good ones, and I hope you will revisit this chapter and this project regularly and check in on yourself from time to time with your goals. When you achieve one, cross it off the list, but then start asking yourself what might be next now that one is done.

Finally, it is a great idea to make what The Thriving Artists call a "dream board." This is where you actually write your goals out on large poster board and you hang it where you will be faced with it every day. A constant reminder of your goals will help motivate you when you start to feel down about how things are going or when you start to derail a bit on your track to fulfillment. It is also a wise idea to share your dream board with others you know and trust, so that your friends and family can help motivate and cheer you on, too.

Once you have your list made and written, you can start to create an action plan for achieving each goal. Ask yourself what the necessary steps would be for you to actually complete each objective. This way, they're not just ideas on paper, they are destinations toward which you are creating a road map. For example:

Goal: To sign with an agent within the next two years.

Action Plan: I will start researching agents in New York and gathering information about the kind of representation I really want. I will talk to all of my friends who have representation and find out if I would be a good fit in any of their offices. I will continue to build relationships with casting directors for whom I audition regularly and get called back or from whom I take classes. I will make it a point to get cast in a showcase or performance venue in the city so that I can invite industry people to see my work. I will take at least two monthly agent classes at Actors Connection.[2]

See how we have now created a specific plan for pursuing a goal? Instead of dreaming about how nice it would be to have an agent and hoping you're in the right place at the right time and the stars align, you have set in motion a specific strategy to ensure that you are in control of your own success. Of course, there are many more steps that could help in getting signed with an agency, but you get the point, right? Create as much of an action plan as you can for each of your goals, and you'll never be caught wondering why they haven't just happened for you. If you don't know what steps are involved in achieving some of your goals, ask for advice from people you trust—particularly people who have already achieved the goal you are setting out to pursue.

Once you have your list of goals clearly defined and you have begun to develop an action plan for each of them, it makes decision making a breeze. From this point on, you will have a litmus test by which to measure every opportunity that is presented to you. If a job opportunity comes your way but you are not certain you want to take the work, just look to your goals and ask yourself

---

2. Actors Connection is one of the most valuable resources for performers in the city. They offer classes, studio space, and workshops daily, and they're one of the most respected, legitimate theatre business companies in the city. www.actorsconnection.com.

if taking that job will bring you closer to any of your stated targets. See how easy that is?

One final word on goals: These are not etched in stone, final, and irreversible. Just like a character in a play that pursues one objective until she suddenly changes course for some reason, we are human and we are fickle. Circumstances change our minds on an almost daily basis. I never would have told you ten years ago that I had any aspirations of being a teacher. Then all of a sudden I found myself creating an auditions course in graduate school and the minute I got up in front of a class, my entire outlook and set of career ambitions changed in an instant. Do not count yourself a failure if you decide to reassess your goals before they are achieved. It is perfectly okay to think you want one thing now only to realize later on that it is not what you want. As long as you are willing and able to sit down and recalculate your route and re-create your goal sheet when things change, so that you can focus your energy on new endeavors, you are not "copping out." Be honest with yourself and don't sell yourself or your aspirations short.

Scene 2

―――――○―――――

What Is Branding?

WHEN I GRADUATED FROM THEATRE SCHOOL, the word "branding" was never remotely associated with actors. Nobody really taught us about how to market ourselves successfully or how to run our own small business. We were taught to act, sing, dance, and audition. Now, however, the business of theatre seems to be heading in a new direction—one that is far more entrepreneurial on the part of the independent artist. Now with companies like The Savvy Actor (www.thesavvyactor.com), performers are being given the tools to really control and manage their careers. Basically, there is a method by which you can guide people's perceptions of you as a person and as an artist, allowing you to gain a great deal more leverage in the "type" game. It can be incredibly empowering, and it can help guide all of your decision making, along with those fantastic goals you just set for yourself. So let us begin by discussing exactly what branding is.

According to The Savvy Actor, your brand is your promise. The brand is everything people associate with your product (you!), and it is your responsibility to deliver the goods and to live up to the expectations that you have established for yourself in the industry. You need to be clear, concise, and specific, and you also need to be realistic about what it is you can actually deliver.

In order to get a clearer sense of what I mean by the power of branding, I want you to do a simple exercise for me. Normally, when I present branding workshops I show images of well-known brand logos at this point and ask the audience to free-associate thoughts with the images they see. However, to go even further in pointing out the strength in good branding, I am not even going to show you images; rather, I am simply going to tell you what the icon is, and your conditioned mind will do the rest. So as I ask you to picture the following four logos, I want you to write down the list of all the words and thoughts you associate with each one. Ready?

1. A golden-yellow letter "M" with the top points curved (like arches!).
2. The inner two rings of a dartboard (red ring, then white ring) with a red bull's-eye in the center, set against a white background.
3. A white check mark (curved at the bottom, rather than sharply angled) against a black background.
4. A sleek, metallic, black and gray apple silhouette (with stem) with an apparent bite taken out of the right side.

Were you able to clearly picture exactly what I described? If so, what thoughts, phrases, or images came to mind with each of those logos? I have done this exercise quite a bit, and I will share some of the common reactions that I hear from people upon flashing each of the images across the screen:

1. McDonald's; Hamburgers; Fries; McRib; Nasty; Fast; Cheap; Greasy; Heart attack; "I'm Lovin' It"; Happy Meal; Ronald Mc-Donald; Childhood; Paul Newman Coffee.
2. Target; "Targét"; Cheap stuff; Better than Walmart; Everything; Junk; Super-Target; Plaid shirts; Video games; Bathing suits.
3. Nike; Swoosh; "Just do it"; Air Jordans; Running; Exercise; Sneakers; Corporate sponsorship; Athletic.
4. Apple; "i-Everything"; Computers; Steve Jobs; Technology; Macs; Innovative; Big Brother; Phone; Essential.

Now understand, these are literally the responses that people have shouted out in my class and my workshops when I have presented this topic. I am neither advocating nor disparaging any of the above brands—I merely chose four of the most recognizable logos that do not have any words etched into them. You will notice that the responses that I charted contained mixed opinions. For each image, some in the audience will respond favorably and others will not. That is par for the course, and you must remember that as you craft your own brand—not everyone will want to buy what you are selling. However, the point here is, the four images your brain conjured on my description are just pictures! They do not represent anything in and of themselves. A bull's-eye does not mean good deals any more than a big check mark signifies excellence in athletics. So why do these images cause our brains to skip a step and fill in their own responses? That is the power of branding.

These companies hire marketing experts to distill their essence into an image, and then they saturate the market with that image, alongside other actual information, so that our brain will eventually do the shorthand work of instantly associating the image with the product. We have been manipulated!

The good news, though, is that as actors we too have the power to create our own individual brands, complete with recognizable images, logos, and catchphrases. Thus we can manipulate people's views of our product just like a corporation does. Let me show you what I mean. I want you to do the exercise we just did with the brand logos; only I want you to do it with a series of actor headshots (which I will actually show you rather than describe). As you turn the page and glance at the photos, I want you to make a list of responses to what you see. Be sure to be honest and do *not* choose your responses carefully; but rather, write down your instant, knee-jerk reactions. This is a private exercise so you will not have to tell anyone what the images made you think. Ready?

1.

2.

Jenna Pinchbeck Photography

3.

Jenna Pinchbeck Photography

4.

Robert Mannis Photography

What did you come up with? Did specific adjectives jump to mind, or did you go so far as to ascribe certain characters to the subjects in the photographs? It would not surprise me if you did. Very often I get responses such as "lawyer," "dancer," "nice girl next door," and so forth when I show these. Some people even start shouting out the names of television shows and movies in which they could imagine these actors. Of course, it makes sense since we are trained to look at actors' headshots and instantly type them. This is what directors and casting directors do for a living, so you can understand the power and importance of a great headshot. But based on this discussion of branding, do you also understand how *you* have the power to control what subliminal message is sent about you?

There's a fantastic book by Malcolm Gladwell called *Blink*, which I highly suggest you read (in fact, read all of Gladwell's books—they're terrific, and they are all on the "recommended reading list" in my theatre class syllabi). In it, the author discusses how major decisions are made in an instant upon first impression—in the blink of an eye, so to speak. In most cases, your headshot precedes you into the audition room. In fact, for appointment requests, you will need your headshot to make a strong enough statement about you just to be invited in to audition. It is not enough to have a good-looking photograph anymore. Your headshot must say something about you; it must broadcast your brand. We will spend more time talking in great detail about headshots in a later chapter, but for now I want you to recognize that your headshot will have the power to do for you what the golden arches, the bull's-eye, the swoosh, and the apple have done for their respective corporations.

You must now begin to think of yourself as a business. My colleague Miles Davis (not *that* Miles Davis!), dean of the Harry F. Byrd School of Business, teaches a lecture for my students every year entitled "You, Inc." He is not a theatre person or an artist, but I find that my students are always moved and inspired by his class because he has a way of empowering them to be entrepreneurs and to take charge of their own marketing schemes and thus, their careers. Dr. Davis tells students to really think about how they want people to perceive them. When their names come up in conversation, what should people associate with them?

You can create a lasting impression that will carry as much weight as your actual talent. In the sections that follow, I will help you begin the process of creating your personal brand. By the end of our work together, you will have a branding statement and a product that is consistent, comprising such elements as your name, your headshot, your resume, your attire, your audition material, and your social media. It is hard work, but I promise you that it will give you much greater control of how people perceive you.

Scene 3

―――――――○―――――――

How Does an Actor
Begin to Craft a Brand?

IN THIS SECTION I WILL WALK YOU THROUGH some exercises to help you determine what your particular unique brand is as an artist. But before we begin, I want to recommend that you go on The Savvy Actor website (www.thesavvyactor.com) and order yourself a copy of *The Savvy Career Manual*. Those guys are the gurus of theatre business. They teach classes, they offer coachings and counseling, and they publish articles, webcasts, and manuals all dedicated to helping performing artists take hold of their careers. I have learned a tremendous amount about the business from Doug, Kevin, and Jodie over the years, and I am proud to recommend them to you. *The Savvy Career Manual* is a hands-on workbook that walks you slowly and carefully through all the steps of creating your own small actor business. I am giving you my take on some of the most basic steps to branding, but if you want to get really in depth, there is no better resource out there than Savvy. Now let us begin our work on figuring out just how to sell "You, Inc."

EXERCISE 1—COLLECT ADJECTIVES

I hate to tell you, but we are going back to making more lists again. This time, we are going to make a list of adjectives that can be used to describe you. I want you to begin this exercise by coming up

19

with eight to ten adjectives that you would use to describe yourself. Avoid blanket physical statements, such as tall or blond or handsome. Think more about how you would describe your essence as a person. Next, I want you to start reaching out to various people and asking them for four to six adjectives that they feel describe you. Make sure that when you choose people to ask, you survey a range of relationships—in other words, you might ask your closest friends, a couple of work or school acquaintances, some teachers and/or directors you have worked with, and any mentors you have. In fact, just for fun, I challenge you to walk up to a complete stranger and ask him to describe you on first impression! (When I teach my workshop, the first thing I do before I introduce myself is ask the class to write down five to ten things they know about me just from me walking in and standing up in front of them.)[1]

You need to be honest with yourself and you need to demand that others be honest with you as well. It does you no good whatsoever to have people trying to flatter you rather than observe you objectively. Let me give you some possible examples of the types of useful adjectives you might find describe you:

Are you bubbly, perky, precocious, curious, or energetic?
Are you mysterious, dark, aloof, thoughtful, or cynical?
Are you intellectual, "geek chic," nerdy, quirky, or goofy?
Are you sexy, vampish, charming, dashing, or seductive?

Obviously, we can go on and on with possibilities, but I am sure you get the point. Go ahead and get started on collecting your adjectives and continue reading below when you have a nice list going.

How did that go for you? Were you able to come up with some good ones? Much like your goals and your self-introduction, this might be an ongoing project for you. It definitely comes easier to some than to others. Do not despair if you were unable to get a good list going; just keep working on it, and keep eliciting others' input to build up your collection of adjectives.

---

1. I totally stole that bit from Dr. Miles Davis. Credit where credit is due.

Once you do compile your descriptors and you get feedback from several other people in your life, it is time to move to the next step, which is to distill the adjectives into the most useful of information. First, take a look at what others said about you versus what you said about yourself. Are there major discrepancies? Do people see you in a way that you did not expect or do not wish to be seen? Did anything really surprise you? Or was people's perception of you pretty consistent with how you think you are presenting yourself to the world? It is up to you to choose which adjectives you want to embrace and which you want to try and shave off of your public persona.

Next, if you have words that could be construed as negative, such as abrasive, bossy, blunt, loud, obnoxious, and so forth, see if you can turn them around into words that can depict you in a more positive light; for instance, direct, determined, trendsetting, energetic, or gregarious.

Also, if you have the word "versatile" or any of its synonyms on your list, cross it off right now. We are trying to get to the core of who you really are on a daily basis as a person. It is so easy for us to get wrapped up in our ability to change faces and personas in order to be "what they want" behind the table, that we lose sight of who we really are and what we have to offer. So I want us to agree that there are probably several sides to you, as you are a real live three-dimensional person. But this process is about looking for the adjectives that really hit on your core being, your essence, and your spirit. What is your "bread and butter"? Because, ultimately, to get started in the business, you will need casting directors to know who you are and how they can sell you to the director and the producers. (More on that process in the second half of this book.)

In the realm of creating a brand for our product, it is important that we try to find what I call a sticky consistency. What I mean is that you must identify those characterizations of yourself that ring clear across different relationships you have (people who know you well and people who just met you) and that have a tendency to be memorable (sticky). For instance, describing yourself as "wise" may be apt, but choosing a word such as "canny" is much more likely to pop in people's memory; it is a stickier word. Avail yourself of the help of a thesaurus as you do this exercise—it will open up a far more interesting list of adjectives, I assure you.

Ultimately, you want to work your way down to three to five words that really hit the nail on the head in describing who you are as a person and as an artist and what makes you tick; essentially, your *essence*. These adjectives will become a part of your brand, and as I said earlier, you must always be able to deliver on them; they are your promise. When people see your headshot or when you walk into a room, they should be able to expect these three to five adjectives to emanate from you without fail. They may be words that you already bring with you 100 percent of the time, or you may need to make a conscious effort to carry them with you, as there can certainly be an element of aspiration in branding (in other words, I want people to think of me as "easygoing," so I will put forth the effort to appear so even when I might not be).

EXERCISE 2—LIST ROLE MODELS

The next step in creating the actor branding statement is to compare yourself to other well-known people in the industry. This can be a comparison of looks, certain traits, or basic essence. Some people balk at the idea of using celebrity actors to draw parallels to themselves, but I will tell you in two simple instances why it can be immensely useful. First, when you meet with an agent, one immediate question she will ask you is, "Who do people compare you with in the industry?" She is trying to get a quick assessment of how she can sell you to casting people and producers, and oftentimes having a famous comparison makes her job easier. The second reason is because many casting calls will actually list names of actors whose type they are seeking in the auditions. For example, "Seeking a female, Madonna-type, sexually charged and confident . . ." or "Seeking a young George Clooney–type with charisma and wit . . ."

So I want you to think about a few well-known actors or performers with whom you would compare yourself or others have compared you. And once again, you can feel free to be specific here. You do not just have to list names; you can qualify them with a statement:

- "I have the acerbic wit of Groucho Marx."
- "I'm like a young Katharine Hepburn, with all that fire and confidence."
- "I have the chin of Jay Leno with the humor to match it."
- "I look like the love child of Kevin James and Jon Favreau."
- "I have the warmth and genuineness of Rachel McAdams."

And did you notice how doing the celebrity comparison exercise can also tend to incorporate the adjective exercise? This list can actually be derived from the previous one—or if you were having trouble coming up with adjectives, try starting with celebrities and then working backward to distill the adjectives from the juxtaposition. Ultimately, you want to have two or three celebrities to whom you can compare at least some facet of yourself.

Now, these celebrities do not necessarily need to be A-list Hollywood megastars. Remember that you are doing this work within the industry, so utilizing newer, up-and-coming Broadway, and indie film actors is certainly fair game. Think outside the box, and just remember that this is only for a frame of reference. You most certainly do not need to become a walking imitation of the actors you list.

EXERCISE 3—BRAINSTORM DREAM ROLES

The next questions I will put to you on our quest for your personal brand have to do with roles and tracks in plays, musicals, or TV shows. I want you to start by coming up with a list of dream roles that you would love to play. Think broadly here, but also think realistically. At first, you do not have to limit yourself to age-appropriate parts, so if there is a long-term goal of playing The Baker's Wife in *Into the Woods* when you are older and more seasoned, go ahead and list it here. Think of plays and of musicals (if you are a musical theatre performer), and really try to come up with a good solid list of characters you can really see sinking your teeth into. Be careful to avoid saying things like "I would love to play any role in _____." Remember, we are trying to be specific here and help you distill your essence in a way that will be marketable for you in the long run. So do not get wistful about how much you love a show to the point where you are unable to identify your part in that particular cast. It is okay to have a couple of different tracks you would like to play, but I am going to hold you to actually naming the roles, rather than being general. (I suppose shooting for an ensemble track is certainly viable, but try to be specific if you can about which track or type of track you could pull off.)

Once you have a list started, go ahead and divide it up between roles you can play right now at your current age and experience level and roles that you want to tuck away for future growth. Do not be swayed by the fact that you may still be in school, where they cast way out of age range; for the purposes of this exercise, I want you to think of the roles you could actually get cast to play in the professional world right now. Maybe it is your dream to be in *Les Miserables*, and right now you see yourself playing Cosette or Eponine, but eventually you would like to grow into Fantine. You get the point.

Next I want you to go one more step for me on the role exploration: I want you to examine what is currently on Broadway, Off Broadway, on national tours, in major regional venues (e.g., Goodspeed, Paper Mill Playhouse, the Guthrie, Signature, etc.), and even what is on television, and I want you to create a list of roles that you could literally step into right now, should the actors or actresses currently playing them happen to quit. I know it is a little more unlikely with television, but knowing that you could play a role of the type that Mae Whitman plays on *Parenthood* (NBC) or that Bridgit Mendler plays on *Good Luck Charlie* (Disney Channel) can be very informative, both to you and to your prospective agent.

See if you can come up with five to ten roles that are out there for you at this moment. This list will serve you in a couple of ways. Number one, it will be another question that an agent will ask you on an interview—"What roles can I submit you for right now?" And number two, it will be a great way for you to seek out audition material. Knowing what is out there for you can lead you to choosing great repertoire. But let us not put the horse before the cart—more on repertoire in a later chapter.

Exercise 4—Put It All Together

So we now have a list of adjectives that describe you; we have a list of celebrities with whom you are comparable in various ways; we have a list of your dream roles; and we have a list of parts in current productions that you can play (these last two lists do not need to be mutually exclusive, by the way). It is now time to start crafting your branding statement based on all the information you have gathered. I am going to offer you three different ways to create your statement, and none of these is necessarily better than the others, nor the "right" way to do this. You will need to play with a lot of different wordings until you find something that fits you like a glove and really serves you in a practical way.

The first approach is to come up with what I call a three-word descriptor. Because information is best served in bite-size portions, the three-word approach keeps it neat and simple. It basically captures your essence in a very short burst, but it can be very powerful and sticky when you get a really good one. It may be three adjectives, or it can also work as adjective, adjective, and noun. Let me give you some examples of my students' branding statements that have used this method:

- Good, Classic Sparkle.
- Charming. Wholesome. Mirth.
- simple. genuine. blissful.
- Polished, authentic charm.

I punctuated and capitalized the statements just as they appear on the actors' websites (we'll get to websites later) or their business cards (we'll get to those, too). Whether you like all four of those branding phrases or not, you must see how the actors have boiled down their essence into a concise phrase based upon the adjective

exercise that we did at the top of this chapter. I can tell you with all
surety that the four actors who created those mottoes live by them
daily. The slogans represent who they are and they serve to guide
the decisions the actors make for their careers. Notice also the way
they took inspiration from corporate marketing schemes and used
periods and capitalization in interesting and unique ways. Again,
there is nothing overly poetic about it, but it does tend to stick a
bit more, I think.

The second possibility for your new brand is to come up with
what can best be described as a catchphrase. Again, this phrase
must be derived from your adjectives and influenced by the roles
you see yourself playing. The catchphrase approach is often more
liberating for people who feel constrained by the three-adjective approach. It allows more room for creativity. As long as you keep it to
those short, bite-size pieces, you should be able to create something
dynamic. Here are a couple of examples:

- Canny meets Classic.
- . . . fearless mensch
- Golden Boy or teenage wasteland (take your pick.)
- Rapier wit for hire.
- Classic charm revisited.

Once more, we have examples from actors who really know
who they are and what they are trying to market to the world. There
is a sense of confidence that comes in being able to make a bold
statement and let it guide you through the process of choosing
clothing, repertoire, headshots, and so forth. Are you starting to
get a preview of how much a specific branding statement can help
make those choices easier? I do not mean to get ahead of myself,
but just think of how much easier it is to choose the right headshot
when you know you are looking for the one that makes your branding statement come to life on the page. More on that soon . . .

The third and final approach to creating your branding statement is to refer to the celebrities you identified in the second exercise and to combine them with each other and with your adjectives
as well, creating a comparison. Let me show you what I mean:

- The boyish outlook of Matthew Broderick meets the humor and style of Ben Stiller. (That's mine!)
- Bass/Baritone down to a Low C with the intelligent charm of Kevin Kline, the physical wit of Groucho Marx, and the sensitive soul (and hair) of Patrick Dempsey. (That is Savvy Actor coach Doug Shapiro's.)
- I have the goofy grace of Mary Tyler Moore and the empathetic determination of Jeanne Tripplehorn.

Obviously this approach is a bit more than the bite-size versions we were looking at in the previous two methods, but again, if you can find something that has a sticky consistency, it should serve you just fine. And as I said, the comparative approach will really give industry people a frame of reference for how they can market you. Some actors I know use multiple branding approaches. Doug Shapiro at The Savvy Actor, for example, uses the Kevin Kline / Groucho Marx / Patrick Dempsey line when he wants to describe to someone in shorthand who he is as an actor, but he uses ". . . fearless mensch" as his go-to slogan on his website and all of his marketing materials. Both work exceedingly well for him, and I hope that one day soon you will take one of his classes and see for yourself!

This business of branding is really starting to take off within the theatre industry. Actors used to select material and attire specifically to suit each individual audition. This meant they were rarely able to be consistent and memorable beyond each singular casting call. But recognizing that casting directors are always balancing a multitude of projects will tell you that it is to your advantage to make a lasting imprint beyond the specific role you are being seen for on any given day. You need to instead become a known quantity. You want casting offices to think of you and call you in even when you have not attended an open call for a particular project. They will do this if you have the bold confidence to state your brand clearly and specifically in your choices. They will do this if you offer them a sticky consistency.

It may take you some time to sort out this branding statement of yours, and you may need to try a few different ones on for size, but you will know it when you hit the jackpot. People will clearly respond to you and things will fall into place.

Scene 4

―――――◯―――――

You Have a Brand; Now What Do You Do with It?

ATTIRE

CREATING YOUR UNIQUE BRAND is the first half of the business puzzle; the second half of the equation has to do with marketing your product. Once you hit on the catchphrase that best represents you, it is time to broadcast it clearly to the industry and to the world. The easiest place to begin to declare yourself is in the physical embodiment; that is, your attire.

When I was coming up in the business, it was common to walk into an audition room and see all the men in nice slacks, dress shoes, button-up dress shirts, and some in ties, vests, and even jackets. It was hard to tell one from the next, but everyone looked "professional." For women, it was bright, solid-colored dresses (lower cut and higher hemmed, generally, for musical theatre gals) and character heels, with the hair perfectly curled. It was a wonder how any casting director didn't just choose their performers at random from the assortment of generically dressed look-alikes.

In recent years, however—especially since the rise in popularity of rock musicals—people have tended to take a more casual approach to audition attire. While you still see the dressed-up formalists of old, it is far more common now to see men in nice jeans and solid, fitted T-shirts, while women are just as likely to wear pants and blouses as they are a dress. Basically, there is a much more "anything goes" kind

of attitude in the audition rooms of the current decade. People are a
lot freer to be themselves, which is immensely helpful. The only caveat is that you must look like you care. In other words, just because
it is less formal now doesn't mean you should throw on whatever is
lying on top of your laundry pile and look like a mess. Actors should
place a great deal of emphasis on choosing their wardrobes wisely.
Even if you are going into the room in jeans and a tee, it must be a
deliberate choice. And guess what that choice is based 95 percent
upon . . . that's right; it's based on your *brand*.[1]

Earlier I mentioned to you that having a career as an actor is expensive. Well, one of the first and most important expenditures you
will need to make is for your wardrobe. It is not okay to wear your
normal street/going-out clothes to auditions. Rather, you must have
a specific set of clothing options dedicated solely to your acting career. For starters, it ensures that you care for and protect the work
attire for longevity; but having a wardrobe for business use only also
provides you with a nice little tax write-off at the end of each year if
you are savvy about keeping receipts and separating work from play.
The other factor in keeping a steady audition wardrobe is that you
will become more recognizable in the room. We will talk throughout this book about how repetition aids in successful marketing.

As I alluded to moments ago, the first step in creating an effective wardrobe is to be clear on what your brand is. What are you
selling? Are you going for casual, boy- or girl-next-door? Are you going for seductive charmer? Are you going for peppy, all-American?
Do you want your clothing to say tough guy/girl or jock/tomboy? Or
are you perhaps going for intellectual, sensitive, and delicate? Notice how we are back on the adjectives here. I really want you to put
some thought into what kind of clothing you buy to represent you.
Look in the mirror with each outfit you try on and ask yourself: (a)
Do I look incredible in this?, (b) Do I feel incredibly comfortable in
this?, and (c) Does this stay consistent with my brand?[2]

---

1. The other 5 percent has to do with the specifics of the audition. In truth, even if your
brand were "clean-cut and wholesome," you would want to make some adjustments for an
audition such as *American Idiot* or *SubUrbia*. Of course, if that really is your brand, you may
want to avoid auditions for those types of shows altogether.

2. I will often refer to brand consistency as staying "on message." So when I say that at
some points later on, you will know what I mean.

As you consider the choice of audition attire, think too about the array of projects for which you imagine yourself going in. If you really plan to do a great deal of Shakespeare and classical work, something with a simple, clean line that allows you to have a full range of movement will be immensely valuable in your closet. If you audition for musical theatre mainly, think about how you will be able to move around in the clothing you pick, should they ask you to demonstrate a little mobility in an audition. If you know you are right for edgier material, think about how you can bring edgy and tough into the room without it looking like utter grunge. Also think about color. Many people look great in black, but it doesn't exactly leave a lasting impression—especially when so many audition rooms are curtained in black. Really explore finding a color palette that works for who you are.

I think at minimum, every actor should have a great pair of slacks that is tailored to fit like a glove, as well as a pair of designer jeans. If you can pull off the T-shirt look, then be sure the tees are fitted and stylish. Otherwise, it is fine to do the button-down as well. Just beware of current trends in men's colors—a few years ago, every man was wearing the bold blue and now it seems they have all shifted to purple. Find a color that really works on you and brings out your best features. Do not be afraid to be a little different, but be sure to avoid patterns and logos. Perhaps come up with several different options so that you have room to adjust according to mood or casting requirements. Sweaters and polo shirts are fine as well; again, as long as they suit your style and your brand. Just take a long look in the mirror before you decide on shirts and be sure that they fit you correctly. Know whether they should be tucked in or left out—whichever way suits the style—and be sure you do not go with clothing that looks too baggy or too tight. We want to see your figure and your physique, but we do not want to be watching you bulge out of something that does not suit your body type. And do be sure to press whatever shirt and pants you plan to wear before you hit the road to the audition. You do not want to look wrinkled and sloppy.

Some men can really pull off the vest-and-tie look in an audition, but I urge you not to go this route unless it really is your personal style to get that dressed up. What we see in the room should be a representation of what we'll get if we hire you. Do be sure to always wear socks (I know there is a fashion movement for men in no socks, but it always looks sloppy in the audition room) and have a nice pair of dress shoes that are not too ostentatious but are simply clean and unscuffed.

There are a few major "do nots" that I hope would go without saying, but I'll say them anyway: Do not wear shorts. Do not go in looking wrinkled and unkempt. Do not wear sneakers or flip-flops or sandals. Do not wear T-shirts with writing of any sort on them. Do not wear sweatshirts or sweatpants. Do not overdress and appear too stuffy and formal for the audition at hand.

Lastly, a word on hair and beards. Some guys can really pull off the long-haired look—it is truly part of their product to look a little shaggy and edgy. That is all well and good, but remember, *we must be able to see your eyes in the audition.* So if you wear your hair in any way that tends to allow bangs to cover over your forehead and get around your eyes, do something about that before you come to the audition. It is imperative that your hair be out of your face and that you do not need to push it back during the audition. As for facial hair, a lot of young men tend to wear a beard or a goatee to appear a bit older. Just remember to market yourself as who you are *now.* There are not a lot of actors who make a living off facial hair (Zach Galifianakis, Chuck Norris, and Tom Selleck come to mind, but really, watch TV and theatre—most actors are clean shaven unless they are required to grow hair for a specific part). If you are a young, twentysomething actor, you are most likely to work within that age range in the professional world, so do not try to appear older because your competition only gets stiffer when you bump up a "weight class," and go up against more seasoned, middle-aged actors. If anything, just keep a short, clean, stubbled look if you wish to appear a bit more rugged, but be sure to keep it tidy.

For actresses, the wardrobe really should contain at least one simple, classic-look dress. Even with all the contemporary, pop-rock, fringe material that is out there, one thing that will never completely go away is good old standard theatre (Rodgers and Hammerstein, Shakespeare, Wilde, etc.). So you should be able to look like a lady when the job calls for that. Just be sure that the dress covers everything it is meant to cover. I suggest that the length come past your knees so there is no worry of exposing anything should you be asked to go to the floor on your knees as part of the audition or callback. And it is also important that you make certain you are not popping out on top, either. Too many girls want to flaunt their figure and they wind up showing so much skin and cleavage that it actually makes us uncomfortable behind the table for fear that something might sneak its way out in a wardrobe malfunction! We want to watch you act and listen to your words, not watch your chest. Enough said?

Take a good look at yourself in the dresses you are considering for auditions, and like I advised the men, make certain that you are not lost in a baggy cut, nor are you squeezing yourself into something that will cling so closely that we can see every bit of you through the dress. I have heard casting directors suggest that women wear Spanx to help smooth out their figures behind a nice form-fitting dress. If that is something you need, it is certainly no reason to be embarrassed—just be honest with yourself. Consider bringing a trusted friend with you to tell you how you really look in the attire you are trying on.

If you do decide to wear a dress to auditions, consider a few things. First, I would suggest you avoid strapless. Even if you are not constantly compelled to be pulling it up over your chest, as most girls do, it never looks particularly comfortable and I think the people behind the table will always be a bit distracted by it. Second, there are simple, pretty dresses that say "I am the ingénue," and that is great if that is what you are selling, but what can you do to make *your* ingénue stand out and *pop* a bit more in the room? What kind of ingénue are you? Are you sassy and witty? Are you a bit bubbly and naïve? Just make sure simple does not translate to generic. And third, what do you want on your legs? Do you have perfectly smooth, unblemished legs worth flaunting? Or do you perhaps need to consider wearing hose to keep from distracting us from the work you are doing?[3] Take a good long look at your legs in

3. I hate to sound so shallow and judgmental, but this is the business we're in. I am just trying to give you every possible advantage when you get in the room so auditors are not distracted from your talents and your charms.

a mirror and make the decision that will prove most advantageous for your particular body type.

Which leads me to your shoes. Many people believe that women should always wear a heel in auditions. Heels certainly accentuate the line of the leg and give you a little more height. But I am not one to say there is a rule for everyone. For starters, if you cannot walk completely normally in heels without making a clumping sound or looking off balance, then definitely do not wear heels in an audition. I see women wearing flats all the time, and as long as they sell it and it is consistent with what they are packaging for me, I am perfectly fine with it. If you do wear heels, though, I suggest not going with extremes in any direction (short, chunky heels are awkward, as are tall, pointy heels); rather, just find a good two- to two-and-a-half-inch heel that does not call attention to itself but just gives you that lift and that confidence that you need to rock it in the audition. I would also be careful with character shoes—particularly beige ones. Yes, they are neutral and professional, but have you ever seen anything as ugly as a pair of tan character shoes? I would say that they can be the death of your beautiful look as our eyes track down your line and take you in.

One more thought on the heel issue—I work with many women who are tall. These actresses often wish to audition in flats because they are embarrassed of their height or they are worried that it will be a disadvantage for them. I say flaunt it proudly! If you are tall, wearing flat shoes is not going to fool us into thinking you are short or average height. Embrace the way you were built and wear those heels and be the tall girl who stands out. You might not be right for every role or couple pairing, but when we want someone tall and striking and leggy we will be able to rely on you.

If you are not a dress kind of girl, then feel free to sport the pants look. Just like the men, you will want a nice fitted pair of slacks that looks stunning on your figure. A pair of designer jeans can be great for you as well. Then look at what kind of top you want to wear that would keep you on message. Just be careful to avoid anything too loudly patterned or frilly—it can be very distracting when women wear blouses with a lot of ruffles and ornamentation. Also, take a good long look at how much skin you are showing in your tops. Do you have incredible arms that find their way to the gym daily and want showing off? Or are you better off keeping your arms covered? Do you have issues with acne on your arms or back? Does your skin tend to flush when you're nervous or stressed? These too are things to consider when deciding how much skin to show. Again, it sounds shallow, but you really need to assess what will draw the attention of the people behind the table in this glamour business.

One tendency that you may also wish to avoid is the secretarial look. Unless you are going in for a film or TV audition that seeks "business professional," do not err too far on the side of high buttoned and stuffy. Quite often, my female students will choose for themselves a "smart" dress or blouse, and it is hard to imagine them in any other situation than behind a desk in a 1950s period piece. There is nothing wrong with that if it is part of your brand (I do have a former student who *lives* in vintage), but just be sure you are being deliberate about those kinds of choices.

I do think that it is perfectly fair game to show some cleavage and skin up top if you have a figure to flaunt—I was not trying to be ultraconservative on that notion. Just do be sure that it is not gratuitous and distracting. And just as with the dress, you will want to be sure that whatever blouse you choose to wear fits you just right so that you are not lost behind it but you are also not busting through it in any area. I will discuss this in more detail later, but for now just think about showing your strengths rather than exposing your weaknesses.

Also of great concern for women is hair and makeup. The same applies to women as men in that we do not want hair in your face, nor do we want to see you pushing it back during your audition. So if you have long and/or thick hair or bangs, do be sure to have a way to pin or tie it back out of your face so that even if you turn profile, we still see you clearly. And I am not completely certain why so many girls feel it absolutely imperative to curl their hair—sure, it looks pretty, but I do not think it is entirely necessary for everyone. If that is your "look" and it represents who you are on a daily basis, go ahead and do it, but remember that when we hire you it is because we want what we saw in the room to be there in the rehearsal process, so what you show us at the open call needs to be what we will get if we cast you down the road.

As for makeup, I do not think there is really an option in audition situations; women need to be wearing some makeup. I love the "all natural" look for sure, and I always respect women who do not need makeup to look beautiful. However, in the audition room it is very easy to get washed out and to appear pale and sickly if you do not have some color in your face. Just try to keep it fairly natural so that it does not call attention to itself. You do not have to look like a harlot! If you are not adept at doing your own makeup just go to any department store or specialty shop and get yourself a makeover. They will help you to find the right colors and products for your particular skin and they will teach you how to apply it to suit your style. You might also solicit help from any girlfriends you know who really seem to have a handle on the makeup business. It sounds a little silly perhaps, but it can be a very valuable lesson to learn how to prep your face to complement your sporty new brand!

Lastly there is the issue of jewelry and accessories. Once again, good taste must prevail, and you must remember that you do not want things that will distract from your work or from your product. I have always heard that a good rule of thumb is to pick one piece of jewelry—a bracelet, a necklace, a ring, a set of earrings—and limit yourself to that. Men and women who come into the room with all of the above dangling and jangling off of every body part often distract the auditors from the work. Be careful too about what features certain accessories accentuate. If you are showing skin around your chest and wearing a necklace that falls right into the open region, it may very well call our attention needlessly away from your eyes. As I said before, just be sure to look in the mirror before you walk out the door and ask yourself if there is anything diverting about your attire.

You also need to consider piercings in the audition room. The big crazes these days are nose rings and tongue studs (I also see a lot of men with upper-ear posts), but if you choose to wear any of these fashions, you need to understand what it might imply for the people behind the table. I have a student who is a sweet ingénue—the picture of innocence and girl-next-door-ism when she comes into the room. Last year she got her nose pierced, but she continued to wear pretty girlie dresses and to market herself as young and girlish. I had to point out to her that even with a little nose stud, there is a mixed message in the packaging and that the piercing was distracting from what she really wanted to say. I do not generally consider myself terribly old-fashioned, but I couldn't quite reconcile the classic ingénue with a nose ring. It is perfectly fine to express yourself through body piercings and tattoos, but you must remember that anything visible in an audition sends a message of sorts and you must stay on your message.

As far as dance attire goes for those of you who are musical theatre performers, I have one piece of advice that is imperative and a second that is more of a subtle, subliminal tip. The imperative word is that you must own professional dance clothing if you plan to make a career out of auditioning for musicals. It is not okay to throw on baggy sweats, T-shirts, and sneakers (and it's never okay to plan to dance in your socks). Nothing looks more unclean and unprofessional. Put some thought and money into your dance gear and come in with clothing that accentuates your line and shows off your physique. Be sure to bring actual dance shoes with you—and bring several types so that you are prepared for anything they may throw at you during a dance call (taps, heels, jazz sneakers, ballet flats). Show the people behind the table that you take your career seriously; it will go a long way toward them wanting to work with you on their project.

The second little tidbit I want to offer you is to try to extend your brand into your dance outfits if possible. I know people who choose a color scheme for all of their audition attire, and they allow that color palette to extend into their dance clothing as well—in other words, their go-to look is mainly a bold green, for example, and they choose the same color green for their audition leotards. When you go shopping for dance clothing, keep your new brand in the forefront of your mind and see if there are options in dancewear that fit into your marketing plan. You never know what kind of impression that will make in the room.

In summing up about attire, just remember that you worked very hard to create a product for "You, Inc." with a unique and specific message that you hope will stick in the minds of directors and industry people. Be sure to be yourself and to express your personality when you dress for auditions. Wear clothing that shows off your strengths and distracts from your weaknesses, and above all, in which you feel incredibly powerful. One other tip I have heard and found to be true is that you should wear underwear that makes you feel sexy. Even though it is underneath your clothing and (hopefully!) will not be seen in the audition, the underwear is literally the closest thing to your skin, and if you wear undergarments that make you feel sexy, it will affect your confidence in the room in a palpable way.

HEADSHOTS

The next important step in crafting your career is to invest in professional-grade headshots. Your headshot will serve as the calling card for your small business, and it will essentially be your "golden arches," so I cannot urge you enough to take this seriously. I get so frustrated with actors who are unwilling or unable to spend the money to get high-quality photographs,[4] or who decide to go into the business and saturate the casting offices with "temporary" headshots. You only get one chance to make a first impression, so I want you to really consider that as you make these decisions. If money is an issue, start making a plan to save up now. Most of you reading this probably invested between $30,000 and $120,000 on your education, so another $500 to get all that training into the room seems like a small expenditure at this point!

We have spent a good deal of time discussing the importance of branding yourself and how much power that can have over your career. If you are not quite there yet on creating your own personal, professional identity, you may wish to hold off on getting headshots. When actor friends come to me to look through their proofs after a photo session, the first question I ask before I will even look at their pictures is: "What are we selling here?" If we do not start from

---

4. And by spending the money, I do not mean $1,000+. Some of the best headshots I have ever seen have come at a cost of $400 or less.

that point, we are likely to get confused by different information, such as which headshot looks the prettiest, which headshot is most artistic, which headshot our mom or our boyfriend likes best, and so forth. In fact, before you even sit for a session with a photographer, you should be discussing your brand with her and expressing what you are trying to capture. Actor pictures are not cheap, so why take the chance on not getting exactly what you need in order to make your business thrive?

The first step on the road to getting brilliant headshots is to find the right photographer for you. It is not enough just to go to anyone who knows how to point and shoot a camera. Theatrical pictures are very different than model photography and artistic photography. There is a style and an approach to these shots that requires an industry professional to truly comprehend. So rule number one is: Do not let just anyone with a camera do your head-shots. I do not care if they are doing it for free or on the cheap. I do not care if they are your cousin or your girlfriend's uncle. And I do not care if they have a home studio where they shoot award-winning still life. You need to go to someone who photographs successful, working actors. Period.[5]

Many schools (my own included) help their students by setting up a group rate with a professional photographer out of New York or Los Angeles or Washington, DC. This way, the young perform-ers can get professional-quality pictures without paying the full industry fee. While this can be an immensely beneficial deal, just be careful that your school is not doing you a disservice by match-ing you up with the wrong photographer for your personal style. You need to do some serious research here and decide on the right per-son to capture your "logo." The headshot will precede you into the room at open-call auditions. It will be what you submit to request an audition appointment. It will be in the playbill of any show in which you are fortunate enough to perform. And it will be the front page of your personal website. Am I conveying the importance of this picture quite enough? You need the person who can capture your arch or your swoosh.

---

5. Can you tell I have strong opinions on the subject?

I highly recommend that you start by going on www.repro
ductions.com and exploring their amazing directory. Reproductions is a company out of New York City that prints bulk order,
professional-grade headshots (among other services), and they keep
a database of photographers on both coasts as a resource for actors
to find the right match for them. There you will find links to dozens
and dozens of professionals' websites where you can view their work
in gallery form. Each photographer will have his own personal approach to shooting actors. You need to find the approach that "gels"
with the product you are selling. Even if you are not getting your
headshots done in New York or LA, the galleries can at least help
you to get ideas about what good headshots should look like. If you
shoot with someone in Ohio, you can certainly show them the work
of others to guide them toward what you are hoping to achieve.

I suggest you start by eliminating any photographers who seem to
place their artistic aesthetic over the importance of featuring the individual actor. Believe it or not, there are photographers who will tell
actors that they *only* shoot one style for all clients. You do not want
to be just another model for someone else's art—you want someone
to capture your personal essence in a unique and powerful way.

As you browse the different websites, take note of which photos
you see that strike a note for you and make you think, "That would
be something similar to how I would like to be marketed." See if
you can compile a short list of three to six different options that
would be viable for you. Then it is up to you to start contacting the
photographers and gathering more information from them. First of
all, know what your realistic budget is. Obviously, price may be an
issue, so I could certainly understand you ruling out exorbitant-fee
photographers from your short list (remember, this does not have
to run you upward of $1,000). But see if you can find one or two
options within your price range. Next, you will want to set up a
conversation with any photographer you are considering, just to
see if your personalities gel together. Remember that you are a
consumer here and you need to be shrewd about business decisions. You are going to spend between two and four hours with
this person and you are going to essentially have to bare your soul
for her lens, so your comfort with her is of the utmost importance.

(This is why I want you to be careful about jumping on the school group rate deal—quite often it works out great, but every once in a while there is an incompatibility issue and cheap unfortunately outweighs practical.)

Find out how each prospective photographer does his or her shoots. How much time will you have? How many "looks" or outfits will you get to shoot? Will you be shooting indoors or outdoors or both? Will the photographer help consult on attire and makeup? In general, find out what his or her general approaches are. I know several photographers who will encourage clients to bring their favorite music to play during the session, just to set the mood for the actor. Some will get you to open up and tell stories as they photograph you casually, so they capture you in a more candid, less posed way. (These are my favorite photographers, personally!) Still others will work in a more artificial way, asking you to pose and either think of something specific or do something physical that causes a certain look to happen for you. There are many approaches to photographing people in these sessions, so you should know going in what you are getting for your investment and make sure it is what you want before you commit.

At this point in time, some basic things to be sure of include:

- The photographs must be in color, not black and white.
- They must be *head*shots, not full body shots.[6]
- They should shoot a mix of landscape (horizontal configuration) and portrait (vertical) shots so that you have options—more on that soon.
- If they are doing your makeup (or subcontracting someone to do it) it *must* look like you! Be very careful not to let someone style you in a way that you won't be able to match at auditions. More on that soon, too.
- You should be on the same page with the photographer from the get-go about what you're hoping to capture and sell with these

6. Some old-fashioned shots used to be either full or three-quarter body shots. With the advanced use of the Internet and online submissions your pictures will be reduced to thumbnail size for many casting offices. The more body you have in your shot, the smaller your face will appear in those thumbnails.

photos. Do not let there be surprises when you get your digital proofs[7] at the end.
- Find out what the photographer's policy is on satisfaction and future shoots. Many will guarantee that you will be happy with the shoot or else they will do a reshoot for free. Also, some photographers will offer a deep discount to clients who return for another session within a certain number of years (since actors tend to need new headshots every few years anyway).

Although it sounds like a lot of information to gather before you even book a session, trust me, you'll be glad you did. I have seen too many actors jump in and pay exorbitant amounts of money for mediocre headshots. When they show them to me and I ask them what kind of research they did before committing to their photographer, they generally tell me that they didn't do much. And of course the unfortunate thing is that they wind up having to go to another photographer and pay to get new shots within a year since the original ones are useless to them. So take control of your career, be a good consumer, and make sure you make informed, strategic decisions on things as important as headshots.

I am going to digress from photography for a moment at this point and expand on this thought of control, which is a notion we will come back to several times within this book. If I can give you nothing else throughout these pages, let me at least give you the gift of empowerment. What do I mean? Well, I know too many actors who view themselves as pawns, doing their best just to book work and relinquishing all control over their careers to the casting directors and the producers. This is how they live their lives on a grand scale as well—never taking the reins on their own lives or valuing themselves as artists and as human beings. I want you to be an empowered artist. I want you to value what you have to offer the world, because believe me; it is a great gift. Do not for a moment think that it is okay to be taken advantage of or that because you may not be a big Broadway star, that means that you are not worthy of be-

---

7. Another result of advanced technology is that most photographers are now shooting digitally and sending you the session via a web link to look at, as opposed to the old proof sheets that people used to get a few years ago.

ing treated with respect. Now, I am not suggesting that you behave like a spoiled diva—that is no way to establish a long, successful career—however, I am suggesting that you do not just assume that whatever the world offers you is all that there is for you. Does this make sense? We will discuss this more, as I said, but for now, as we are talking about setting up headshots for you, I wanted to open up this idea of empowerment in order to encourage you to feel like you have some real power over what your photos will look like and how your session will go. Too many actors just want to pay their money and have the photographer tell them exactly what to do, no questions asked. I am encouraging you to make it a collaborative experience! This way, you will be able to look at the results feeling confident in your options because you led the session from the beginning toward your desired goal.

Now that I have said that, let's get back to the process of getting your incredible headshots taken.

Once you have settled on a photographer with whom you "gel" and feel comfortable and confident, and you have established a sense of what you want from her in the session, and you have scheduled a shoot date, it's time to get prepared for that appointment. You will notice that in structuring this book, I began with attire before I discussed headshots. This is because I want you to have a strong sense of physical identity before you try to get someone to photograph you. The easiest answer to the question of "What should I wear?" is "Wear your brand." At this point, you have created some looks for yourself that align with how you want to present yourself to the industry, so what to wear in your headshots should be a simple no-brainer. I think it is perfectly fine when people wear some of their audition attire in the shoot. One powerful technique of marketing that I briefly mentioned earlier and that we will continue to discuss later is repetition, so having a picture with a certain outfit or "look" and then walking into the room with that same look can be a strong memorable device for you.

Think clearly about what physical attribute(s) you really want to feature in your photos (e.g., Do you have stunning eyes, lips, hair, cheekbones, teeth, dimples? Do you want your figure accentuated—as long as it is done in a tasteful way?), and choose clothing that helps you make those features *pop* in the picture. That can be done with color and cut of clothing, and it can also be done through the use of makeup and personal styling. Just be sure that whatever you do to yourself on the day of the photo shoot is what you plan to do on the morning of any audition—even if we are talking about five a.m.! Because the single most important aspect of your headshot is that *it must look like you.* I see too many women get overly made up for their pictures, to the point where it looks like someone else. I also see women feel the need to curl (or straighten) their hair to look great in their pictures, but then they walk into auditions with their hair completely different. I have seen men take headshots with a beard to appear older, but then they show up completely shaven to the audition, or vice versa. All of these instances are major faux pas on actors' parts.[8] The bottom line is that your headshot is your brand logo. You send it ahead so that we have an expectation of what will walk in the room. We have called you in based on that expectation. If you cannot match the brand (remember, your brand is your promise!), then it does not matter how talented you are, you have already lost us at hello. So think carefully about how you want to look for your photo shoot because you absolutely must be able to deliver on whatever those pictures advertise.

Just as we discussed with attire earlier, be sure that the choices of clothing you bring to the headshot session point out your strengths and your brand attributes. Do not plan to accessorize in your shots because very often a pair of earrings or a necklace will completely distract from your own physical features. So think clean, simple looks. Pick colors that go great with your skin tone and your hair, and avoid patterns and logos and frills. And just like choosing clothing for an actual audition, make sure that your level of formal versus casual is reflective of who you are and what you wish to present to the world (I very often see men do an entire session in a suit and tie and I ask them if they are trying to sell themselves as an actor or as a young lawyer). The underwear trick is also particularly

---

8. The exception is if you are altering your look for a specific role you have been hired to play and you plan to return to your headshot look after the job is done; in which case you would make that clear to the casting team when you walk in. If it is a long-term contract, you may wish to get temporary headshots to use while you are sporting the different look.

useful for a headshot session. Wear undergarments that make you feel incredibly sexy and powerful and your confidence will shine through in the pictures.

A lot of young actors tell me that they like to change their look with a certain amount of regularity. They like to cut or color their hair or grow or shave a beard because they get bored with maintaining the same exact style year-round. So they want to know what to do about headshots. Should they have several different headshots to cover any of their particular moods or whims? To this I say: You have to create some consistency. Remember, it's part of branding and marketing to create a *sticky consistency*. If you are constantly changing from long to short hair, from straight to curly, from blond to red, from beard to clean, and so forth, it is going to be that much harder for people to identify you in their minds. So as hard as it may be for you, I think the strongest marketing tool you can utilize is one of steadiness and reliability. Choose an identity and wear it out for a while. See what it gets you. After a couple of years, it is certainly acceptable to reevaluate and rebrand yourself (look at any major corporation—they go through rebrands all the time, but they do it strategically). But just realize that changing looks and rebranding means entirely revisiting the branding steps as well as attire and headshots, and so forth.

Finally, it is very important to take pristine care of yourself in the days leading up to your headshot session. You are making a substantial and pivotal investment in your career, and you cannot afford to have it marred by exhaustion or poor physical health. I would urge you to avoid alcohol and large amounts of caffeine the week of your shoot, and be sure to string together several consecutive nights of solid sleep. If exercise and good diet are part of your normal routine (which they should be if you want to be a success in this industry!), be sure to stick with that routine so that you enter your photo day feeling great about yourself physically. If, for some reason, good health is not something that is normally of high priority for you, you may wish to make an extra effort that week, just so that you bring a glow and energy with you into the room when you go to get photographed. Spend a few days revisiting all your work on branding and repeating your phrase or statement over to yourself like a mantra in order to psych yourself up for a successful and fun photo shoot.

Hopefully, this will be a very exciting endeavor for you. Some people get scared to be in front of the camera—they get nervous and retreat back into their heads, which can be deadly, as you can well imagine. But if you have really planned a step-by-step approach and you have been clear about what it is you want to capture and you are solid on who you are and what you have to offer the world, you should approach this day with eagerness and anticipation. This is the day that you get your "swoosh" on!

When you arrive at the studio (or whatever the shoot location happens to be), take a moment to reestablish rapport with the photographer. Show her what you brought for outfits and explain once again what you are looking to have your shots say about you. If you have hired a hair and makeup artist to prep you for the session, be sure to clearly communicate how you need to appear in the photos so that you can match it for every audition. Again, let them know about the brand you have chosen to market, and also let them know if there are any particular physical elements you would like to accentuate in the photos.

From this point on, you must begin to trust the photographer. All the encouragement I gave you about controlling your career should have happened earlier on in the process as you screened and interviewed potential photographers. Now you are there and you have established a specific goal in terms of what you want to convey with your shots, so you have to allow the photographer to help you make that come to fruition. She will talk you through the shoot and (hopefully) keep you relaxed and comfortable. Hopefully you will have a lot of fun and you will really open up and be yourself and as I said earlier, bare your soul for the lens. Try to offer the camera opportunities to catch you really being yourself in a raw, candid way. If something strikes you as funny, laugh and enjoy it. I guarantee you that if you let yourself go in this way, the results will be much more magical and useful to you than if you simply pose, smile, look serious, and so forth.

And just remember, these photos must capture *you* and *who you are*. We are not going for a specific character (I have heard photographers tell clients things like, "Give me your best 'Hamlet' look for these shots," and inevitably the results are just plain absurd). So be yourself, relax, and enjoy the process.

Generally speaking, about a week or two after you complete your photo session, you will receive the proofs of the shoot to go through, share with others, and narrow down your best options. As I said earlier, most photographers are using online, digital proofs these days, which makes it especially easy to show your photos to people whose opinions you value. In most cases, the session you paid for will include two touch-ups. This means that you will pick the two photos that you like best and the photographer will enhance them so that they look perfect,[9] and then they will give you 8 × 10 prints of those two photos for you to reproduce.

Before you make the mistake of launching your pictures all over Facebook for the world to post comments, I want you to make a strategic plan. Create a list of the most valued advisors you have *within the industry*, and plan on going directly to them for feedback on your headshots. I specify people within the industry because you need to be sure you are getting good information. I do not mean to disparage the importance of your mother's or your girlfriend's opinions, but it is often hard to get objective information from people who are just looking to help you find the prettiest picture of you. You need to seek out teachers, mentors, and directors (certainly agents and casting directors if you have access to any) who can offer you specific reactions to what they see when they look at your headshots. It is more than a matter of like or dislike; rather, it is about finding out what message each of your prospective shots is sending (remember our branding exercise in the first chapter?). You need to choose a headshot that will make an impact in the room, so I suggest you begin by leading the people from whom you are seeking advice—tell them your branding statement and what you are going for with your photos, and ask them to respond with that in

---

9. Be very careful about the touch-ups. Remember, these must still look exactly like you. I suggest that touch-ups include eliminating flyaway hairs and minor blemishes and possibly making minor color and contrast adjustments. But I have seen photographers doctor photos to the point where the actor's skin tone is altered and features such as beauty marks and freckles are wiped completely out. This is no good. Also, be sure that any background "stuff" is blurred out of the final photo.

mind. Ask them to objectively assess which photos stay consistent with the message you are trying to send with your headshots.

I have a student who got headshots recently and came to me for a review of her proofs. When I asked her what she was going for in her photo, she told me she wanted to continue to trade on her youthful looks and her ability to play young teenagers, even at the age of twenty-one. Adjectives she was using to describe herself included innocent, sweet, precocious, and wholesome—all of which were perfectly in line with her looks, her abilities, and other people's perception of her. That said, one of the most beautiful shots in the bunch (and her absolute favorite) happened to be a very sultry, seductive shot. She wanted to know what I thought of her using it as a possible alternative, since it was so sexy and mature and it really would have made a great impression and got her appointments. I had to discourage her from making this her primary or even her secondary headshot, simply because as beautiful as it was, it did not represent the product she was selling. I suggested that she keep the picture on file in case she decides to change directions in the next couple of years. I also told her it might be fine to have that kind of photo in a gallery on her website; but as far as sending it into the room for auditions, I warned her that it would send the completely wrong message. Could she be sexy and sultry? Absolutely. But is that really what she is going to make a living doing? Absolutely not. This is the type of consideration you need to make when choosing the best shots for you. (I have another girl who is in the same boat; only she is fairly busty. We had to make certain that her headshots did not contain cleavage, in order for her to maintain that "girlish" message.)

Ultimately, you want to come up with *one great shot* to represent you and your business. That shot needs to make a bold statement about who you are, and it needs to entice us to want to call you in and meet you. The shot might say, "I've got a secret, and wouldn't you like to know," or it might say, "I am such fun, you really want to get to know me." Just be sure it says something other than "Hi, I'm nice." (Boring!) There is an old school of thought that an actor needs a "smiley" and a "serious" headshot. I could not disagree more with that notion. It basically implies that directors are not creative enough to imagine you in a lighthearted play if you are serious in your shot or that you could not possibly do serious drama if you are smiling in the photo. Remember, this picture is not representative of what you can do; rather, it is representative of *who you are*. You have worked so hard to brand yourself, so trust that you will be able to rely on the one shot that broadcasts your brand, rather than trying to have different pictures for every different type of project or every emotional state you might need to play. I mentioned the importance of repetition in marketing before, and this goes right along with that notion. You want your photograph to become a recognizable "logo" for you, and it is hard to make that stick if you are saturating the market with multiple different headshots.

I will tell you, however, when it becomes useful to have an alternative headshot or two: if you plan to split your interests between theatre and film/TV/commercials. There is a bit of a different aesthetic in the world of film work, and oftentimes an actor can benefit from distinguishing between a "theatrical" shot and a "filmic" shot. It is hard for me to explain this in a scientific way, but I will try to expound. For starters, in theatrical photos, the configuration of your shot (landscape versus portrait) does not really matter. Sure, everyone has his own opinion, and someone will tell you that vertical is the only way to go, while others will respond much more to horizontal. But really, there is no rule when it comes to a good theatrical headshot. For film and TV, though, I would recommend that you lean toward a horizontal or landscape configuration. There is a simple, psychological reason that this is effective: it is how we see your face when we look at it on film. Think about it—television and movie screens are rectangles in which we tend to look at faces close-up and just off center. If you can find a great shot that emulates that setup, it can provide a subconscious advantage for you as it makes it easier to picture you on-screen.

Secondly, whereas your theatrical headshot needs to broadcast exactly who you are as a person, a film and TV shot should put you more into a box, typewise. As it turns out, in theatre we really want to know the individual actor and we want to cast a great person who brings a lot to the table and who can work his way into a believable portrayal of a role. On camera, however, it is much more important that we cast someone who is genuinely, believably the role being cast. It is much harder for great acting to compensate for wrong type on camera. If they need a lawyer, they want someone who really broadcasts "lawyer." (Now those suit shots might come in handy!) To that end, you should be sure you do your homework and watch a lot of television and movies and know where you fit into that market. Are you a half-hour sitcom type? Do you belong in the world of *Law and Order* or *CSI* and other such prime-time dramas? Are you an indie film type? Can we see you as a young soccer mom selling hand soap? These are important questions to ponder if you are going to approach the world of on-camera work. And once you know where you really fit in, choose a secondary shot that really makes a clear statement.

Beyond that, you will not have a need for more than one head-shot to represent you, theatrically speaking. Once you have gathered feedback from your trusted advisors, hopefully you will have been able to choose the go-to photograph for your new logo. Be sure that you are truly happy with the one you pick, because it becomes a very expensive endeavor to change your mind after you have had prints made. For these photos, you want to make certain that you choose a high-quality printing company. Again, it makes me ill when young actors spend hundreds of dollars on great photographs, but then they go to their local Walgreens or Costco to have reproductions made. A high-quality print for your high-quality photo is of the utmost importance, so do not do this on the cheap. There are plenty of companies available to you online that will take your proof and have bulk copies sent out to you within a week at a very affordable rate. Just be sure that you are getting the best quality possible. Three companies that I have found to be very reliable are Reproductions (www.reproductions.com), Precision Photos (www .precisionphotos.com), and Argentum (www.argentum.com). All three specialize in actor headshots, so you know they understand your business and not just the business of photographic reprints.

You want to make sure that you print your shots in matte finish (as opposed to glossy) and 8" × 10" (as opposed to 8½" × 11"). You also want your shot to be surrounded by a solid white border, and your name should be printed inside that border. Do not have your name printed directly on the photo, and do not skip the border—it is just standard practice, it looks clean, and it makes the casting offices' lives easier.

The other thing that we need to consider here for the first time in our discussion is how your name relates to your brand. Once you have established a marketable product for your own little company called "You, Inc.," you need to realize that your name will go hand in hand with your headshot in representing you to the industry. That said, be sure you are happy with your name before you emblazon it on hundreds of photos, business cards, and a website. I suggest you check with Actors' Equity Association as well as Screen Actors Guild to be sure a member of those unions does not already have your name. (Names are exclusive in the actors' unions.) Even though you might not need to worry about joining the union for a few years, you certainly do not want to have to change your name once you have established yourself. Not to mention the fact that you may not like your given name. I have two graduating seniors this year who were both very unhappy with their last names. One of them decided to create a new last name for herself, and the other decided to drop hers and just use her first and middle names. But both of them have felt much more confident in their brands since committing to the name changes. The sooner you realize you wish to go by a different name, the easier it will be on your career and your brand.

Decide what you want people to call you when you walk in the room and when you take a job. Look back at your branding statement and make sure your name rings consistent with that.[10] There is nothing that says being formal and using three names makes you somehow more appealing. Sometimes the three-name thing can get obnoxious with actors, especially if it makes for a very long name. But if you really want to be known as a three-named actor (and there are some very good, successful ones), then by all means go for it, just as long as you are not doing it just for the sake of being pretentious. Finally, if your name is Christopher but nobody calls you that, it is perfectly acceptable to call yourself Chris on your

---

10. I had a student named Jonathan, who often went by Jon or Jonny. When we talked through his brand and looked at his shots, he decided that Jonny was the most suitable name for how he was trying to present himself to the world, so he went with that, and it helped determine which photo was best for him.

headshot. Remember that whatever you print on that picture is what people will call you when you walk in the room, and it is what they will associate with your brand.

Now that you have given your name full consideration, you have only to choose the font you want to carry that brand upon your headshots. It is shrewd marketing to find a font for your name that will be consistent on your headshot, your resume, your business cards, and your website. Once again, it is another opportunity to find a sticky consistency. One of my former students is extremely artistic and has a very pristine and attractive signature. She found software that allowed her to sign her name personally and save it as a computer file, so that she could use her own handwritten signature as her name on all of her actor business materials. It is unique and quite handsome and it really speaks to who she is as an artist. Think about how you want your name to appear when people see it for the first time.

RESUMES

The flip side (literally) of your shiny (but not glossy!) new headshot is a polished resume. Now before we launch into the how-tos of crafting your stunningly professional resume, let me tell you a few things that the actor's resume should *not* be:

- It is not a standard business resume. So do not use a template from a word processor to format it like you would if you were applying for a job at an office.
- It is not a laundry list of every single performance you have ever done since birth. Quantity does not make this document more impressive (unless you have done multiple major Broadway-level gigs).
- It is not a dumping ground to list all your work experience, both in and out of theatre (e.g., "day jobs," technical theatre and/or directing, etc.). There is a way to cover some of that important, related stuff, which we will discuss soon, but let's really focus on making this an acting resume.
- It is not a place to lie or embellish *anything*. You will get caught!

Good—I am glad we got that out of the way. Now, let's start from the beginning and help you design a killer, eye-catching representation of who you are.

The first question to ask yourself is: What is the purpose of a resume? If you answered, "To tell them what shows I have done and what roles I have played," you are only partially correct. While that is most actors' main concern when designing their resumes, I can tell you that unless you have big Broadway, tour, or regional credits to your name, the shows and roles are really just a small percentage of what we are looking at as we scan down your page.

The real purpose of the actor's resume is to give us a glimpse into who you are as a person and as an artist. A well-designed resume will continue trading on your branding statement (that's right—another opportunity to broadcast your brand), and it will give us all sorts of clues as to where you have come from, what you have done, what you value, and what you bring to the table when you approach your theatrical work. Can you believe all that information can be conveyed in a one-page document that looks like a bunch of lists? Well, trust me, it can. It does not always work out that way for everyone, but if you follow my advice and put the time and thought into this project, you will find that the back side of your headshot will pack much more of a punch than the performers who simply build off of a template and list things without any heart and thought invested.

As we walk through this process, I will offer you a number of pointers about what really looks attractive and what really does not work when we look at actors' resumes. But I am not going to give you *the way* to design yours, because I want you to have a little creative freedom of expression within the parameters of professional expectations. I will show you some examples of good and bad resumes, which you are more than welcome to reference and steal from (only copy the good ones, though, please!), but I want you to know that as long as yours is clean, well formatted, and professional, you can create a document that really conveys your own personal aesthetic.

We begin with your name. Remember how at the end of the last section I told you that your name is of major importance to your brand and your marketing scheme? Well, just as we want to see your name printed boldly in the border of your headshot so that it carries a bit of punch to it and jumps off the page, we want to see that name hollering out to us at the top of your resume. I see too many actors choose to print their names in a small font, comparable to the size of everything else on the resume. This is a huge mistake. My advice to you is, as I said before, find a font that you can use as your go-to style for anywhere your name appears, and use it on the top of the resume in a text size that really makes it stand out. I have seen some formatted with the actor's name left justified, and I have also seen it front and centered (this is more common). Neither is right or wrong; you get to make a choice.

And if I may digress for just a moment—let us talk about one of the most important factors in your perfect resume: format. At the end of the day, you will have a lot of choices to make in terms of how you want to lay things out and how you want that page to look, but no matter what, it *must be clean and eye catching.* As a director, I must first be able to see your organizational skills and your ability to put the time and effort into creating a slick, polished document; but I also need the resume to function properly in order to make my job easier. I need to scan down quickly and find the most important information in a simple, structured manner. I often suggest that to test the quality of formatting, either look at a resume from a great distance or blur your eyes when looking at one up close. The idea is to ignore the actual information listed and to be able to see the resume as more of a picture. Is it attractive? Does it flow? Are the columns evenly spaced? Does it appear organized and not too cluttered? When looking at it from a distance, does the name still jump off the page? This is all very important.

Take a look at the example on page 56 of a horribly formatted resume. (This was a real resume I received from a student of mine before she had taken my class, but I changed the name and all the information to protect the innocent!) Notice how when you hold it at a distance or squint at it, the name is too tiny to be seen. This actor also does what many novices do, which is to use text boxes with visible borders to separate information. I cannot tell you how unattractive that is. I also want you to observe the cramming of everything up into the top half of the page. We want you to be able to cut your resume down to an 8" × 10" size to line up evenly with your headshot, but the information you provide on the resume must utilize the page. I do not mean that you have to add filler and have information crammed into ten inches of paper; rather, you must space it in such a way that we are not looking at four to six inches of blank paper. In other words, let it breathe. Can you also see how bad her columns are? Because she used the space bar to move the cursor across the page, her columns are all uneven and wonky (that is a term I love to use—it is not technical nor particularly eloquent, but it conveys exactly what I need it to say). Using the Tab key instead would have fixed this problem. Finally, how many typos can you count? Not even knowing whether or not she has spelled people's names correctly (which is absolutely *vital*—people get very touchy about having their names spelled right!), I count at least five misspellings. Take a good look and tell me if this resume makes you want to get to know this girl.

Mary Perkins

(555) 555-5555
singdiva@comcast.net

Height: 5'7"		Hair: Blond
Weight: 150		Eyes: Hazel
	Soprano	

REGIONAL THEATRE:

The Vagina Monologues	Ensemble	On Fire Theatre ProJect, VA
(LaTasha Jones, Dir.)		
The Little Princess's Birthday	Dragon	Shinig Star Productions, IL

EDUCATIONAL THEATRE:

A Turn for the Nurse	Sylvia Crane	Downers Grove North HS
Anton in Show Business	T-Anne	State University of State
The Visit	Frau Schill	Western America University

EDUCATION:

Working on: BFA, Music Theatre: State University of State
    Acting: Sally Anders, Mark Kintney, Dr. Joe Frandsen
    Voice: David Newstead, Dr. Eric Kim
    Dance: Jesse Gorney, Alex Arnold, Robert Scherholder
Western America University (no degree earned, transferred to State University)
    Acting: Billy Kind, D.C. Winslow
    Voice: Matt Bearn, Kit Kameron
    Dance: Harvey Clemmons, Dennis Barksdale

SPECIAL SKILLS:

Dialects (Cockney, Standard Brittish, American Southern, Receptionist Voice); Willing to
dye/cut hair; Can quickly memorize music; Alphabetising

Pretty bad, huh? It's actually laughable—I show this resume as part of a presentation I do all over the country, and it always gets a reaction of disbelief. People think I am making this up. But you must trust me when I tell you that there are many "actors" who even call themselves professionals who think that this sort of nonchalance is acceptable. They feel that what they have to offer is their talent and that no matter how they carry themselves professionally, once they get in the room, their skills will speak for themselves. But remember, friends, that you make a first impression well before you walk in the room. You have either submitted this resume in order to request an appointment, or the monitor at an open call has sent it to the artistic team in advance of you coming in so that they know something about you when you walk into the audition studio. If I received this resume before I met you, I would be far less inclined to be rooting for you. I would make assumptions about your training and about your level of commitment to professionalism.

In my first book, *Get the Callback* (Scarecrow Press, 2009), I open by equating a production to the director's baby. I advise that actors find ways of being worthy of "holding the baby" and gaining the trust of the production team. One solid way to start down the right path to gaining our trust is to demonstrate that you are serious about this business and that you are committed to excellence and to hard work. You can go a long way to showing that through your headshot and your resume.

And so, back to the process of crafting your winning resume . . .

Once you have chosen a font for your name and you have set it atop the page, it is time to fill in each of the standard requisite sections of the resume. Although I told you there is not a singular way that these must all look (format-wise) nor a specifically required set of information, there are some basic criteria that will be expected, and you would be wise to cover each of the following areas to an appropriate degree:

1. Contact information and vital statistics
2. Related performance experience
3. Training
4. Special skills

Contact Info and Vital Stats

It seems quite logical to begin with this section so that no one has to search far to find out how to contact you. In a sense, this is the most important information on the resume, which is probably why it normally stands at the top (just below the name, of course). Over the years that I have been in the business, the expectations for this section have changed and evolved. And while there are no hard and fast rules—and by the way, everybody you speak with will have a different opinion on what should and should not be included—we can certainly discuss what might go in this section.

The first question is, are you a member of any of the actors' unions or of the Equity Membership Candidate (EMC) program? If you are, then you are required to list that on your resume, and the rule of thumb is that it immediately follows your name. If you are not a member of the unions, then do not put anything down; I've seen actors write "Non-Union" on their resumes, and that is completely unnecessary. However, you may need to list any of the following if they are appropriate to you: AEA; SAG-AFTRA; EMC (Actors' Equity Association; Screen Actors Guild–American Federation of Television and Radio Actors; Equity Membership Candidate, respectively).

Not long ago, performers would always have an indication on their resume of how exactly they would rank or tout their skills; for instance: "Actor" or "Actor/Singer/Dancer" or "Actor/Singer," and so on. However, it seems as though there is a movement away from having this information on the resume. When you really think about it, it's fairly useless. We know you are an actor; otherwise you would not be submitting this headshot and resume. And as for your other performance skills, we will get an indication of where your strengths lie from reading your credits and from seeing you in the audition room. A lot of actors found themselves pigeonholed because they considered singing or dancing their strong suit and so they put "Actor" lower on the list, only to find that many directors do not want to work with people who do not consider themselves actors first. So perhaps it is best to dispense with the label.

If you have agent representation, that would be the next point of information below your name. Check with your agent to find out how he wants you to list his information; but generally speaking (particularly if you are signed with an office, as opposed to freelancing) your agent's contact information would be the primary way for directors and casting offices to get in touch with you.

I am sure that many of you reading this have your name written and nothing else so far. Perhaps you are not at the stage where you have joined the unions or landed an agent. Do not let either of these factors worry you in the least. It is absolutely possible (and quite common) to build a career for yourself without having an agent, and everyone who sticks it out finds his way into the union when the time is right—we will talk more about unions in a later chapter.

So now let's add your contact information to this page. The three imperative sources of contact that I want you to have listed on your resume are phone number, e-mail address, and website.[11] Whatever you do, do not list your home address on your resume. It is totally unnecessary, and you do not need it floating around out there in an industry in which not everyone is on the up-and-up, so to speak. For phone number, I suggest you list your cell as opposed to your home (if you even still keep a home phone—I know I do not!). The other option is to enroll in what is called a service. Basically a service is just a voice-mail system where people can leave you messages, which you can retrieve at any time. Using a service puts a little buffer between you and the people whose hands might wind up holding your resume. It allows them to contact you and leave any pertinent information in a message, but they would not be able to get you directly on the phone. The advantages are that you will never have to worry about less-than-savory people hounding you on your cell phone; you will never worry about taking an important phone call while you are running from place to place or while you are getting into bad-cell-reception land (more about taking calls later); and you will never be put in a situation in which you are asked to make an important decision without getting to process the information and think about it a little. So a service is definitely something to consider. Some people even list both cell and service numbers on their resume, just to give directors and casting offices

---

11. Do not worry if you don't have a website up yet. By the end of our work together, you will. For now, you can leave that off if you're not ready.

the option of talking to them or leaving a message. The service is not vital, nor is it even industry standard anymore, but it is certainly an option to consider.

Next, include your e-mail address. Do yourself a huge favor and create an e-mail account for your professional career, separate from your personal and/or school e-mails. This e-mail should be easy to remember (not too many numbers) and it should have your name either as the address or included in it. For example: John.Doe@ yahoo.com or Doe_Jane@hotmail.com or JohnDoe21@gmail.com. Notice how these are all simple variations on the actors' names with very little else to confuse the situation and keep it from being memorable. I also want you to avoid the temptation to be cute and clever in your professional e-mail address. Do not use things such as BroadwayBaby214, LovesToSing99, BigBelterGurl1991, and so forth. If you feel the need to use such cutesy handles for your e-mail, then keep them for personal use and not for business. Finally, if you are still in school, do not list your school e-mail address (ending in .edu) on your resume. Remember that school is a finite endeavor, and you will not be using that e-mail much longer. However, your resume can be sent out and referenced months and even years after it lands in a casting office. You do not want someone trying to contact you at your school address if you have long since stopped checking that e-mail.

Before we move on to vital statistics, I want to remind you to play with formatting here. Depending on whether or not you have a website up, you may want to space all the contact information across one line. You may want to have the contact information stacked in a left-hand column and the vital stats stacked in a right-hand column. You may want to split phone number and e-mail address over center and then have the website centered on the line below. There are a myriad of permutations possible here, so you need to just play and find out what looks best to your eye.

Now we get into some pretty contentious ground as we begin to talk about vital statistics. Industry people all have strong opinions on what should and should not be included in this section. I do not believe that there is a definitive right or wrong answer, but I will list for you all the items that *might* be included and I will leave it to you to decide what you use and what you omit. I will also explain to you the argument on either side for having or deleting each piece of information. In the end, think about what you are trying to sell and what you want people to know about you before they even call you into the room. And of course, if you should be fortunate enough to have an agent shepherding your career forward, you can consult with her about what she wants you to list on your resume.

The following pieces of information are or once were standard practice for listing on the resume: height, weight, hair color, eye color, and voice part. The obvious reason behind this section is to give us a better, fuller picture of who you are, since we are only seeing a close-up of your face on the other side. However, some things have changed in recent years and there are conflicting views about the use of several of these statistics.

As a director, I like it when an actor lists height and weight. If I do not know you and I am only seeing your headshot, it helps me get a better picture of what you will bring into the room physically if I should call you in, so there are fewer surprises. I might know that I have cast a leading lady who is 5'11" and I cannot possibly have a shorter leading man, so knowing that you are only 5'6" can save us both the time of scheduling you for an audition that you could not possibly book, based solely on your physicality. Conversely, I might see that you are 4'11" and a short person might be exactly what I am looking for in the role. Most of the time you will not know exactly what they want (unless they list it specifically in the casting call, which does happen on occasion), so instead of trying to guess, I suggest you just tell them up front what you have to offer and if it is what they want, they will call you in; otherwise, you spare everyone the time.

And yet, there is a reverse argument on the height and weight issue, which is totally worth considering. Many agents have told their actors not to list this information because it can type them out of an audition before they even get a chance to be seen. These agents feel that getting you in the room, even if you are ultimately not going to be physically right for a part, is of great value to your career, and they do not want you being turned away on account of your height or weight before the creative team even gets to meet with you and see what you can bring to the table. A close friend of mine had a horrible experience because of height being listed on his resume. He was perfect casting for the lead role in a pretty major musical based on the life of a real person. That real person happened to be part of the creative team and he got final say over who would play him in the stage production. Even though my friend was the exact height of the celebrity, this man had a bit of a complex and wanted someone a little taller to play him in the show. So my friend never even got into the room to audition, simply because the real person saw his height on the resume and vetoed him up front. Can you believe that?

I will be honest with you; I do not think that story is terribly common. I think more often than not if you list your height and weight, it is glanced at and considered but it is not generally a make-or-break factor in you getting an appointment. In most cases, it probably does not matter one way or another if you choose to include this information or not. So use your best judgment and decide for yourself whether to list it.

The history behind having hair and eye color listed really stems from the fact that only a short time ago, all headshot photography was done in black and white. So we actually needed you to tell us what color your hair and eyes were since they could not be determined through the picture. Now, of course, all headshots are in full color, so we should be able to see clearly the color of your hair and eyes. That being said, many actors still list this information. Again, it is completely up to you—I do not think you will be kept off any lists just for choosing to include or not to include your hair and eye color on your resume. I suggest you take a look at the overall format and determine if having this information keeps a nice flow to the page or if it adds clutter. I would also say that if you have a particularly unique hair or eye color, it might be worth having it on there, just as part of the brand. For instance, I had a student who was a redhead, and she always listed her hair color as "Spicy Chestnut." That becomes interesting and it makes a bolder statement than "Hair: Red."

If you are a singer, you will want to provide some information about your voice type. There are a couple of ways to go about this, but

I would suggest that you do not get too complicated. The simplest method is actual voice part: Soprano, Mezzo, Alto, Baritone, Bass, Bari-Tenor, or Tenor (or any other variation that you could imagine). Some people have a wide range and can sing in multiple styles and registers so they choose to get a little more fancy: Mezzo-Belter; Soprano with Belt; Tenor with Rock Falsetto; and so forth. There is certainly nothing wrong with being that specific—it will really help us to know if you are possibly right for what we are casting. Just be sure that whatever you list you are able to deliver in the room.

The other way to list vocal ability is to use specific range terminology. Some actors will list things like "F#2–A4" to indicate the outer limits of their range. Although this indicates a great deal of musicality and voice savvy, I do warn you about this approach for two reasons: First, most people (at least the ones who get the first look at your resume) do not know how to interpret this data. A competent musical director would understand what that means, but the average director (like yours truly) just wants to know what kind of voice is going to walk in the room with you. Secondly, you are setting yourself up to potentially have to prove yourself every time you walk into an audition. You are likely going to list the most impressive high and low notes you have so that they really know what you can do should they decide to call you in, but the reality is that you will have good days and bad, and I do not know that you want to set up an expectation that on any given day you can hit those notes. My suggestion to you is that if you wish to specify your range, you should also include the voice part; for example: "Bari-Tenor—F#2–A4 + Falsetto to A5." This will satisfy my limited knowledge of vocal range while also looking impressive to a musical director.

There really is not anything else I can think of that you would need or want to list for your vital statistics. Some people will put age or age range, but I cannot emphasize enough what a *bad idea* that is! For starters, your age does not matter (unless you are a minor and it becomes about a labor issue, in which case they will ask you about that). Putting your age on the resume is the quickest way to be typed out of tons of work. And as far as an age range, why would you want to tell me what you think you can play? Why not let me decide. Maybe my view of you is different than how you see yourself. Maybe you give yourself a range of twenty-two to twenty-six, but I could have used you to play the thirty-year-old in my show had you only not typed yourself out. Suffice it to say, you do not want to mess with ages and dates on the resume.

Related Performance Experience

The next section to tackle is the one in which you list your performance experience. There are many ways to approach setting this portion up, and I will try to cover all possible bases for you, depending on your level of experience. We will start with the simplest and then add in complexities as we go. Just remember that we want to think of this as *related performance experience*. As I mentioned earlier, it is not about quantity and filling up the page to be impressive. You have a brand you are selling and you want your experience to be consistent with what you are trying to make us think of you. So before you list any credit, ask yourself if it stays on message or if it will be confusing. Also ask yourself if it represents you well.

In this section, I want you to get used to using the Tab key to move your cursor across the page to create even columns (the space bar will never line up—just look back to the sample resume a few pages back). I strongly urge you to use the three-column approach, where you list show first, followed by the role you played, and then the theatre venue or the company where you did the show. Some people like to have a fourth column for directors, but I really feel like that makes the page too cluttered, not to mention that listing every director is gratuitous. More on that soon. Show titles should be in italics (not underlined or all caps!), and all other information should just be in normal font. The other thing I want you to think about is priority of credits. Some people tend to list their performances chronologically, but I would suggest you lead with the most significant (and best representative) roles so that they catch the eye first and foremost. Just realize that casting directors will be looking at stacks of hundreds of resumes and will often do a quick scan, so you want your most pertinent information near the top where they're more likely not to miss it. Remember to lead with your brand!

It is general protocol to title each part of the resume once we get below vital statistics. In its simplest form you can title this section "Theatre Experience" or "Performance Experience," either of which can be a catchall for any level of productions you have attained. The next possibility is to split your credits into different categories if you have multiple productions on a variety of levels. Some examples of these groupings include: "New York (or insert other major city) Experience," "National Tours," "Broadway and Off Broadway," "Regional/Stock Theatre," "Professional Theatre," and "Educational Theatre."[12] Just be sure that you only split the credits into subcategories if you have more than one performance to list under each heading. Also, be sure that you only use "Professional" as a label if "Educational" is your other set. You do not want to have a group of professional credits and then another group of noneducational credits—this just screams out community theatre, and we are building you a professional resume. Community and high school theatre have no place on this document for professional actors beyond the college level.

I can think of several other possible types of experience you may want to list on your resume, and again, with each of these, I urge you to consider whether you are listing them to fill space or whether they really represent who you are and what you are selling. The most obvious to me is "Film and/or Television Experience." If you have done student film, independent film, television episodes, and so forth, you certainly would be wise to list them on your resume—especially if you have had featured parts, if you have reel footage of your work, and if you hope to continue working on camera. Typically, this section would also follow the three-column approach where the title of the film comes first (in italics), followed by the character you played (some people will also add "lead" or "featured" in parentheses next to the character name), and then the production company or the director. I do not recommend that you include extra work or commercial work on this resume. If you have

---

12. This is where you list college credits if you are in school or recently out of school. This will be the first category to go once you start amassing professional credits. And just be careful that you're not listing too many out-of-type credits that will confuse your branding mission. How you get cast in school is not necessarily accurate to how you will be seen in the "real world."

built up experience in those areas, you can have a separate list of your work and make a note on your resume saying, "Commercial [or Extra] experience list available upon request."

Many young performers have also done work in variety settings, such as theme parks, cruise ships, Renaissance fairs, comedy or improvisational troupes, or vocal performance groups. Any of these types of credits can certainly be listed on the resume if you feel that they will really illuminate who you are. You can either create a specific category if there are multiple credits in a single area, or you can make a general heading and call it "Related Experience" or "Other Performance Experience." But at the risk of being redundant once more, I would only list these types of performances if you really feel that they enhance or support your brand.

So in theory, right now you should have a resume with your name boldly shouted from the top, followed by your contact information and your vital statistics, organized in a neat, clean fashion. Then we should see your performances listed under headings in three columns, all evenly spaced across the page. Are you with me so far? In the pages to come, I will show you several different examples of resumes, so that you have some possible models if you're not getting a clear picture in your head of what this should look like.

The one other item I wanted to cover in your performance experience section has to do with special cases that are worthy of mention, such as a well-known director or choreographer, a world premiere, or an award-winning performance. Earlier I mentioned to you that I am not a fan of the fourth column that many actors use to list every director (unless every one you list is A-level, Broadway caliber, with a name). I told you that I thought it was cluttered and gratuitous. The other problem with listing every single person with whom you have worked is that then the important ones get lost in the mix—one loses the ability to see the forest for the trees, so to speak. The truth is that while every person you work with is important in terms of contacts and the growth of your reputation, not every director's name is going to be one that catches the attention of the casting team. I advise you to limit the directors and choreographers you mention to those who are well known within the industry. Or in some instances if you know you are going in for an audition where a director's name would carry some weight, you can add it on. My preference for these types of situations is that you do not create a new column on the right; but rather, you drop down to the line below the show title, decrease the font slightly, indent the tab, and possibly even parenthesize what it is you want to say about that performance. This will truly make the additional information stand out and it will give you the pop you are looking for in including the extra detail. This method can work for directors, choreographers, premieres, awards, and so forth; anything out of the ordinary that you want to point out. Here are some examples of what I mean:

Dirty Rotten Scoundrels	Freddy Benson	NCCA Papermill Theatre
(Kevin P. Hill, Dir./Choreo.)		
Amour	Dusoleil/	Goodspeed Musicals
(World Premiere)	Passpartout	
Pop!	Candy Darling	Studio Theatre, DC
(Helen Hayes Award, Best Supporting Actor)		
Crossing	Soldier	Signature Theatre, DC
(Staged Reading; Eric Schaeffer, Dir.)		

Don't get me wrong, you certainly do not want a drop-down explanation for every credit you list, but do you see how clean the columns are and how the additional detail for each one jumps out a little clearer by the way I have separated it? This is the kind of consideration I want you to pay to formatting. And if things do not fit the way you need them to fit, I want you to keep exploring different fonts and different sizes. Just as long as it stays clean and readable, you should be good to go. (And speaking of readable, make sure that for directors whose eyes are getting on in age, such as mine, you choose a font that is big enough to read without the aid of a magnifying glass. Some actors use microscopic fonts just to accommodate the quantity of credits they feel the need to list. Please do not do that.)

In addition, if you worked in a capacity above and beyond your role in the show (e.g., dance captain, understudy, swing),[13] you can either list it right next to the role you played:

Ragtime	Ensemble, Tateh u/s[14]	Shenandoah Conservatory
Ragtime	Evelyn Nesbit/Dance Cap.	Shenandoah Conservatory
Ragtime	Judge/Male Swing	Shenandoah Conservatory

Or you may choose to list it the way I just explained for directors, awards, and so forth:

Ragtime	New Rochelle Ensemble (Dance Captain)	Shenandoah Conservatory

Or, if you have multiple instances of doing work such as dance captaining, you can put an asterisk (*) beside each of the corresponding performances and have a footnote at the bottom of your resume saying, "*Denotes Dance Captain."

You know my feeling by this point—as long as it is clean and organized, you can have the freedom to choose how you want to format the resume. Remember to step back and look at it before you print fifty copies, and make sure that if it landed on your desk at a very busy time, the most important information would be quickly attainable.

Training

Once you have finished adding all your relevant performances, you are ready to create the third section of your resume under the title of "Training." Some people choose to use the word "Education," which is fine as well, especially if you have a degree besides theatre. I know some actors who began studying another subject altogether, such as biology or English. There is no shame in that, so if it is applicable to you, do not be afraid to have it on your acting resume. If anything, it creates a real conversation starter and it tells us something about you as a person.

---

13. A swing is someone who learns multiple tracks in a show and must be prepared to cover any of them, should the actors cast in those roles need to step out for any performances.
14. The shorthand "u/s" is the traditional abbreviation for understudy.

The obvious purpose of this section is to tell us *what* you know; but the true underlying importance of the Training/Education portion of your resume is to clue us in about *whom* you know. We want to know where you studied and what your degree is (assuming you completed a degree, which is not even necessarily vital). We want to know in which performance areas you have training. But perhaps most importantly, we want to know who taught you. We want to know whose styles you had exposure to, and we want to know who you know in common with us that we could call for a reference about you.

That's right . . . I have just hit on one of the most underlooked (by actors) and yet most useful elements (for directors) of the resume: your references. Once again, I will make an important digression from our discussion on building the resume. I need to let you know that in almost every case where you are auditioning for a team that does not know you or your work, they will scour your resume for directors or teachers whom they know and they will most definitely call to get the inside scoop on you and your behavior. No matter how talented you are, if you have a reputation for being difficult to work with or if you left a job or a school on bad terms, that information will work strongly against you when you are trying to get cast.[15] It makes perfect sense, of course, but so many actors do not acknowledge that their reputation carries so much weight. Trust me, though, it does. So before you list a production credit or a teacher with whom you have studied, ask yourself what this person would say about you and her experience with you if someone should call for a character reference. This business is so darn small, that there is very little possibility of stringing together a career if you burn bridges along the way. Of course, we have all had bad experiences that blew up into something bigger and we have all made tactical mistakes in the short term that we neglected to consider in the long term; but you must trust me that in those instances, it is best to leave it off your resume rather than chancing someone investigating and digging up dirt on you.

---

15. The good news is that the opposite is also quite constant. I have been on the fence about an actor's abilities and after calling someone on their resume to find out all the wonderful things about him, I have offered him the job based largely on his reputation!

So now that you have considered who you might *not* want to have on your resume, let us build the training section. Typically you would begin with your school and your degree as a header, followed by a list of what you studied with whom. It is easiest if I show you an example of what I mean.

BFA Musical Theatre—Shenandoah Conservatory
Acting: Jonathan Flom, Tom Brooks, Carolyn Coulson-Grigsby
   (Classical/Masque), Kirsten Trump (Accents)
Voice: Matt Edwards (Contemp./Pop-Rock), Byron Jones
Dance: Linda Miller (Ballet), Alan Arnett (Jazz/Tap), Elijah Alhadji
   Gibson (Jazz/MT Styles)

Allow me to point out a few different things that I did with the above example. First, I did not use complete sentences to list my educational experience. (I have seen people write "BFA in Musical Theatre from Shenandoah Conservatory" and this is not necessary.) Second, I indented each subsection to make it easier to read. Third, I chose in some cases to expound on what specific subject was covered by certain teachers—this is totally up to you whether you want to or not. Fourth, I left out all doctoral titles. (It is pretentious and unnecessary to call people "Dr. Byron Jones," etc., on your resume.) Fifth, I limited the information to performance-specific training, as opposed to including dramatic lit, history, tech classes, and so forth. And finally, I checked to make certain that I had spelled everyone's names correctly.

As with everything on this resume, there is no singular way to create this section. There are many variations, but the above example is one of the simplest versions I can offer you. If you want to be even simpler (as in fact I am on my directing resume), you can notate your degree and school, followed simply by a list of names of those with whom you studied, sans subjects. You can also go into greater detail if you wish, including the number of years you studied certain areas, such as ballet, or the specific unique training you may have received, such as pointe.

You may also have training outside of your college degree or certificate program. If so, you can create an additional subheading for that other institution or studio. Just be careful that you do not list so much training that this section becomes the largest part of your resume. Remember, it is mainly about giving us some names to look at and giving us an overview of the type of instruction you have had.

One other useful subsection that may well apply to you is one we can call "Workshops and Master Classes." Here you can list well-known people with whom you took a class but who would not be called upon to necessarily remember you and act as a reference for you. The reason this section is useful is that it tells us whom in the industry you know and it indicates that you are aware of those people's teachings. You can either create a blanket list of names of people from whom you have taken a class, or you can list the specific subject matter. Here are some examples:

WORKSHOPS/MASTER CLASSES
Stephen Schwartz; Nikole Vallins; Jason Robert Brown; Anne Reinking; Sheri Sanders; Joy Dewing

WORKSHOPS/MASTER CLASSES
Rachel Hoffman (Audition Technique); Julio Agustin (Fosse); VP Boyle (Pop/Rock); Joe Deer (Acting the Song); Ronn Burton (Alba Emoting)

Get the point? I figure you do—and as I said, there are some samples coming up.

Special Skills

The final section of the resume is called "Special Skills." It is pretty self-explanatory, I would think—this is where you list (literally, in list form, separated by commas or semicolons) any additional skills you bring to the table that might be useful or might at least be great conversation starters. I have seen special skills that range from the entirely practical to the entirely ridiculous, but you never know what will spark the attention of the people behind the table. Let me give you some common examples of the kinds of skills most actors tend to list:

Foreign languages (including the level of proficiency—beginning, conversational, fluent, etc.); Accents or dialects (list specifics); Character voices and impersonations; Improvisation or stand-up comedy; Musical instruments (include years and/or proficiency level); Ballroom dance training; Cheerleading; Sight-reading; Tight harmony skills; Athletic abilities or sports; Acrobatics or tumbling; Circus skills (such as fire-eating, juggling, contortion, etc.); Certifications (such as SCUBA, rock climbing, CPR, etc.); Odd and quirky physical abilities; Unique mental abilities (e.g., naming all the presidents of the United States in order in thirty seconds); Additional theatre skills (here is where you can list things such as carpentry, stitching, electrics, stage management, choreography, etc.).

It always makes me sad when actors tell me that they do not possess any special skills worth listing. Everyone has some quirky hidden talents! Think outside the box, and if you really cannot come up with anything, then start training yourself in some of these areas so that you can eventually add things to your list. Make it your goal to learn to juggle or to balance something on your nose or to perfect your George Clooney impersonation.

The other common items I see listed on actors' resumes under the skills section are: Valid Driver's License and U.S. Passport. There are differing opinions on this, but I will give you mine (it's the least I can do since you are reading my book!): I think it is a space filler and a waste. The school of thought was always that if an actor were auditioning for a film in which she may be asked to drive a car, or if she were auditioning for a small touring company that required the actors to drive themselves around, listing driver's license would indicate that the actor could do the job. And if the gig included an overseas leg, listing U.S. Passport would indicate the actor's ability to fulfill that contract. But I do not see license and passport as skills so much as they are possessions. I mean, you wouldn't list owning tap shoes as a special skill even though they may be required for a job, right? My feeling is that if I am a director and I need someone to drive or go to China, I will ask in the audition if the actor is able to operate a vehicle or if she has a passport. Again, that is just my opinion. Putting those down on your resume will certainly not keep you from booking work (I would hope!), but in the grand scheme of things, if you have plenty of other skills that are useful, do not waste the ink on letting us know about your driving and traveling abilities.

The real key to the successful special skills section of the resume is making sure that everything you put down is tested and foolproof. You *must* be able to demonstrate anything you indicate in a moment's notice, the only exceptions being things that require outside props or preparation, such as fire-eating or playing a tuba. We do not expect that you will have those items with you at every audition you attend, but you should definitely be able to provide a demonstration of those types of skills at a callback if they ask you to do so. I do an exercise with my students every year where I collect their resumes early in the semester, and on some random day I pull them out and make them get up and show off the special skills on their list. Anything they are unable to achieve with absolute impressive proficiency, the class tells them to strike from their list. It is a good way to keep them honest and to be really sure that whatever they write down can be done at the drop of a hat. You would not believe how frequently you will be called upon to demonstrate your skills—and fortunately or unfortunately, it is usually just for the amusement of the creative team!

And speaking of amusement, I would encourage you to think of one thing to include at the end of your skills that might either be a conversation starter or just a cute button to your list. This last item does not necessarily have to be a skill, but rather it can be a quirk or a gesture that might make them smile or laugh at reading it. I have a friend who includes "Can catch small food in my mouth," and he has had many an M&M and a grape tossed at him in auditions. I also have a friend who lists "Gives great hugs," and once in a blue moon someone calls on her to prove it. Things like that, which are not exactly marketable theatrical "skills" per se, but that will catch the attention of the creative team in a positive way, can be a benefit to you. You just have to be sure that it does not become gratuitous. One funny or quirky skill at the end is all you need.

The last thought I have for you on the subject of special skills has to do with listing languages, dialects, or impersonations. You *must* have something prepared to say when you are asked to demonstrate any of these abilities. I cannot tell you how often I ask an actor to show me his Irish or his Russian accent or to let me hear his Gilbert Gottfried impression, only to have that actor ask, "Okay, what do you want me to say?" This is your show, buddy! Do not ask me what you should say—have something ready. Assume I am going to ask. For accents, you may wish to have a monologue that you can do in perfect dialect. For foreign languages, get ready to have a conversation if you say you speak French or German. For impersonations and character voices, have something to say that really hits the nail on the head for that character.

The special skills parade, as I call it, is a great opportunity for you to show off your abilities and to showcase your personality. I have seen actors get job offers solely on the fact that they killed it in the room when they were asked to demonstrate these skills. You have got to put a lot of thought into this section and make sure that you are coming up with fun, useful, dynamic skills to list. And at the very least, be sure that you can craft a short list of practical, demonstrable talents. Do not put pressure on yourself to be funny or unique for now—just give us some things that we can talk about with you, ask you to show us, or consider useful in our production.

Has all of this detail about resumes made your head spin? Can I remind you of one more little thing before I show you some different examples? You know what I'm going to say. . . . Remember to review every inch of the resume for its consistency with your branding statement and your marketing scheme. How do you want people to think of you? What do you want the first impression of you to be? What does this resume do to represent you to the industry? Are there credits that are going to confuse me as I compare your headshot or your actual appearance (typewise) to roles that you have listed? We are talking advanced stuff here, so I am asking you to use a fine-tooth comb to make these decisions and these edits. But I promise you it will be worth it in the long run. Now let's look at some examples:

PROFESSIONAL ARTISTS
~a talent agency~

• Phone: • Fax:

Jessie Hooker

AEA

Email:	Cell:	www.jessiehooker.com
Height: 5'9"	Hair/Eye color: Dark Brown	Voice: mezzo-sop.(belter)

Off-Broadway

Sistas	swing Gloria(perf), Tamika	St. Luke's Theatre
(in production)	Roberta, Simone	

National Tours

Legally Blonde	Judge/Ensemble	Troika Entertainment
(dir: Marc Bruni)	u/s Pilar (perf)/Paulette	

Professional Theatre

Company	Jenny	Geva Theatre Center
(dir: Mark Cuddy)		
Rent	Joanne	NCCA Papermill Theatre
(dir: Kevin P. Hill)		
I Love You, You're Perfect..Change	Woman 2	NCCA Papermill Theatre
Something's Afoot	Lettie	Great Plains Theatre
West Side Story	Consuela	Shenandoah Summer Theatre
Hairspray	Lorraine/Ensemble	Shenandoah Summer Theatre
God's Favorite	Mady	Great Plains Theatre

Educational Theatre

Ragtime	Sarah	Shenandoah Conservatory
The Wild Party (Lippa)	Kate	Shenandoah Conservatory
Kiss Me, Kate	Hattie	Shenandoah Conservatory
Working	Heather/feat.solo	Shenandoah Conservatory
Two Gentlemen of Verona (musical)	Ensemble	Shenandoah Conservatory
(dir: Lara Teeter)		
The Robber Bridegroom	Ensemble	Shenandoah Conservatory
(dir: Lara Teeter)		

Training

BFA, Musical Theatre- Shenandoah Conservatory
Acting- Jonathan Flom, Lara Teeter, Thomas Albert, Sally Anderson, Stephen Levi, Jason Sherry
Voice- Medea Ruhadze **Ballet, Jazz, MT Styles-** Robyn Hart Schroth, Alan Arnett, Lara Teeter, Elijah Gibson
Workshops/seminars: Theatre: Joy Dewing, Jillian Cimini, Eric Woodall, Aaron Galligan-Stierle, Nikole Vallins, Diane Riley, Doug Shapiro, Ed Linderman, Gary Krasny, Pat McCorkle Chris Nichols (The Krasny Office), Michael Goddard (Nicolosi & Co.) **Commercial:** Allynn Simons, David McDermott, Michael Guy, Tisha Ioli

Special Skills

Winner of 2011 Telsey & Co. youtube competition (RENT audition), accents: (British/Cockney, Southern, NY), Tonal Memory, Sight Reading, Jumping Rope

AARON GALLIGAN - STIERLE

BROADWAY

Ragtime	Henry Ford	Neil Simon Theater, dir. Marcia Milgrom Dodge
Dr. Seuss' How the Grinch Stole Christmas	Papa Who	St. James Theater, dir. Matt August

PLAYS

The 39 Steps	Clown #2	Utah Shakespearean Festival, dir. Eli Simon
The Merchant of Venice	Launcelot Gobbo	Utah Shakespearean Festival, dir. Sharon Ott
Room Service	Leo Davis	Utah Shakespearean Festival, dir. Mark Rucker
A Midsummer Night's Dream	Flute	Utah Shakespearean Festival, dir. Kathleen Conlin
The Merry Wives of Windsor	Slender	Utah Shakespearean Festival, dir. Kate Buckley
Measure for Pleasure	Will Blunt	Florida Studio Theater, dir. Russell Treyz
The Taming of the Shrew	Hortensio	Pennsylvania Shakespeare Festival, dir. Russell Treyz
Broadway Bound	Eugene Jerome	Pennsylvania Centre Stage, dir. Brant Pope
The Tempest	Stephano	Pennsylvania Centre Stage, dir. Bob Vernon
Twelfth Night	Feste	Penn State Theater, dir. Mark Olsen
Noises Off	Lloyd	Penn State Theater, dir. Dan Carter

MUSICALS

Curtains	Daryl Grady	Papermill Playhouse and TUTS, dir. Mark S. Hoebee
Ragtime	Henry Ford	The Kennedy Center, dir. Marcia Milgrom Dodge
Dr. Seuss' How the Grinch Stole Christmas	Papa Who	1st National Tour, dir. Matt August
She Loves Me	The Busboy	Westport Country Playhouse, dir. Mark Lamos
Cinderella	The Herald	Broadway Asia International Tour, dir. Bobby Garcia
Forever Plaid	Frankie	Utah Shakespearean Festival, dir. Russell Treyz
Camelot	Mordred	Utah Shakespearean Festival, dir. Brad Carroll
White Christmas	Phil Davis	Arts Center of Coastal Carolina, dir. Russell Treyz
The Last 5 Years	Jamie	Pennsylvania Blackbox Theater, dir. Bob Vernon
The Secret Garden	Dickon	Shenandoah Summer Music Theater, dir. Linde Herman

FILM

Suicide	George (lead)	Independent Short
Paradise	Roger (lead)	NYU Senior Thesis
Making Space Nazi	Cort (lead)	USC Graduate Film
Looking for May	Clerk (supporting)	Columbia University Graduate Film

TRAINING
MFA Acting Degree at Penn State University

SKILLS
Accent/ Dialects: RP English, Cockney, Irish, Scottish, New York, German, Southern, French
Sight Reading, Basic Guitar and Piano, PADI Scuba Certified, Excellent Poker Player

*Note—Aaron's resume does include the contact information for his agency, but they requested that it not be published. That is why there is no phone number or e-mail.

MEGAN NICOLE ARNOLDY

AEA

Height: 5'7"
Weight: 125 lbs.
Hair: Blonde
Eyes: Blue-Green

THE LUEDTKE AGENCY
████████
NEW YORK, NY 10019
TEL (212) ████

LAS VEGAS/TOURS

Jersey Boys (Las Vegas)	Lorraine	dir. Des McAnuff
The Drowsy Chaperone (1st National)	Swing/Janet, Kitty u/s	dir./chor. Casey Nicholaw
Fame (South Korean Tour)	Serena	Phoenix Productions

REGIONAL THEATRE

The Drowsy Chaperone	Janet/Asst. Choreo.	Human Race Theatre/Kevin Crewell
Cabaret	Frenchie/Dance Capt.	Milwaukee Rep/Mark Clements
The Drowsy Chaperone	Janet	Ogunquit Playhouse/Casey Hushion
Minsky's (World Premiere)	Sunny/Mary, Flame u/s	Ahmanson Theatre/Casey Nicholaw
42nd Street	Peggy Sawyer	Tuacahn Center for the Arts/Deanna L. Dys
Grease	Sandy	Marriott Theatre, Lincolnshire/Marc Robin
42nd Street	Ensemble/Peggy u/s	Walnut Street Theatre/Charles Abbott
Grease	Sandy	Carousel Dinner Theatre/Ray DeMattis
The Sound of Music	Liesl	Helen Hayes Theatre Co./Richard Sabellico
The Music Man	Ensemble	Sacramento Music Circus/Leland Ball
Aida	Ensemble	Sacramento Music Circus/Gary John LaRosa
A Musical Christmas Carol	Caroler	Pittsburgh CLO/Rosemary Newcott
Annie	Boylan Sister	Pittsburgh CLO/Charley Repole
My Fair Lady	Servant	Pittsburgh CLO/Glenn Casale
Funny Girl	Vera	Pittsburgh CLO/Richard Sabellico
She Loves Me	Ensemble	Pittsburgh CLO/Van Kaplan
Singin' in the Rain	Ensemble	Pittsburgh CLO/Charley Repole
Fiddler on the Roof	Ensemble	Pittsburgh CLO/Glenn Casale
George M!	Secretary	Pittsburgh CLO/Richard Sabellico
Guys and Dolls	Ensemble	Pittsburgh CLO/Van Kaplan
Jekyll & Hyde	Ensemble	Pittsburgh CLO/Robert Cuccioli
Good News!	Pat	Struthers Library Theatre/Kevin Hill

NYC READINGS

The Gypsy King (NAMT FESTIVAL 2007)	Marc Robin, dir.

INDUSTRIALS/BENEFITS

Mercy Foundation's Reindeer Ball, UPMC Children's Ball, Kidapalooza-RWS and Associates
Unsung 2006: "Sex, Love, and Lies"-Fantastic Feats Productions directed by Phillip George

COMMERCIALS

Penn State Bookstore- Wix Pix Productions
Brusters Ice Cream Jingle- New Perspective
Tony Awards 2010 Print Ad

TRAINING

B.F.A. MUSICAL THEATRE PENN STATE UNIVERSITY
Voice-Mary Saunders, Beverly Patton, Roseanna Irwin, Matt Farnsworth
Tap,Jazz,Ballet,Modern-Kevin Hill, Spence Ford,Sandra Clark, Tera Clark,Gerard W. Holt,Jill Brighton
Acting-Charles Dumas, Peg French, Tammy Backeris, Richard Nichols, Jane Ridley, Barry Shapiro

SPECIAL SKILLS

Trumpet, German, Walking on Hands, Cheerleading, Yoga

Matthew DeLorenzo

Email: matthew.delorenzo@▮▮▮▮▮   Cell: ▮▮▮▮▮▮   www.matthewdelorenzo.com

Height: 6'1''   Hair/Eye color: Brown   Voice: Tenor, Sopranist

PROFESSIONAL THEATRE/ SUMMER STOCK:

*Pop!**	Candy Darling	The Studio Theatre
Seussical	Wickersham	Imagination Stage
The Music Man	Ensemble	The Kennedy Center
(w/Marvin Hamlisch & Shirley Jones)		(dir. Patrick Cassidy)
Show Boat	Ensemble	Shenandoah Summer Musical Theatre
White Christmas	Ensemble	Shenandoah Summer Musical Theatre
Into The Woods	Jack	Encore Theatre

EDUCATIONAL THEATRE:

Angels in America: Part 1	Prior Walter	Shenandoah Conservatory
Assassins	Charles Guiteau	Shenandoah Conservatory
Noises Off	u/s Gary	Shenandoah Conservatory
Damn Yankees	Ensemble Swing	Shenandoah Conservatory
Anything Goes	Ensemble	Shenandoah Conservatory
A Midsummer Nights Dream	Lysander	Oakton Theatre

CONCERTS:

Handel's Messiah	The Washington Chorus	The Kennedy Center
2009 Christmas Gala	"	"
Music for Christmas	The City Choir of Washington	National Presbyterian
Mozart Requiem	"	"
Broadway Rocks 2009!	"	Wolf Trap

AWARDS: *denotes Helen Hayes Award

TRAINING:

BFA Musical Theatre - Shenandoah Conservatory (2012)

Voice- Donna Gullstrand, Robert Shafer, Tiffany Powell, Michelle Kunz

Acting- Sally Anderson, Mark Kittlaus, Jonathan Flom, Marcello Rolando, Vanessa Lock

Ballet, Jazz, Tap- Robyn Hart Schroth, Linda Miller, Alan Arnett, Elijah Gibson, Jereme Goshorn

Workshops/Seminars- Jow Dewing, Nikole Vallins, Diane Riley, Alice Ripley, Aaron Galligan-Stierle, Doug Shapiro, Natalie Weiss, Ed Linderman, Gary Krasny, Pat McCorkle, Julio Agustin, Ed Herendeen, Joshua Finkel

SPECIAL SKILLS:

Accents (Southern, NY, NJ, British, Cockney), Musician Skills (Tonal Memory, Sight Reading, Learns Quickly), Jumping Rope, Perform in Heels, Funny Faces, Celebrity Impressions

Now I grant you, not each of these examples of resumes have followed every "rule and regulation" I laid out to you down to a T, but as I said earlier, this is all very subjective. I wanted to show you samples of several different actors I know who are at different phases of their careers, all of whom have taken variations in their approaches to building their resumes, but all of whom have had success in the industry. And each one of them has considered what he or she included in the resume along with what format was used to provide the best representation of personality, organization, and professionalism.

With these examples, you should have plenty of ideas on which to model your very own dynamite resume. You will see these four actors coming up in the actor profiles that I have spread throughout the book, so you will learn more about them and how they have branded themselves. The first of these profiles is below.

PERFORMER PROFILE
Jessie Hooker, Actor

Meet Jessie Hooker!

Jessie is a graduate of Shenandoah's Musical Theatre Program, and she has been making waves in the industry since moving to New York a few short years ago. I asked Jessie to allow me to profile her as an example of a young, up-and-coming actor living in New York City. Although she has yet to earn a Broadway credit (at time of publication), she has done a national tour (*Legally Blonde*) and an Off-Broadway show (*Sistas*), and she signed with a major talent agency. A few pages back, you saw Jessie's resume as an example. Take a look at her headshot and answer the earlier branding questions I asked about what that photo says about her.

JF: *How long have you lived in New York City?*
JH: As of now one year and a couple months.

JF: *How long did you live in New York and audition before you booked your first professional work?*
JH: I was in NYC for about one month before booking work but both projects I booked early on I ended up not taking due to bigger things in the works (Broadway callbacks, etc.) that I (with my agent and other mentors' advice) felt would further me as a person and performer. It was seven months total before I booked a gig that I *took*, which was *Company*. Which is how I got my Equity card.

JF: *How long did it take you to book your first Off-Broadway gig?*
JH: I booked my first Off-Broadway show after a year in the city (after *Company*).

JF: *How long did you stay non-Equity before joining the union and what made you join it when you did?*
JH: I was non-Equity for almost two years after school. I did my first non-Eq. tour for nine months and while it was a dream I knew after that experience the next tour and work I wanted to do was Equity. I felt like it was "time" to join the union after being called in for professional/ Broadway shows and watching how I "held up" with the other actors that were my type. I felt (with the guidance of my agent and other mentors) that the fact that I was getting called back was a good sign that I could hold my own in the union once I was offered my card.

JF: *How did you get an agent? Did you book work without representation or has your success come since you've had an agent?*
JH: I met my agent during a class/workshop held in NYC. I had booked previous work without my agent and now have booked work with her as well.

JF: *You are in a committed, long-term relationship. Anything you want to share about how you balance life in show business with that relationship?*
JH: It's a hard thing and you have to *want* to be in a relationship. My boyfriend and I *started* our relationship long distance. He's also a musician/actor and knows and experiences the ups and downs of the business that can be hard if you're experiencing the total opposite at the time. You learn how to help each other with the ups and the downs and you *constantly communicate*. As much as I *love* it there's so much more to life than performing and I'm happy that I can share that with my man.

At the end of the hard tiring days in the city it's so nice to have someone to come home to. That's what I love at the end of the day—no matter how good/bad that audition, callback, or performance went.

JF: *Any "pearls of wisdom" that you'd like to offer to young actors planning to make a go at this industry? Maybe share the biggest lesson you've learned since being in the biz?*
JH: One thing I've learned so far is that you can't try and be anyone else. I know it sounds cliché but once you truly let go of the other people in the audition who went in before you or the people going in after you it takes the pressure off. You walk into the room and say "Hi, this is *me* and I'm gonna show you the best *me* I have today and you'll want to work with *me*" and truly believe that. If you hear something back, great; if you don't you will—plain and simple. Someone somewhere wants to work with *you*, not a carbon copy of anyone else.

JF: *Any commentary on the biggest mistake you made along the way? Or anything personal from you to the readers?*
JH: The first thing that sticks out to me is worrying. I waste *so* much energy worrying—whether it's about what the people behind the table want, the rumor that everything is already cast (Why should I even go to that audition?), worrying about the other people auditioning (These people look *fierce*. Are they even going to cast black girls?), or even after that final callback thinking through everything *after* it was done. Did I look the right way that last beat of the song? They were looking at my resume the *whole* time—did I just disappoint them? You just gotta take a breath and do what you've been trained or called to do. That's all we're really asked for. So I'm working on the not worrying.

COVER LETTERS

I do not generally like to speak in absolutes. It seems that the moment you say, "Never do this" or "Always do that" someone will give you three examples to contradict your position. That said, I will tell you with no hyperbole involved that you must *never* submit a headshot and resume without a cover letter. That is right, I am telling you to *always* accompany your materials with a brief and specific letter when submitting yourself for an audition appointment. *Always*. Get it?

As directors, producers, and casting directors, we behind-the-table folk see a lot of submissions. I mean, we could be talking hundreds a day when a project is going into preproduction. The envelopes (or more typically today—the e-mails) pile up, and someone has to weed through all the actors vying for the gig in order to narrow down the few that fit the type and vision for the show and call them in. One thing that the casting team hates is when actors blindly submit themselves for every job posting in *Backstage* or *Playbill*.[16] Many "actors" are so desperate to be seen, and so ignorant of the notion of branding and marketing strategies, that they decide to cast the widest net possible by sending in their picture and resume for every job out there, even if there is not a part for them.

I cannot encourage you enough to avoid this tactic. Although it may seem like a mathematical advantage, I assure you it will keep you out of more auditions than it will get you into. By simply sending in a picture and resume for every job, casting directors will start to remember you—and not in the way you want them to remember you. They will consider you unprofessional and ill trained, and they will feel you are wasting their time if you do not consider and directly address their stated casting needs.

What you *should* be doing is looking for the casting opportunities that are really a spot-on match for your brand and your abilities. Who is casting a role that you have right in your "bread basket"? I mean a role that you could walk right in and play convincingly now. As you begin to identify your perfect casting opportunities, you submit yourself (assuming it's not just an open call)[17] and you give the casting people a little introduction to who you are and why they should call you in; this is the cover letter.

Before I get specific about what should be included in the cover letter, let me warn you against one other common faux pas among

---

16. *Backstage* is a subscription-based trade paper for the performing arts. Based in NYC, it advertises jobs and auditions across the country for actors in both paper and online forms. Playbill.com is another phenomenal (and free) online theatre source. All actors should read it daily to keep up on industry news. They also offer free job listings and audition information without needing to be a member.

17. You will notice that on *Backstage* and *Playbill* there is probably an even split between auditions that you just show up and attend (open calls) and auditions that are "by appointment" and require advanced submissions. In this section, we are specifically discussing submission calls.

the unwashed masses of actors. Almost as bad as not sending a cover letter at all is sending the form or template cover letter. It generally reads something like this:

Dear Sir or Madam:

I saw your posting in *Backstage* and I would very much like to be considered for an audition. I am a hardworking, punctual actor and I think I could bring something exciting and special to your production. Please contact me at your earliest convenience if it would be possible to set up an audition appointment.

> Yours truly,
> Generic Actor

I say it generally reads like that, but sometimes it is even less specific—sometimes it just says, "I saw your ad and I would like to audition." Once again, these actors tend to blindly submit for everything and they feel as though adding the cover letter makes it seem more personal, but in this example, it certainly does not. The actor who writes that kind of letter is just going through the motions. But this *business* is all about a personal touch. I hope that this far into my book, you have realized that much!

Your cover letter needs to reflect . . . (drumroll please) your brand! It needs to say something about you. It needs to tell us why you are sending in your picture and resume for *this specific* job, and it needs to give us a reason to think about calling you in for an audition appointment. In essence, if I have two hours of time set aside to cast a certain role, you are asking for 5 to 10 percent of that time. It does not sound like much, but when you think of the hundreds of actors who will be asking for their chunk of that time, it really does become precious. While a casting director may be willing to take a risk or two and look out-of-type if an actor seems really interesting, by and large, they do not have time to waste inviting in every person who sends them a photo. You need to grab their attention in a professional (and appropriate) way and help them do their job.

The first "rule" in crafting a cover letter is that it must have perfect spelling and grammar. If you are in school for acting and you think that taking English Composition is a waste of your time, think again. I am so terribly turned off by actors who cannot compose a short letter and take the time to check their spelling and usage. It can really become detrimental to your career, as directors want to work with smart actors. I highly recommend you get yourself a copy of the book *Eats, Shoots and Leaves* by Lynn Truss. It is a grammar guidebook with a terrific sense of humor. Truss hits on many of the common errors (their/there/they're; your/you're; its/it's; use of the comma, semicolon; etc.) and she does it in a way that is engaging and fun to read. I keep a copy of this book nearby whenever I am writing, and it has served me quite well.

So assuming you will be sure not to get eliminated from the pile for weak writing skills, generic form letters, or no letter at all, let us discuss what makes a great cover letter. In the beginning of this section, I told you a cover letter needs to be both brief and specific. Specificity begins with the opening address. "Dear Sir or Madam" and "To Whom It May Concern" are about as generic as you can get. I urge you to know whom you are targeting in your submission. If there is a casting director, an artistic director, a company manager, or a director listed in the audition advertisement, address them directly and professionally. "Dear Mr. Flom:" is a suitable opening. If you have a relationship with the person casting, you can address him by first name. In the unusual case that there is no person listed in the ad, do your research. Try to find the theatre's website and discover who does their casting so that you can address your letter to someone by name. And if you are really stuck for figuring out who is in charge of the casting decisions, at least address your letter to the specific company that is seeking actors (e.g., "Dear Bay Street Theatre Casting:" or "Dear Joy Dewing Casting:"). Being this precise in the address of your letter will go a long way to showing the artistic staff that you are interested in their particular project, not just any old acting job you can get.

In the body of the letter, you want to craft a brief ("brief" being the operative word!) statement that reflects your personality, addresses the needs of the production, and touts you just enough without being cocky. Avoid getting too long winded and replicating your entire resume in paragraph form; rather, if there is something germane to the production that you wish to highlight on your resume (such as a specific special skill you possess that would be useful in this show), mention it. Otherwise, simply explain what you are interested in and keep it concise. Here are a few examples of cover letters that take slightly different approaches and address various possibilities:

Dear Ms. Dewing:

I saw your ad today seeking the role of "Flower Girl" in the Miami production of *Orchid* and I am very interested in being seen. I have extensive training in a variety of styles, including 12 years of ballet and pointe. Pop music is my strength as a singer, and I think I'd be a great fit in a "*Moulin Rouge*, cabaret-style" show. I would love to set up an audition appointment to come in for you. Please feel free to reach me by e-mail (jane.doe@yahoo.com) or by cell phone (212-555-5555). I look forward to hearing from you soon.

Best,
Jane Doe

This letter addresses some of the specific needs of the call as per casting director Joy Dewing's ad (this is a real casting call, by the way). It tells Joy exactly which role this actress is targeting and it addresses the special skills the actress possesses that are called for in the production. Note that it is short, to the point, and professional. Also see that contact information was included in the cover letter. I know it will be on your resume as well, but it is wise to include it either in the cover letter body or in a letterhead, just in case your resume gets separated from the cover letter. If this actress were submitting a hard copy of the headshot and resume, she would want to be sure to hand sign the letter as well. However, if it were an e-mail submission, the signature would be understood.

And speaking of e-mail submissions, many people ask me if they should attach a cover letter in file form or make it the body of the e-mail. I highly recommend that you make the e-mail body your cover letter when submitting electronically. Chances are, if you attach a file with your letter, it will never get opened because the casting office simply does not have the time. Here is another example:

Dear Jeff,

It was so great meeting you last week at Actors Connection! I loved your class and I really appreciate the feedback you were able to offer me on my song. I see that you are casting *All Shook Up!* for North Shore, and I would relish the opportunity to come in with my guitar and audition for "Dennis." I know it's a different side of me than what you saw in the workshop, but it really is where I live. My contact info is in the letterhead above as well as on my attached resume. Please let me know if it's possible to schedule an appointment.

All the best,
John Actor

This letter is clearly more personal and less formal. It assumes a relationship with the casting director and it reminds him how he knows the actor.

The one other approach I want to suggest to you is a technique I learned from my friends at The Savvy Actor, so I credit them for this fully. They suggest referencing a relationship and a success in your letter when possible. This approach is great when you do not have a direct personal connection to the casting director but you want them to feel they have a strong reason to consider you. It looks something like this:

Dear Mr. Clemmons:

I see that you are casting the new production of *Jekyll and Hyde* for Broadway. I just finished VP Boyle's Pop/Rock course and he suggested I reach out to you as he thinks I'd be a great fit for your ensemble. I was recently cast in *The Scarlet Pimpernel* for Ogunquit's summer season, so I'm no stranger to Frank Wildhorn's style. I'll be in Maine until July 15, but I'd love to get in to see you on the July 17 session if you have any openings.

I've attached my photo and resume and I hope that you'll consider contacting me for an audition.

Sincerely,
John Actor
john.actor@hotmail.com
(917) 555-5555

Are you starting to understand what I mean by brief and specific? Did you notice that each of these letters contains only a few short sentences? Do you see how the relationship/success model (VP Boyle, *Scarlet Pimpernel* gig) can be implemented? You may even wish to throw something about your brand into the letter:

Dear Pat McCorkle:

I see that you are casting Hartford Stage's production of *How to Succeed in Business without Really Trying*. As an actor I have the boyish outlook of Matthew Broderick with the humor and style of Ben Stiller, and I would love to be seen for the role of J. Pierpont Finch. Please let me know if I may set up an appointment to come in and sing for you. My contact information is listed above as well as on my attached resume.

Regards,
John Actor

I hope that you have enough examples and variations to get you started. And I hope you can see that you must not underestimate the importance of the cover letter. As you continue submitting yourself for audition opportunities, you will find what works for you and what does not. As I have emphasized over and over throughout these pages, you need to be consistent with your brand and stay on message in every aspect of your business. The cover letter is no exception. If your brand reflects a version of polished professionalism, your letter should and will sound different in tone than if your brand were more along the lines of quirky and fun loving.

Take some time now to look on Playbill.com or Backstage.com and craft some sample cover letters for yourself. What kinds of skills are you finding relevant to mention? How is your personality able to shine through in your letters while still maintaining professionalism? Show your letters to people to get their opinions on your effectiveness.

REPERTOIRE

Without a doubt, the stickiest area for most of the actors I work with is in building a solid repertoire for auditions. I have people ask me all the time for help and suggestions. They want to know what pieces are too overdone. They want to know how to find good pop/rock cuts. They are afraid they will not have the perfect song or monologue for every single audition possibility. They want to find the hidden gem of a song that no one has ever heard before. Generally speaking, they approach audition rep with trepidation and confusion.

I can certainly understand where the fear stems from—the business is ever changing, and a piece that one director loves, the next one is absolutely going to hate. So guess what I'm going to tell you . . . do not try to please everyone! Do not try to have a song for every single casting director and for every role in every show. Russell Simmons wrote a great book called *Do You* (which I highly recommend you read), and that is my advice when it comes to filling your book with audition material: do you.

You have worked so hard at this point to create a marketable brand for your actor business; I have guided you through the process of choosing clothing, headshots, and resume formats that support the product you are selling. You should take the same approach to choosing repertoire. With each piece you decide to tackle, ask yourself if it communicates your essence in some palpable way. Now clearly, you will need different song types (ballads, up-tempos, traditional musical theatre, pop/rock, etc.) and different monologue types (classical/verse, contemporary, dramatic, comedic, etc.), but somewhere in each era and in each genre, you should be able to find something that shows us a good bit about who you are and what you bring to the table.

So often actors tell me they want to have an expansive repertoire that really demonstrates their extreme range—a song that shows off their highest note; one that shows off their lowest note; a monologue that shows them spewing their emotions all over the floor; another that attempts to "slay 'em in the aisles" with comedy. But again, I say to you that your job in the audition room is to strip away the masks that amateurs layer on, get present in the room, and trust that what *you* have to sell is the best *you* there is and that no one else will bring what you bring, even if they've chosen the same piece as you have. We all admire actors like Meryl Streep and Denzel Washington for their versatility, but they did not make a career by trying to be versatile. Rather, they each began (as all successful actors do) by marketing themselves for targeted, specific roles, after which they were stretched, once they had become proven commodities. Even now as they are known for their versatility, both of those actors still convey a certain essence of self through any role they tackle. Think about it: What is the essence of Meryl Streep? Of Denzel Washington? I know you do not want to be put into a box and pigeonholed, but I also know you want to work. If you didn't you would not be reading this book. So trust me when I tell you that McDonald's really nailed the hamburger and fries long before the McRib and the McNugget came along, and you should follow suit.

So just to reiterate, you want the repertoire book you build to have a variety and range of genres and styles, but somewhere in each piece, a bit of your humanity and your brand must be revealed. Does that make sense? I suggest you begin your journey to find repertoire by going back to our early work on branding in the beginning of this book. Remember when I asked you to name roles you could see yourself playing? Well, where better to begin selecting audition material than from the shows that contain roles that seem to have your name emblazoned on them already? So you think you should be playing "Nina" in *In the Heights*? Great, put "Breathe" in your book. Is it overdone? A little. But things go in waves and phases, and it will work its way out of the audition rooms soon enough. Although, if you are perfect for "Nina" and you do that song incredibly honestly and it tells us something about you, then who cares if it is overdone? Ultimately, the casting director's job is to put aside his or her opinion of your material and focus on finding the best talent for the project.[18]

I think the best way to find great audition rep is to follow this method of reading and seeing plays and musicals and identifying roles for which you are suited, both typewise and talentwise. This way, it is never about finding something clever and show-offish, but

---

18. I cannot tell you how many times someone has walked into an audition, announced that they will be singing a song that I *hate* and then blown me away by making me hear that song in a different way than I ever have before. It's all about honesty and connection to the material. I love it when that happens!

rather, it is about helping the casting director do her job by walking in and making a clear statement about who you are.

Please do yourself and anyone behind the table a favor and avoid finding audition pieces from monologue books or song collection books (unless you read and know the source material!) or off the Internet. There are plenty of writers who publish contentless monologue books, designed to give actors either great stand-alone moments of drama or comedy in the room. But these always fall flat because there is no full story behind the monologue. In addition, these pieces tend to be speeches or stories. I suggest that your second biggest criteria (second to the piece revealing something about you) behind choosing any material, song or monologue, is that the piece is *active*. What do I mean by active? I mean one of the purposes of seeing you do solo work in an audition is for us to imagine how you would interact with another onstage. You should look for material that engages an imaginary partner (with whom you have defined the specific nature of your relationship) and which begs the question: What do you want from that partner? This is Acting 101 material, and if you have ever taken a course in acting, you have no doubt heard a variation on this idea—what is your goal, objective, and so forth? You need to apply that line of thinking to auditions as well. Be prepared to tell the casting director to whom you are speaking in the piece and what you want him or her to do.[19] And yes, this applies to both songs and monologues!

One other way to seek out repertoire is to look back on one of our other branding exercises and to do something I call "chasing the carrot." I asked you earlier to think of other actors to whom people compare you. Let's say that you really fancy yourself a young Aaron Tveit. You saw him in *Next to Normal* and you really thought that was a role you could nail. Great! Now put something from *Next to Normal* in your book and look up what other shows Aaron has done. You can use the Internet Broadway Database (IBDB.com) for a lot of great source information. You will find that he was in *Catch Me If*

---

19. Note that I say, "What you want him or her to *do*," as opposed to just "what you want." This keeps it even more active since it eliminates intangible, inactive objectives such as "I want to be happy" or "I want to tell him . . ." Approach each and every song and monologue you do by deciding what you are going to get your scene partner to do by the end of it. That is how to activate a monologue.

You Can, so you go look up that show and seek out repertoire material from it as well. And as you're investigating *Catch Me,* you notice that a guy named Brandon Wardell was Aaron's understudy in that show. Suddenly you get "sidetracked" and you look up Brandon on IBDB and you find out that he has done *Good Vibrations, Thoroughly Modern Millie,* and *James Joyce's "The Dead"* on Broadway. So now you go investigate those shows, look at/listen to clips and find that there are roles for you in them as well. And this process can go on and on without end. Follow an actor to a show, follow the show to other actors, follow those actors to other shows, and so forth. Isn't that a great way to hunt for audition cuts?[20] This is a far better method than simply starting with someone else's suggestions of monologues and songs because it begins with what attracts *you* to a specific character.

Now that you have some methods to approach finding audition repertoire, let's talk categories. I'll begin with monologues since (like it or not) all actors must have them.[21] At an absolute minimum, I would urge you to have four pieces memorized, analyzed, and at constant performance level. These pieces should comprise a classical dramatic, classical comedic, contemporary dramatic, and contemporary comedic monologue. Just to add a little clarity to the terms, classical generally means something pre-1800s in verse, such as Shakespeare or his contemporaries (and yes, there are other classical verse writers besides Shakespeare!) or something from the Greek or Roman canon, while contemporary generally means something from the mid-twentieth century (e.g., Arthur Miller, Tennessee Williams) or later. Playwrights such as Oscar Wilde, George Bernard Shaw, Henrik Ibsen, and Anton Chekhov do not really fit neatly into either category. In fact, they would provide great additional pieces for your repertoire in a fifth category of early realism.

As you read plays from each classification, continue seeking out the characters that you could play *right now* if a company were casting that show. Look for scenes in which your character engages

---

20. The answer is yes!

21. It is more and more common that you will be asked to read from the script rather than perform a monologue for auditions, but you still need to have monologues at the ready for those occasions—such as agent interviews—when they are still required.

in active pursuit of an objective from another person and see if you can't cull a monologue from that. It is probably in your best interest to have at least one of your pieces be Shakespearean, since his work is so commonly produced, and one be from a very contemporary play (as in something written in the last three to five years).

One other thing I want to clarify for you is that comedic doesn't necessarily mean "ha-ha funny," nor does dramatic necessarily indicate weepy death-cancer-suicide emoting. Remember when I told you that we want to see you being honest in the room. When you think of comedic pieces, just look for something light and possibly humorous, as opposed to a stand-up routine. And when you look for dramatic, think of finding something where your character absolutely needs her imaginary partner to do something urgently and sincerely (this is where stakes are found). Again, avoid the common temptations to break down crying in the audition or to tell a super dramatic story about something that happened in the past (e.g., anything from *The Laramie Project!*). This is not what we want to see in an audition.

It would be impossible for me to give you a list of monologues that are good in auditions. No sooner would this book be published than all of them would be overdone or yesterday's news. In the appendix of my last book, *Get the Callback*, I offered some suggested repertoire both by actor type and by genre. You are welcome to refer to that list as a jumping-off point. I also encourage you to contact the Drama Book Shop in New York (www.dramabookshop .com) and publishing houses Samuel French (www.samuelfrench .com) and Dramatist Play Service (www.dramatists.com) and make monthly investigations of newly published plays that have characters in your age range. You should also regularly be trolling Playbill .com to keep up with the latest news in Broadway, touring, and regional theatre. You will find lots of ideas for repertoire simply by following what is being produced around the country. The best thing you can do is read, read, read. Do not take shortcuts and snag audition material from collections of audition material. These are overdone and inevitably story pieces. Rather, read plays, educate yourself on the business to which you have decided to dedicate

your life, and stay current. You will find that finding audition monologues becomes a by-product of this kind of engaged, active work.

As for music, there are some fairly standard song types required
in auditions, which you should have represented in your book at all
times. Generally speaking, you will be asked to perform some variation on the following: standard ballad; standard up-tempo; comedy
song; contemporary musical theatre; pop; rock; country. While
there are countless other possibilities called for in casting ads, these
are the big ones upon which most casting directors rely. So you are
generally pretty well covered by representing at least one piece from
each of them in your audition book.[22]

Standards generally mean Broadway show tunes taken from
the Golden Age or the Jazz Age of musical theatre—this repertoire
includes anything from Rodgers and Hart, George and Ira Gersh-
win, Cole Porter, Harold Arlen, Jerome Kern, Rodgers and Hammerstein, Lerner and Loewe, Frank Loesser, Leonard Bernstein,
Betty Comden and Adolf Green, and other contemporaries of those
writers.[23] Basically, this period begins in the early 1900s and goes
up to about *Fiddler on the Roof* in 1964. The plots were simple, the
structure formulaic, and the American musical identity was beginning to form in this era. You will find more traditional song forms
with recognizable melodies throughout these composers' works.
And no matter how much rock and other contemporary styles infil-
trate the Broadway stage, the work of the Golden Age writers will
never go away; thus their audition material will always be part of the
expected repertoire. So make sure you have at least one ballad and
one up-tempo from this period.

Just keep in mind as you dig for material in any of these genres,
it is not about conforming you to any particular style or sound; rather,
it is about finding the characters and the songs from each period that
strike close to you as a person. I mention that now because I know a
lot of actresses who are more or less contemporary belt singers and do

---

22. In *Get the Callback*, I walk you through the process of building a rep book if you've
never done that before.

23. Again, in *Get the Callback*, I have recommended repertoire by genre and by actor type
in the appendixes, so I will not repeat rep lists in this book.

not consider themselves adept at performing "legit" or classical styles of singing. Legit is a weakness for them, yet they feel required to have some legit songs in their book for those occasions when standards are requested. But standard and legit are not synonymous. There are plenty of saucy, early belt character types in standard musicals (Ado Annie in *Oklahoma!*, Lois Lane in *Kiss Me, Kate*, and Reno Sweeney in *Anything Goes* to name just a few). So always remember to show your strengths in auditions rather than exposing your weaknesses. If you do not sing legit soprano, do not have legit soprano music in your book. If a particular audition is seeking legit sopranos, you are probably not going to compete in that category anyway, right? It comes back to being authentically you.

When it comes to finding comedy songs, I am going to ask you to think outside the box. The fact of the matter is, although many songs are funny within the context of the shows from which they originate, almost no songs are naturally funny in the audition room. Why? Because we know all of these standard show tunes, and what makes comedy work is the element of the unexpected. To that end, I am going to share with you a little project I do with my beginning Acting through Song class (and in the spirit of credit where credit is due, this was passed down to me by my professor, Cary Libkin at Penn State) that generally leads to some pretty great comedy audition material.

The exercise is called the "Wrong Song" exercise, and the assignment is this: Choose a song and create an utterly wrong context for it. You can bend gender, you can alter tempo (as long as you communicate this to the pianist), you can even change the key (as long as you have the music in the new key for the pianist and do not ask him to transpose on sight!). But you cannot change the lyrics. You must use the original text to create a character and a scenario completely unintended for the song. And here is the kicker—it must work for the entire song; meaning that you cannot just create something clever that works with the chorus of your song but makes no sense in the verses. It is a challenging little project, and it forces you to really examine the lyrics and create a very specific moment-to-moment circumstance and reason for every word.[24]

---

24. And really, isn't that what you should be doing with every song anyway?

I have seen some great successes with these presentations, from a man standing on a window ledge about to jump off singing "Defying Gravity" way under tempo, to a blind girl singing "Where Is Love" from *Oliver*, to a rendition of "Till There Was You" sung by a girl in solitary confinement of an insane asylum. I have even seen some bold choices that are a little too adult for this book! Now, the assignment criteria does not include being funny, yet most of these presentations tend to be hilarious. Why? Because they give us something unexpected. And also because the actors are so committed to their scenarios.

At the end of the presentations we discuss why we do the assignment. We discover that it is a great icebreaker for the first singing assignment in front of one's classmates. We discuss the aforementioned attention to detail and specificity of lyrics that it requires. And we also find that the more successful concepts lend themselves exceptionally well to comedy audition cuts! We then go around the room and tell each student what auditions his or her wrong song would be perfect audition material for.

If you try this approach to finding comedy songs, you will never have to worry about your piece being overdone! Even if you choose a common song, it is doubtful that anyone else will have presented it in the way you have chosen to present it. (There is a very manly Broadway veteran who is over six feet tall and as masculine as they come who has made a living auditioning with "I Feel Pretty.") So do some thinking and see what you come up with as your "wrong song." Start with your own repertoire and see what you can do with a song you already know. You can really do this with any genre of music from standard Broadway to pop music, so think big. And have fun.

Contemporary musical theatre is a pretty broad category. Just as I recommended with monologues, I think you should have something in your book from the last three to five years for sure. However, in truth we tend to consider anything from *Hair* to the present-day contemporary material. So again, it comes back to showing off what you do best. Do you soar on the broad, epic style of Schönberg and Boublil (*Miss Saigon, Pirate Queen, Les Miz*) or Frank Wildhorn (*Jekyll and Hyde, The Scarlet Pimpernel*)? Or do

you really excel at the poppy musical theatre sound of Stephen
Schwartz (*Godspell, Pippin, Children of Eden*) or Maltby and Shire
(*Closer Than Ever, Baby, Starting Here, Starting Now*)? And of
course, you can never go wrong with Kander and Ebb (*Steel Pier,
The Rink, Kiss of the Spider Woman*)![25]

But what about the really contemporary composers—Jason
Robert Brown, Adam Guettel, Laurence O'Keefe, Ahrens and
Flaherty? And there's an even newer wave of composers who are
not necessarily producing full musicals but rather song cycles and
cabaret/concert material, such as Jonathan Reid Gealt, Carner and
Gregor, Kerrigan and Lowdermilk, and the list goes on and on.[26]
Just visit www.newmusicaltheatre.com to see what I mean.

The answer is that all of this falls into the category of "contemporary musical theatre." You just need to do your research and find
what really speaks to you. As I said, some people will really find
that one composer's style really hits home for them while another's
just does not. I just need you to keep a couple of things in mind as
you explore the myriad composers out there: First, remember that
the audition song must meet that criteria that I laid out for monologues—it must engage you in speaking to another person from
whom you want something. So avoid story songs, just as you would
avoid story monologues. Second, it must be something that will
not make an accompanist's eyes cross at trying to play it. You may
notice that I left Sondheim out of our discussion. This is because
his music is famously hard to play. Jason Robert Brown and Adam
Guettel tend to produce very challenging accompaniments as well.
I would recommend that before you put a selection in your audition
book you set it in front of a pianist and ask her if it is playable on
sight without preparation.

One final word on the contemporary category of repertoire.
My friend VP Boyle, who has experience at all levels of Broadway
theatre, from performing, to casting, to teaching (he wrote the
incredible book *Audition Freedom*, which you must read!), goes

25. I purposely omitted *Cabaret* and *Chicago* even though they are Kander and Ebb's most
popular shows. In fact, that is why I omitted them!
26. Do be careful with song cycle and cabaret material. Although singers love to sing it,
it is not always the most effective in the audition room due to its frequent lack of character
and context and its often-meandering melodic structural nature.

so far as to create a subcategory of contemporary music, which he calls "driving dramatic." I love this! It means that something in your book requires you to really attack a song and to increase the stakes based on the circumstance and the accompaniment, but it really does not count as either a ballad or an up-tempo. Some examples would be "Back to Before" from *Ragtime*; "Gethsemane" from *Jesus Christ Superstar*; "Finishing the Hat" from *Sunday in the Park with George*; "Willing to Ride" from *Steel Pier*; and "Forest for the Trees" from *Spitfire Grill*. This type of song can be very effective in the audition room. See if you can find one sung by a character you might play.

And now we touch on the type of music that is really the most commonly required in auditions today: popular music. You may read ads in the trade papers that call for "pop," "pop/rock," "rock," "country," "R & B," "disco," "blues," "gospel," or even "club/dance." All of these subgenres are considered to be forms of pop music. Basically they are asking you to sing a song that is not part of a musical theatre piece. Let me repeat myself so that you are quite clear on that point: When they ask for any form of popular music, they do *not* want you singing from a show! (*Hair, Jesus Christ Superstar, Rent, Spring Awakening, American Idiot, Movin' Out, Jersey Boys*, etc., are all shows. You cannot sing that material when an audition calls for a pop song!) If I have not mentioned it already, this leads me to a very important piece of advice as you plan repertoire for any given audition. Be sure that you read the casting call very carefully and give them what they ask for. If they want pop music, do not sing from a show score (even if you are using music that was originally pop but later integrated into a show, such as *Rock of Ages, Mamma Mia*, etc.). If they want Broadway or show music, do not sing pop. Even if you think you have the perfect song for the show they are casting but they have asked that you do not sing that kind of song, do not sing it. Trust me, following guidelines tells us a lot about you as someone we do or do not want to hire.

I suspect that some of you reading this book are greatly relieved by the movement toward popular music in auditions today, while some of you feel cheated and frustrated by the diminishing call for old standards. But you are a professional, and part of your work is to be ready for anything that comes your way. Just remember to stay on message with your brand as you seek out material of any genre.

So let us begin by thinking about what music you love. Some people really truly love country music. I am not one of those people. So country would not be the first piece of the puzzle that I would tackle. I grew up on classic rock tunes that my parents used to play for me, and I also enjoyed the music of the '80s and the '90s (when I saw *Rock of Ages* for the first time, I don't think I have ever had so much fun in the theatre!). So if I were looking to start working on some pop repertoire, I would probably start with artists such as Chicago, Fleetwood Mac, the Eagles, REM, Bryan Adams, and maybe a little Huey Lewis and the News. These are artists that can cover both "pop" and "pop/rock" calls and I enjoy singing their material. For something a little more contemporary, I might look into Rufus Wainwright or Jason Mraz's catalogs. Even if you do not know me, you are probably getting a sense of my style by the list of artists to whom I gravitate. It is really important to start with what you love because this will help your humanity shine through ever so much more. (The caveat is that just because you love it does not mean you should sing it. It may be out of your range or it may not demonstrate any particular vocal prowess.) Among all the subgenres of pop, this is the area where I really live.

But what if an audition call is asking for country music, which, I mentioned earlier, is really not my thing? Does that mean I skip that audition all together? Possibly; but I think there is an alternative solution, which requires thinking outside of the box again. If my goal is to show them who *I* am in an audition while still giving them what they have asked to see, I may need to tweak something in my repertoire to meet the audition requirements. As it turns out, the Eagles, although considered a great California classic rock band, happen to have many songs with a southern bent to them. In fact, country artists have covered many of their songs. So, instead of torturing myself trying to fit a square peg into a round hole and coming up with a killer Keith Urban or Clint Black song (no judgment on them, it is just not my preference), I can go in with a tune I really enjoy and connect to and sell that. For example, I could easily bring "Take It Easy" or "Peaceful, Easy Feeling" as a country song and still feel like I am being true to myself and to my sensibilities as an artist. Likewise, if the audition required a blues song, I am never going to pull off a Robert Johnson or a B. B. King song, but I can probably find something by Eric Clapton that I can really put over.

What I find immensely fun about the invasion of popular music into the theatre world is that it really opens the door for people to showcase their personalities in ways never before possible (just go be a fly on the wall for any *Mamma Mia* audition!). And the choices are limitless, since new music is released constantly. You should get yourself on Spotify and Pandora radio if you have not already. Both of these websites are terrific sources for finding new and exciting pop music ideas for auditions. You can do a variation of "chasing the carrot" on Pandora, simply by typing in an artist you like and then listening as the magic of the Internet finds you tons of other artists similar to them. Then once you find a great song for you, you can either go to www.sheetmusicdirect.com or www.musicnotes.com to seek out the printed music. Just beware that many of these songs are not in very piano-friendly arrangements. If you are serious about this career, it is totally worth the investment to have a professional create great piano audition arrangements for your pop songs. This way, what you hear in the audition room will come much closer to the feeling you got from hearing the song on the radio.

Speaking of piano arrangements, one other factor you might consider when looking for pop—particularly rock—audition material is how it will sound played on a solo piano. If you are coming up with real guitar-driven songs, you may be very disappointed and thrown off when you get in the room and the accompaniment sounds like some other song you have never heard. Look for music that is based in piano and get someone to play it for you before the audition so you know what it will sound like without the other instrumentation. And here is a piece of sage advice: Let the percussion section of the music live within you during your audition. Even though nobody in the room will hear it, you should have the drumbeat going in your head, and you should let that driving beat emanate from within you as you perform your audition.

When VP Boyle teaches his remarkable pop/rock class in New York, he talks about the pop section of your audition book being an expansive portion containing a variety of "colors" within the genre. It is up to you to find which colors work for you, whether you excel at country, grunge, bubblegum pop, folk, or scream metal. Work on finding a variety of pieces that showcase your personality as well as your vocal chops for any pop-rock audition that might come up. I highly recommend that you check out Sheri Sanders's book *Rock the Audition*. To my knowledge it is the only book out there that actually walks you through finding and performing pop music throughout the eras and genres, and it even comes with a DVD to help you hear and see some examples. Like VP, Sheri is one of the biggest names in the industry today helping actors prepare to give killer auditions for the contemporary theatre. Read her book and take one of her classes if you can.

There are plenty of resources out there for you to find great material for your audition repertoire—the best of which are, of course, play scripts and musical libretti. I did not intend this to be a book about helping you seek out specific pieces; rather, my work with you in this book is in regard to creating and marketing your own personal brand. And so I must sum up this section on repertoire with one vital reminder: Make sure that every piece you choose to work on and bring in to auditions speaks to you in some real way and reveals some of your soul to the creative team behind the table. Make sure as well that it stays on message and conveys something of that brand you worked so hard to create.

Be especially careful when teachers assign you material to learn—particularly voice teachers, whose agenda might be to find you material that makes your voice grow or soar in some wonderful way, rather than giving you material that hits close to your heart and to your type.[27] Make sure you are not sending mixed messages to the people in the audition room (as in, looking like a sassy best friend, having a headshot that represents that type, but choosing to sing classic ingénue material). And above all, make this an ongoing project that never ends—continue to refine your repertoire and expand it. Keep reading plays and seeing productions and looking for material that would really work for you. And if you ever get the opportunity to do so, for goodness sake get

---

27. Voice teachers, I love you. I am generalizing here, so please do not be offended. But if you choose material for your students, consider their type and branding message in addition to the sound of the voice.

yourself into an audition room behind the table as either a monitor, a reader, an assistant, or an observer. This way, you can see what people do well and not so well; what the casting people really respond to; and of course, what material people are coming in with that you might be able to steal!

Business Cards and Postcards

Two additional powerful marketing tools for actors are the business card and the postcard. They are both smaller, more portable ways to broadcast your brand beyond the headshot in the audition room. For starters, it is great to have a postcard with your headshot and name across the front and your contact information plus room for a personal message on the back. After a particularly successful callback or a terrific class or workshop, it is nice to drop a postcard in the mail to the casting director or to the person who taught the class and thank them for their time. As with cover letters, we want to be brief and specific (the nature of the postcard certainly forces brevity), touching on something they did for you or something you learned in your time with them. Here are two examples:

Dear Joy,

Thank you so much for taking the time to work my cut of "The Day after That"[28] with me in the audition room for *Ragtime* today. You really helped me make some great discoveries with the piece. I look forward to hearing from you again soon.

Best,
Jonathan

Dear Ashley,

Thank you so much for all your insight tonight at your Actors Connection class. I enjoyed working through my monologue from *Seminar* with you, and I hope that we might work together in the future.

Warmest regards,
Jonathan

---

28. Great driving dramatic Kander and Ebb song for men!

Again, notice that I specify exactly what they did for which I am expressing my gratitude. I do this for two reasons: First, it reminds them of exactly who I am since they may have seen hundreds of people that day; and second, it makes the postcard correspondence more personal and less formulaic (as in "Thank you for your time today."). In short, it shows that what they did for you was worthy of you taking the time to specifically acknowledge them in a note with postage paid!

The other great use of the postcard is to announce a performance or a success to people in the industry with whom you already have some established relationship. As opposed to a mass e-mail, the postcard is much more personal and it literally puts your face and your brand into their hands. Here is what I mean:

Dear Diane,

I wanted to let you know that I will be appearing as Dwarf #3 this holiday season in *Christmas Dwarves on Ice* at the Dive Theatre, from November 30 through December 29. Please let me know if you have a night free to be my guest and catch a performance.

All the best,
Jonathan

Dear Nikole,

I'm pleased to announce that I have just signed with Joe Thompson at the Talent Bunch. I wanted to let you know since I've had some terrific callbacks with you. Having representation is a real boost to my career, and I look forward seeing you at more auditions as a Talent Bunch client.

Sincerely,
Jonathan

It is important that when you order postcards, you use the same photograph and name font that appear on your headshot. There used to be a notion that you could send them a postcard that shows them a different look than your headshot that you gave them at the audition; however, it is not hard to see how this can get us away from our consistent branding message. Instead, we want to saturate their minds with our image like a corporation does with its logo.

The other wonderful marketing tool for your actor business is the good old business card. Nowadays it is not an expensive endeavor to order large quantities of cards in full color with your headshot on one side and your information on the other. The business card should be carried around with you at all times. You never know when you might be at a restaurant or a party or a Laundromat and meet someone who could help your career in some way. While it is very easy to exchange phone numbers and e-mail by whipping out your smartphones, it is a far better marketing strategy to put your face and your brand into their hands by passing them a business card.

I recommend that the side with your photo be just that—your photo. While on the back, you should include your name, your phone number, your e-mail address, and your website. You can even include a little branding phrase if you like. I have a former student named Vassiliki whose name is a bit tripping on the average tongue, so her card is marked with a big "V" on the back, which has really become her nickname as well as part of her brand. I have another former student who includes "Quirks for hire" on the back of her card. I even have a student who has a caricature sketch of himself on the back of his card, demonstrating his sense of humor and charm. You can be creative on this as long as you remain professional.

In Keith Ferrazzi's terrific book, *Never Eat Alone*, he refers to the "Networking Jerk" who is in a hurry to press his card into as many hands as possible at a business event. I echo Keith's sentiment in warning you not to be this person. The business card exchange comes at the end of a discussion, after you have made a real connection with someone new. It should really only be given out when accompanying a dialogue that includes something to the effect of, "We should get together sometime" or "Let me get your number and I'll give you a call" or "I can send you the information about that class—what's your e-mail address?" You should not, on the other hand, be walking up to people and passing off your card to everyone you meet and exchange pleasantries with.

One other use of the business card can really replace the postcard altogether. I know many actors who, instead of sending out a postcard to say thank you, prefer to send out an actual "Thank You" card on stationery. They will buy cards in a color/design scheme that really matches their personality, their brand, and their website design, and when they send out the personalized cards, they will insert a business card inside, so that the recipient is still getting a photograph with the correspondence. This method is certainly as effective as the postcard—it is all a matter of personal preference.

There are dozens of websites that offer mass quantities of high-quality postcards and business cards at a very low rate. I have found www.vistaprint.com to be reliable, inexpensive, and quick on delivery. Just be sure to choose a template and a color scheme that stays consistent with your brand and your web design (which we will be discussing momentarily) so that the power of branding can continue to work in your favor.

PERFORMER PROFILE
Aaron Galligan-Stierle,
Actor, Director, Audition Coach

Laura Rose Photography

Meet Aaron Galligan-Stierle!

Aaron is an actor, director, audition coach, and creative consultant. His Broadway credits include *The Phantom of the Opera*, *Ragtime*, and *Dr. Seuss' How the Grinch Stole Christmas*. Other major credits include the international tour of *Cinderella* staring Lea Salonga; four seasons at the Tony Award–winning Utah Shakespearean Festival, and major roles at regional theaters across the country including the Kennedy Center, Papermill Playhouse, TUTS, Westport Country Playhouse, Pennsylvania Shakespeare, and many more. Aaron is a faculty member in the Musical Theater Division of the New York Film Academy and has taught workshops and acting classes across the country. Aaron also co-owns the film production company Lonely Planet Productions. He received his BFA in Musical Theater from Shenandoah University and his MFA in acting from Penn State University. More information can be found at www.aarongs.com.

JF: *How long have you lived in New York City?*
AGS: Seven years.

JF: *How long did you live in New York and audition before you booked your first professional work?*
AGS: I was booking work before I moved here. Throughout high school and college I did professional summer stock each year, followed by two seasons at the Lost Colony. While in grad school, I worked at the Tony Award–winning Utah Shakespearean Festival for two seasons, and then I moved to New York (and did one subsequent season at Utah). After moving to NY, I did a showcase in the fall and one in the spring. Then I did a nonunion, paid understudy job. All of those happened within the first nine months. Then I went to Utah. Upon returning, I got my Equity card doing *White Christmas* (one year after moving here).

JF: *How long did it take you to book your first Broadway gig?*
AGS: Two years, almost to the day. I moved to NYC in September and booked *Grinch* in July two years later, but it began rehearsing in September. Fun fact: each of my subsequent Broadway gigs has happened almost exactly two years to the day later!

JF: *How long did you stay non-Equity before joining the union and what made you join it when you did?*
AGS: I stayed in the nonunion world because every professional job I was taking gave me points toward the union. I always was looking toward joining the union. I turned Equity for two reasons: (1) it is impossible to make a living in the nonunion world; and (2) after the third season at Utah Shakes, I simultaneously received my last required point[29] and was offered my first Equity contract within one week. I took that as a sign.

JF: *How did you get an agent? Did you book work without representation or has your success come since you've had an agent?*
AGS: I had work before I had an agent (Utah). Once I moved to New York, I got my agent through the Penn State MFA showcase. I was asked to sign immediately. Essentially I was with them for four years, during which (with the exception of one small regional job) I booked every job on my own. I had the agent but they did not submit me for any of the jobs I took (including two Broadway shows, a national tour, an international tour, and countless regional gigs). Then I changed to a different agency that I could not have gotten without the previous representation or the previous credits. This new agency has gotten me every job since I signed with them, and they have introduced me to a huge amount of

---

29. It takes fifty weeks of working in an Equity theatre under Equity Membership Candidate Program guidelines to earn your way into the union. More on that later.

contacts and booked me for countless auditions that I would not have been able to get without them.

JF: *You are married with a child. Anything you want to share about how you balance life in show business with that relationship?*
AGS: It is very hard. There is a conflict. That being said, the most important things are: (a) a partner who understands your career and passion at an incredibly deep, visceral level (possibly a former performer); (b) a commitment to making that relationship work even if it at times causes conflict or your career to be challenged; and (c) a lot of luck.

JF: *Any "pearls of wisdom" that you'd like to offer to young actors planning to make a go at this industry? Maybe share the biggest lesson you've learned since being in the biz?*
AGS: Get your finances in order. Do not rack up debt of any kind for any reason. Save everything—as much money as you possibly can. Keep your living expenses as low as you possibly can at all times. Because even if you have a huge success, that success will end and you'll be back to making no money. So save the money while you have it, rather than spending it, and you'll survive the inevitable dry spell.

WEBSITES

We have reached an age where it is virtually unacceptable for an actor not to have his own website. It is simply too easy to build, design, and maintain a presence on the web and so the expectation is that everyone will do it. Websites have become essential marketing tools for artists. I have personally steered casting directors to several actors' websites on their search for a particular role. On the website, one can find the actor's resume, headshots, and media clips, along with contact information. When well maintained, the actor website is another ace branding method that can really provide an edge in the industry.

The good news is, if you are a technophobe (like me!) there are simple click-and-drag templates available that will make it easy as pie for you to craft a very adequate website. The other good news is that you can always hire someone to do it for you. You will most likely get a better, slicker site, although you will have to budget to have it built and maintained. The trick is to make it user friendly, eye catching, and consistent with your branding statement.

Whether you are going to do it yourself or hire a designer, if you are going to call yourself a professional actor, you must get moving on this right away. I suggest you begin by seeking out and purchasing your domain name. The domain name is basically the web address where your site will live. The reason I start with this is because you want the website to be as simple to find as possible—best-case scenario, it is your name (e.g., www.jonathanflom.com). However, your name may already be taken. The easiest way to check for your domain's availability is to visit a site such as www.godaddy.com. When you arrive on the website, you will see a box that says, "Search for a new domain." Type in your name as you would have it appear and it will give you results. It may say that the domain is already taken, in which case it might offer you other suffixes, such as .co, .org, or .net. You can either go with one of those or you can play with variations on your name until you find something easy to remember and marketable. For instance, some people use a hyphen (www.jonathan-flom .com); some people will use their middle name (www.jonathanseth flom.com); some will use initials (www.jsflom.com). The trick is not to stray too far from your actual name, as we want instant recognition with your web address—something sticky that people will remember.

Once you find a match for your domain name, I suggest you purchase it immediately so that you own it and nobody else can take it from you. You do not have to have content for a site yet, nor do you have to be ready to launch it, but purchasing the domain ensures that when you are ready to design and go live with your site, you will have a place for it on the Internet. At the time I am writing this, the going rate for a two-year contract on domain with GoDaddy.com is $25.34. Now you may be able to seek out even cheaper rates, but what I like about GoDaddy is that it is simple to use and it is one-stop shopping. They sell domains as well as templates, hosting (we will get to that soon), and other great services.

Now that you have become the sole owner of your very own domain, it is time to start building an eye-catching, slick actor website. Before we get into the ways of going about building the actual page, let's discuss what content we want to have present on a great site. First, we will begin with the essential items:

1. *Your name and headshot.* Remember, this is all about branding. You want your "swoosh" to be the first thing people see when they log on to your site, so put it front and center.
2. *Current news and announcements.* You want to be able to report any successes, such as shows you will be in, conferences you will be attending, awards you have won or for which you have been nominated, agent signing, etc. Just remember to keep it related to your business.
3. *Headshot and resume.* Because so much of the casting process is done electronically now, you will want to have both a viewable and a downloadable version of your headshot and resume available on your website.
4. *Contact page.* Most websites have a "contact me" tab through which a person could type in her e-mail address and a message to you without having to leave your web page and copy your e-mail address into an actual fully composed message. That message will be relayed directly to your inbox, as any other, and it will include the return address of the sender.

Those are the four absolutely necessary items on your website. At minimum, you could launch a successful site if you had the above information ready to go. However, as you get creative and personalize your web page, you may consider the following as possible content as well:

1. *About Me.* Many people like to include a brief biographical page on their site. This might sound a good deal like the "sixty-second pitch" we did at the beginning of this book. It might showcase your sense of humor, and it should certainly tell us more than your life as a performer. It can be casual and should really ring out with your personal voice. Keep it consistent with your brand, and find at least one or two unique things to highlight. You may even choose to include a childhood photo of you on this page.

One thing to avoid is date of birth—remember, we do not want to indicate your age anywhere on the resume or website.

2. *Photo Gallery.* Remember when you were going through your headshots and, even though you had to narrow it down to the *one* singular best shot for your brand, you found so many great photos of you that you just wanted to use? Well, here is your chance. A photo gallery might include other shots from your session (oftentimes, photographers will take some silly, candid pictures during a shoot, and those can be used here to showcase your personality), photos from productions, behind-the-scenes or backstage shots (keep it tasteful!), or even photos of you doing things other than acting—such as playing a sport or demonstrating one of your special skills. Again, just remember that this is business, and it must all have a purpose.

3. *Media.* This gets a little sticky because of copyright law. We have former students asking us all the time for archival footage of them performing in shows at Shenandoah, and we simply cannot share it with them, due to licensing arrangements. However, if you have video of you in rehearsals, in concert or cabaret settings, in an arranged studio setup, or magically in some publicity recording of a production, you may wish to post *short* (no more than thirty-second) clips on your website. It is all well and good for a casting director to see your picture and read your resume, but it can really make a big impact if you have some really great video (or even audio, for that matter) clips of you performing. And again, that performing does not need to be in a stage production. It can be reel footage from film work or voice-over demo; it can be special skills (e.g., fire-eating or tumbling); it can be concert footage; it can be original songs that you write and perform. See if you can come up with three or four short media clips that really show you off *well*. That is really important—they must be high quality and you must be at your absolute best, or it is not worth posting them. Also, if you have a YouTube channel (more on that in the next section), you can include a link to that as well.

4. *Reviews.* If you have had newspapers review your work favorably, you may wish to have a page that includes these reviews,

either partially or in full. Just be sure to cite the source and the production information.

5. *Other "Services."* If you do something other than perform (e.g., costume design, graphic art, coaching, web design!, Pilates instruction, etc.), you may wish to include either a page about it on your actor website, or a link to an external site if you have a separate one for your other business.

6. *Links.* Many actors choose to include external links to their Facebook, LinkedIn, YouTube, or Tumblr pages. In addition, you might link the theatre(s) for whom you are working currently, the photographer who did your headshots, or the professional whom you may have hired to design your website.

Take a look at the following actor websites and navigate your way around them to see what they have done. See where you can note elements of their personal brands within the design and content. Notice what they have chosen to include and how they have formatted their sites. This should give you some clearer ideas of what I am talking about.

www.jessiehooker.com
www.aarongs.com
www.dougshapiro.com
www.matthewdelorenzo.com
www.emilykayelynn.com
www.ehlersonline.com (with this one, just let the photos scroll to the music for a while and you will really get a taste for who this artist is!)

So, are you ready to start building your own killer website now? You may have noticed that with several of the above examples, as well as on my own website, when you first enter, you see a logo that says "Wix.com" as it loads the page. Wix.com is one of the easiest, most user-friendly site builders, and I highly recommend it.[30] You will not need an instruction manual or a detailed step-by-step from

---

30. As a matter of fact, you can even purchase your domain directly through Wix and have everything through one company, rather than using GoDaddy *and* Wix.

me to figure out how to build your site on Wix. It is all right there for you. You simply choose a template (remember your brand!), and you begin to load content by either typing it in or clicking and dragging files and photos from your computer. I have built several sites on Wix and most of my students have used it as well, to great success. It is easy to design and it is just as simple to maintain, so you can really keep it up to date. You will inevitably find some challenges along the way in formatting, but be patient, and remember that this takes some time. Be creative and try to solve any problems you encounter as gracefully and artistically as possible so that you create something that really represents you clearly.

Other possible options are to use the template design settings available through GoDaddy.com or to use iWeb, which comes standard on MacBooks. All three of these options are template based and require no experience in web design or coding. The only downside is that you are limited to the predesigned templates, so you may feel a bit restricted artistically.

Let's take a little bit of time and walk through the early phases of building a Wix.com site. Once you have established an account with them, you will begin the process by clicking "Create" along the top tabs. Browse the templates and find one that speaks to you. Realize too that the templates are just placeholders—all the photos, layout, and information you see on the premade Wix designs are editable. You can change the color scheme, the background, the page arrangement, and so forth. But starting with a blueprint might just make it that much easier for you in the beginning. You can also choose from among "Blank templates" if you want a little more personal creative freedom.

You will note in the examples I provided that Matthew's is very professional, simple, and clean, while Jessie's leans more on the side of fun and colorful. Michael's is energetic and edgy (I mean, come on, his branding statement is right there on the home page!), while Aaron's is slick and cool.[31] What is your personal brand? Which template style stays consistent with the product you're selling? Try to find one that works. (You will notice under the "Music

---

31. And just as a point of information, I should point out that both Aaron and Doug have professionals design and maintain their websites—they are not done through templates.

and Entertainment" tab on Wix, there's even a specific set of categories for actors.)

Once you have found the template that works for you, choose
the "Edit this site" option. And voila! You get a brief, instant help
video from the fine folks at Wix to get you started and you are on
your way to customizing your web presence. Just remember that
you can click on the help option at any time to get advice on how
to navigate the process. Also, be sure to save your work regularly.
When I was designing my site, every once in a while my computer
would freeze up, and if I had not saved recently then I was redoing
design work that I had already done.

I suggest you begin with the home page. Create something eye
catching and functional. Some people have a brief news feed right
there on their home page, while others choose to make "News" a
tab-click option. Some people have the home page include all the
tabs to navigate the site, while others simply open with a name
and photo and you have to click to enter the full site. I have shown
you examples of both. I have also given you an example of someone who incorporates music into his home page. Whatever you
do, try not to clutter the home page with too much information.
Another solid piece of advice is to try not to make people scroll
down the page to see everything. It is better if it is all viewable in
the single screen shot.

Once you have your home page built, it is time to start adding additional content. You may as well start with the essentials I
listed a couple of pages back: News, Headshot and Resume, and
Contact. As I said, you may have already included a newsfeed on
your home page, but if you have not, you will need to create a page
for it. Do so by clicking "Add Page" under the page manager on
the right side of the screen. Then choose your layout (again, you
can customize it so don't be deterred by the limited style options),
and you are off and running.

Each time you create a new page, you will want to be sure to
name it. Whatever name you choose is what will appear in the
clickable tabs on your site, so keep it short and precise (News,
About, Resume, Media, Contact, etc.). Also, do not worry about
the order in which you create the pages as you build your site. You

can always shuffle the order of the pages (and their respective tabs) by moving them within the "Page Manager" box.

Remember when I told you that you might encounter some challenges in the process? Well, no portion of this process is likely to be more frustrating than creating the cleanly formatted resume page. I am going to offer you two suggestions, either of which should save you at least some of the innumerable hours I spent experimenting with ways to make things line up evenly! It is important that the resume be both viewable and downloadable on your website. You want someone to be able to obtain and print a copy of your resume, but you do not want him to be required to download it just to see it. The downloadable file is simple to create. We will start with that.

First, once you have a beautifully formatted resume, save it as a PDF file instead of a DOC (this allows people to get a copy but not to edit it). Go ahead and save your headshot (which is most likely in JPG form) as a PDF as well. Next, go to the "My Files" tab on the left side of your Wix page. Click on "Upload," and then find your resume file from among the choices on your computer. Upload the PDF copy of your headshot, while you are at it. Then once you have them both uploaded, you will see under "My Files" that it tells you to "Click an item to add it to your site." So go ahead and click both the PDF for your headshot and for your resume, and you will see the buttons added to your page. Once they are on there, you can move them around, you can change the image that appears on the button, you can rename the file. Just play around with it and come up with something that you like.

Now comes the difficult part. You need to make your resume appear on the page in full view. If you were to hand type the entire resume, it would be a painstaking process to make all of your columns line up perfectly; yet they must. Unlike our work on your actual resume document, where the Tab key replaces the space bar for formatting purposes and clean lines, that will not work on Wix. I have found that the only way to guarantee everything lining up beautifully is to put each individual section and column into its own text box. It is simple to get the boxes lined up perfectly (as you move a box around on a page, measuring lines will pop up to show you how that box lines up with the others), then you can just type one column into each box and the information will surely format correctly. You may need to condense the resume or make a sort of "highlights" version so that you don't have to mess with scrolling, which can become insanely complicated when dealing with multiple text boxes on a single page. So try to fit as much as you can onto the single page and save yourself some headaches!

Go ahead and try this. Create a text box for your name first. Move your cursor over the "Add" button, and then click on "Text." For your name, you can use a "Title," but for the rest of the information, you will want to use "Paragraphs." Remember to find a font for your name that closely approximates what is on your headshot and your actual resume. Then just continue to add text boxes for each component of the page: Contact information and vital stats; "Theatre Experience" (can be a "Title" as well); show column (in italics!); role column; theatre/venue/company column; "Training" title (list of all your training); "Special Skills" title (list of all your special skills). As I said, it is quite a bit of work to format this way, but it will look good once you put all the work in.

The other option for you to make your resume viewable is to take a screenshot of it and then upload it as a photo on your web page. On a Mac, you do this by holding down Command+Shift+4, after which you will see a target cursor appear. Drag the area you want to save, and once you release the mouse you will hear the sound of a photo being taken and then you will find a "Screenshot" file on your desktop. From there, you can upload it into Wix just as we uploaded those other files, and then you can add the screenshot onto a page like a photograph.

The downside of using the screenshot method is that you cannot scroll at all for the shot—it will only be able to capture as much image as is on the screen at one time without scrolling down. So you may have to shrink your resume view down to about 80 percent in order to capture it all in one image. Try that method and see if it works for you.

Are you still with me? Do you have a page now that shows your resume and also includes buttons to download both the resume and the headshot? Great! If you got through all that work, then you deserve a reward. Get a latte or an ice cream or go take a nap or read a chapter or two of a great book (other than this one!). Just remember to save your work before you close out!

When you are ready to continue, why don't you make your contact page, since that is incredibly easy to do? Simply click on the "Add Page" button on the right, and choose one of the "Contact" layouts. Then you can customize it and make it your own. If a contact form does not automatically appear in the template, you may have to add it. To do so, scroll over to "Add" on the left side, and choose "Widgets" as your option. Then choose "Contact form" and select which variation you would prefer. Once your contact form is added to the page, be sure to link it to your e-mail so that anyone sending a message gets routed to you properly. Do this by clicking on your contact form while in the edit mode and selecting "E-mail"; then type in your e-mail address and all memos will go straight to the address you provide.

By the way, if you should want to have a "Contact Me" button on any or all of the pages of your website, that is easy to do. On any given page, simply go to "Add"; choose "Navigation" then "Buttons"; select the button you would like and edit it to say "Contact Me"; then click on where you laid the button and choose the option that says "Link." Select "E-mail" and add your e-mail address, and once again, anyone who clicks that button will be able to route a personal message to your e-mail.

By this point, you should be getting the hang of how to use this Wix thing. You will probably not take long to surpass my own knowledge of the site, and the more time you spend playing around on it, the more likely you are to discover new and exciting things. You will notice that there is an option at the top of the editing page that says "Preview" (right next to the all-important-yes-I'll-repeat-myself-once-more *Save* tab). You can click on the Preview tab at any time to get a glimpse of what your website will look like and how it will function once it is live online.

The only other functional piece of information I want to share with you about building your website on Wix is how to link something to an outside web page. For instance, if you are appearing in a production and you want people to be able to go to the theatre's website and purchase tickets, you can create an announcement on your newsfeed with a note that says "Click Here for Information and Tickets." After typing that (or whatever you want it to say), highlight the particular text you want to link, and then click the Link symbol at the top right in the text edit toolbox (it looks something like a diagonal number 8). You will get a pop-up window that asks you to choose the type of link. For an outside website, select "URL," and then either type in or copy and paste the website to which you want to direct people. You will notice there is also an option for linking a Wix page—this is how you will help people navigate between pages on your own website, if you have not figured that out already.

At this point, I am going to leave you to figure out the rest on your own. I have gotten you started, and hopefully you are well on your way to building the quintessential actor site. Trial and error is your friend throughout this process; so do not get discouraged if it does not come together exactly how you imagined after just one sitting! I assign this project to my students about halfway through the semester (as it appears about halfway through this book), and it is the final culminating project of their Preparation for the Profession course, so they are expected to work on it for about seven or eight weeks (or a few really late nights, as the case might just be with the few procrastinators I have!).

Once you have the entire site designed and ready to launch live to the world, you need to purchase what is called "hosting." This means you are paying for space on the World Wide Web to hold your site, to keep e-mails (that's right, you can create e-mail accounts directly through your website, such as jonathan@jonathan flom.com), and so forth. To give you an idea of the cost of hosting, it can run anywhere from $4.50 to $8.99 a month on a yearly contract for 150GB of space, plus your e-mail addresses and the ability to host multiple websites. Basically, this type of plan is more than sufficient for your actor website. Depending on when you sign up and which company you go with, there are usually multiple promotions going on (today GoDaddy is giving away free domain names with the purchase of hosting).

As I indicated earlier, you can buy the hosting through one company and build the site on another, or you can go for the one-stop-shopping approach. Either way, once you pay to have your site hosted, you should get an e-mail with explicit instructions on how to connect your site to the live domain on the web. They will send you your DNS host number and your DNS IP, which you will use to link the site with the Internet. I designed my original site with iWeb a few years back. Then I bought the domain and the hosting with GoDaddy and found it incredibly easy to link the two. Then, last year when I redesigned my site on Wix, I found it equally easy to switch the site over. Again, I am a technological idiot, so you should have no problem whatsoever if you just follow the instructions on the e-mail you get or utilize the online help options. I also recommend that you save any e-mails you get from Wix or GoDaddy regarding your setup, so that way if you need to change anything, you will have all the original information handy.

Best of luck creating your stunning website! Remember to have fun and really let your creative personality shine through. Once you have it up and running, you can always play around with new designs, additional pages, updated information, and so forth. And do be sure that you upload a new resume whenever you add a credit to your list.

SOCIAL MEDIA

I want to spend a little bit of time talking about social media, its power, and its dangers with you. I am specifically going to address Facebook, Twitter, and YouTube since those are the big three for performing artists at the time of writing this book. But what I have to say about them should apply universally to any other myriad trends that pop up between when I write this and when you read it.

The first, biggest, and most hard-and-fast rule I must lay down for you is that *nothing* is private. And your reputation is everything. You must remember that mantra every time you go to post something on social media, be it a photo or a "tweet" or a video. No matter how private your settings are, you should just assume that someone from the industry will see what you have posted, and you *must* ask yourself before pushing "post" whether it could reflect negatively on you.

I know many potential employers, both within theatre as well as in the world of "day jobs," who will look a possible employee/ company member up on the Internet before offering them a job. They will search you on Facebook and they will also Google your name to see what comes up. We even do it now when we are re- cruiting prospective students for the conservatory—as they send in prescreen audition videos, we often see if they have additional material posted on YouTube that can give us a further indication of their talents (for better or for worse). It may sound invasive and a bit like stalking, but with all the information available, why wouldn't one do his research before offering a person a job or admittance to a school? The bottom line is that if you have anything online that paints you as wild, difficult, inappropriate, or negative in any way, it could adversely affect your chances of getting hired. Furthermore, if you have low-quality videos of you performing in which you are not at your best, they could also leave an irreparable first impression.

So the first thing I am going to ask you to do at this point is to take some time to go in great detail through your social media. Review every photo and posting of you (or about you) on Facebook and remove anything that makes you seem unprofessional or too much of a party guy/girl.[32] The next step is to increase your privacy settings to the maximum. Make sure that only your friends can view your profile, your photos, and your wall posts. Also ensure that you must approve anything to be posted on your timeline by someone else. And finally, make sure your phone number is not readily avail- able on your Facebook page. While this will not completely keep your page private, it will certainly limit the amount of access that people get to your postings if they are not your friends. Once you have enhanced all of your privacy settings, you must still use great tact when deciding what to post on your page. Everything is fair game for scrutiny.

I want to share a brief story with you to illustrate my point fur- ther. I was shown a video on YouTube of a Broadway-level actress performing "Defying Gravity" from *Wicked* in Chicago, and I agreed

---

32. I know, you might say that Facebook is personal and it is only for your friends to see, but trust me, everyone sees it, and in this business you do not get to have that kind of personal space online. If you really need that personal page, consider using an alias, instead of your real name.

with the person who showed it to me that it was the best rendition of the song that I had ever heard. I went ahead and posted a link to the video on my wall with a note about how great I thought it was. As is often the case with Facebook, this led to a lively conversation about what others thought of the performance—most were in agreement that it was stunning, but a couple of people questioned what made it any better than other versions and some even went on to pick apart this particular singer. Well, you can probably guess that within a few degrees of "friend separation," the actress in question saw the post via my original friend who showed me the video in the first place. (When he commented on how much he loved her interpretation, her name got tagged and thus she could follow the entire thread.) The next day, she had commented on the post, thanking those of us who praised her work and agreeing with others that it was not the perfect performance. (She did say, however, that she learned to always call out of *Wicked* on the day when you have strep throat!) Mantra number two—recite it with me: The world is small!

Next project: If you have any videos up on YouTube, please review them and see that they are videos that you would be happy representing you to a potential agent. Enough said? You have to control what is out there about you because your reputation must be within your control. You should also just do a Google search of your name and see what comes up, because you know someone else will do that. And my rules for Twitter use are the same that apply to postings on Facebook.

Well, now that I have been a social media humbug, I will tell you that there is a great deal of virtue to these Internet outlets. For starters, I do not know how any of us would know what is happening in the world without Facebook and Twitter! While I have not crossed over into the Twitter world yet, many actor friends in New York swear by it—not just for the ability to share constant updates of what one is doing at any given moment but also because there are audition services posted (such as when there are short lines at certain calls in the city, or when an Equity call may be seeing nonunion performers). In addition, as impersonal as it can be, Facebook does make it much easier to stay connected to far more people. Sometimes just "liking" or commenting on someone's posts from time to time is enough to stay in their consciousness, and that can be a big part of the game. Just recently I was trying to gather some actors for a reading of a script I was writing. I went right to my Facebook page and scrolled through my entire list of friends for ideas. I'm sure if I do it, others are doing it as well.

It is also great to be able to share production announcements, major career milestones, successes, and photos with a large group of people at once. You may even choose to create a fan page for yourself as an actor and invite people to "like" your page. This can be the outlet for all your business-related announcements, while your personal page can be just that: personal. (Again, observing the rules of good taste and decorum.) I do think it is important to have a presence on Facebook, as long as you are careful to maintain it in an appropriate way.

As for YouTube, its effectiveness is apparent in the number of people who have become "YouTube sensations" almost overnight. People have literally built careers from regular postings of great material on YouTube. The key is to make sure it is great. Sure, you could take the horrible postings route and get famous just as quickly, but I do not think that is what you really want to do. Nor should getting famous be the goal. Rather, the objective is to have some stellar representations of your talent (and your brand!) searchable on the web. When you meet an agent at a class or at a party and you hit it off, you want to be able to give them your business card with your website listed on it, so they can view your site and click on links to your YouTube postings and see you perform.

Most actors now are beginning to create their own YouTube channels, which I highly recommend. This way, someone can search your name and instantly find all of your videos grouped together. These clips still need to be careful to observe copyright laws, but they can range from cabaret/concert performances to special skills demonstrations to promotional video from a show to you in a studio setting performing an original song of yours. The sky's the limit on what you can do. Just remember once more that the videos should be high quality (as opposed to someone sitting far back in a theatre taking shaky video on her phone); the performance *must* be high quality; and it should tie in to your brand somehow—tell us something about yourself and your product through this video.

ATTITUDE/REPUTATION

We have discussed many different elements involved in broadcasting your brand to the industry and to the world, from the way you dress to the headshot you choose to the credits on your resume to your repertoire and your web presence. But there is one more vital piece to the puzzle of marketing your actor brand: reputation. I know I have mentioned it in passing here and there, but I think it deserves an entire subchapter because it is really that important.

Your reputation can really be the make-or-break factor in you getting work and having a long, successful career. It can be the decision maker in whether or not an artistic team is ready to give you your first big break. It can also be the component of the audition that keeps you from getting a job.

I cannot even tell you the number of times I have heard about or personally been a part of a creative team trying to decide between two actors. One of the actors is clearly more talented (or at least better suited for the role) than the other; but the second actor is so lovely to work with, while the more talented is a pain in the behind. Almost without fail, the choice will be the more pleasant of the two actors. Because unless there is a gaping hole between their abilities or there is serious question as to whether the nicer actor can actually perform the role, we would *always* prefer to work with nice people. The rehearsal process is long and emotional. You have been in shows before—you know how you become like a family with the cast and crew. Would you want some jerk invited into that family when you could have a kind, hardworking, generous person instead? Of course not!

To that end, you must keep a great attitude as you go about your business. It begins with the way you treat even the assistants, the interns, and the monitors[33] at auditions or in agencies. Be careful not to lose your temper or act like a jerk, even when you are under pressure. Everything you say and do can and will come back to you. When you get into the room for a musical audition, treat the pianist

---

33. In Keith Ferrazzi's fabulous book, *Never Eat Alone*, he refers to these types of people as "Gatekeepers." You must treat them well because they may very well be the barrier between you and the people higher up on the "food chain," whom you want to meet.

like he is your friend and scene partner, rather than as if he were hired help just there to do your bidding. When a director or casting director asks you to make an adjustment in the audition room, say yes and try what they ask you to do, no matter how much you might disagree with it. And when you are waiting in the lobby or the holding room for an audition, do not get involved with speaking ill of anyone. I have seen it a hundred times—someone in that room is pissed that the audition is going so slowly so they try to engage others in negative talk. It is not an activity in which you want to participate; trust me.

You know, there is an old joke that goes, "How do you make an actor complain? Give him a job." Unfortunately for so many, that rings true. And I must advise you to be mindful of the black hole of negativity that often creeps into a cast or a company. It can not only tear the artists apart and affect their performances, but it can also wind up getting you blacklisted for your attitude.

It is so easy to let it happen virtually unnoticed. The director extends rehearsal beyond the originally scheduled time; the costume that was built for you does not fit right; another actor has not memorized her lines; the company has not paid the actors on the agreed-upon day. I am not saying that all of this is fine and that you should just let everything roll off your back—sometimes actors allow themselves to be walked upon like doormats! I hate seeing companies take advantage of artists. However, there is a right way and a wrong way to go about dealing with problems in the workplace.

The wrong way is anything that has to do with talking in whispers with other cast members about how bad things are; speaking behind someone's back about her; blowing up and walking out of a rehearsal or talking back to the director or choreographer. The wrong way is posting things on Facebook or Twitter that announce your dissatisfaction with the play, the company, or the management. All of these are self-destructive, and while they may feel good in the moment—you may feel righteous and vindicated for any wrongdoings—I assure you that behavior will only serve to attach itself to your reputation.

I had the misfortune to be involved in such a toxic situation recently. As a director, I like to keep things positive and optimistic, as I think it simply makes for a better artistic collaborative environment. However, sometimes things happen beyond your control. As it turns out, the company for whom I was directing was having some issues in upper management and it was affecting the actors in a pretty serious way—from contracts being broken and salaries not being paid to actors being "volunteered" to do extra work not previously agreed upon. You can imagine how this changed the energy in the room when we would take to rehearsing—the actors only wanted to gripe about the company. I had an arduous task of keeping them focused on the great work we were doing on the show.

As we progressed, more and more little things built up that were unacceptable to the actors. Fortunately, I was able to keep them positive and productive during rehearsal time, but in the evenings all they wanted to do was complain. I suggested a method of taking their grievances forward to the managing director in a professional and courteous manner, but that never seemed to happen for some reason. My show opened the season and things were pretty good when I left, but when I returned to check in on the show a month and a half later, the cast was in tatters. Some were not talking to others; most would arrive at the theatre exactly at the required call time and not a moment before; a few were even angling to get out of the contract and not finish the season. It was a mess.

I had kept in touch with a few of the cast members throughout the run, and I cannot tell you that their issues were unfounded. They had every right to feel mistreated and used; however, the way many of them chose to deal with it was a real shame. By the end of the season, I can assure you that almost none of those actors would ever be hired back by that theatre (one of them did in fact break the contract and leave a few weeks early). And while none of those actors probably would want to work there again anyway, what they needed to take into account was the fact that three directors were jobbed in there, as were numerous other artists, such as stage managers, designers, choreographers, and so forth. All of those hired artists will work at other theatres, and in no uncertain terms, they will encounter those actors again (remember the small world mantra?).

Can you see how your behavior in one specific situation can have a lasting effect on your reputation down the line? Now, it is only fair to say (especially since I'm still close with several of those actors and they may be reading this section right now) that not everyone in that company behaved poorly. I could see that several of them just went about their business and did the job they were contracted to do. Was it ideal? Of course not, but those actors remembered how lucky they were to be able to make a living going out on stage and doing what they loved every night. Were they happy to leave town when the season ended? You bet! But they made sure to leave on good terms, having done what was asked of them in spite of their disagreements with the management. These are the kinds of actors who will always work. Why? Because they will come to be known for their reliability through good and through difficult times. They will be remembered for their positive energy and their commitment to the show. And their good attitude will attach itself to their brand and become a part of the product they are selling.

So let's talk about the right way to handle negative situations. The first step is to breathe, distance yourself from any other negativity in the company, and reflect on whether the "issue" you have is really worth pursuing or if it can simply be chalked up to a bad day at the office and promptly forgotten. If it is a recurring situation or something that cannot be left unaddressed, the next step is to ask yourself who is actually in control of what is causing your dissatisfaction. (Too often, actors will complain to other actors or to the stage manager about an issue with the director or the producer. What good does this do? It breeds negativity and solves nothing.) Once you pinpoint the person or people who are responsible for the issue, calmly request a private meeting with them outside of rehearsal time. It is important that it not be on a break in rehearsal or during rehearsal, as the process must be kept sacred and your personal issues and concerns must not bleed over into the work.

Spend some time decompressing before you meet with the person, so that you are not driven by anger and emotion when you meet with him. Think about what you want to say and think about how you can express your feelings in an honest, nonaggressive way. Nobody wants to be yelled at or have a finger pointed at him. Besides, you are calling this meeting in order to solve a problem, so (just like you do in acting) you need to play to win. How can you get what you want? By attacking or by reasoning with the person?

Once you have said what you have to say, be open to hearing what the other person says in response. You may have opened her eyes to something she was not aware of. You may also not know the circumstances behind her actions, which she may have the chance to explain to you (e.g., you did not get paid because the company is struggling financially, but checks will be cut tomorrow). You may find that a compromise or an understanding can be reached right then and there. Or you may also find that you have someone who is not able to give you satisfaction after the discussion. When that happens you need to take some more personal breathing time to consider what you want to do next.

Ask yourself if the issue is really just an inconvenience or if it is worth going to battle and possibly staking your reputation on it. Ask yourself if there is some other method of friendly intervention—perhaps someone higher up in the company, or maybe further discussion over a drink with the person with whom you are having the misunderstanding.

If you are a member of Actors' Equity and rules are clearly being violated, your next step is to contact the union for them to intervene. If you have an agent, you can always complain to your agent and let them negotiate on your behalf. But if you are just starting out in the world of nonunion work and you have no representation, you are really on your own. You are going to have to deal with some less than pleasant situations; I can promise you that. And yes, sometimes you are going to have to suck it up and just get through a job even under unfavorable circumstances. I do not want to see you taken advantage of, but I also want you to look always at the big picture of your career.

Is this situation really so bad that I am willing to stake my reputation on it and make a stink? Will it keep me from getting hired by anyone involved in this production? Will breaking my contract and walking away cause more problems than it will solve? Will it come back to bite me later?

These are the questions I need you to answer for yourself in any negative situation. We are all human and we all, especially actor types, are driven by our emotions and our impulses. But I want you to learn how to pause, breathe, and reflect when it comes to any kind of an adverse circumstance. Give a second thought before you act rashly, and remember that just like with social media, someone is watching. What you do today will be remembered by someone tomorrow, be it good or bad.

And so as you move through this career and through life in general and you have big decisions to make, remember that you are not just making decisions on behalf of you as an individual; you are making decisions as the CEO of a corporation—"You, Inc.!"

Scene 5

─────────○─────────

The Six "Be's"

When I created my "Get the Callback: Success through Branding" workshop, I came up with six dictates or principles, if you will, that I feel summarize the things an actor must be in order to find success and well-being in the industry. I want to wrap up this first part of the book by sharing them with you.

Be Consistent

I have said this over and over to you (consistently, one might say!) throughout these pages. It is so important for your actor business—as for any business—that you are able to deliver time and time again with great consistency. You set an expectation in the headshot and resume you send out, in the clothes you wear, and in the material you choose. You also have a reputation and the assumptions that are based upon that. You have to trust that you are enough and that what you have (your product) is special and unique. Some people will want to buy what you are selling while others will not. That is the nature of the business. You have to keep your head on straight and "stay the course" through the ups and downs. You cannot change up the game plan after every rejection. Stay consistent. Stay "on message" with your brand, and when the time is right, you will work. If you stick with your brand and it does not pay off after a

127

long time of trying (and you have been as undeviating as the North Star), then it may be time to rethink and to rebrand. But until you make that decision, just be sure to stay true to the image you have created for yourself.

BE SPECIFIC

Nobody ever gets cast for being general. Part of branding is committing to the type and the energy and the style of your personal product. If you second-guess yourself and try to broaden your auditions to be more generic in order to have wider appeal, you will find yourself struggling even to get called back. People will not know what to do with you. You cannot be afraid to assert yourself in a direct and specific manner and proclaim, "This is who I am" to the industry without fear or concern of rejection. This specificity begins in the branding process—getting you to really home in on what *specifically* your product is. It applies to headshots (it is not sufficient to choose a photo that simply shows you as "nice" or "pretty"; you must make a more precise statement about who you are). And it certainly applies to repertoire—targeting particular roles for which you are right, rather than just singing a nice song that shows off your vocal abilities. Always ask yourself how you can be more specific when you are preparing audition material. Go back to the fundamental questions of "To whom am I speaking?" (e.g., "I'm speaking to Jim. He is my older brother by six years, and we have never had much of a relationship. He is like a stranger to me, but our blood ties us together. He has always resented me for being born and I have always tried to steer clear of his temper") and "What do I want from him?" (e.g., "Our father just died and we are settling the estate. I want him to give me Dad's school ring, which was always his prized possession, but Jim does not want to give me anything, since I moved away when I was twenty-two"). Do you see how you can go deeper? You can be more specific by expounding on the *nature* or *essence* of your relationship and the details behind your objective. That is what specificity is. It will always strengthen your audition work.

Be True to Your Word

You have heard the saying "Your word is your bond." Reliability is a tremendous factor in reputation, and it most definitely becomes attached to your brand. If you say that you plan to be somewhere or to do something for another person, you have to follow through. Committing to a project, whether it is paid or unpaid, the lead or a small walk-on part, is committing to a project. Treat every job as if it were the lead role in an Equity performance and you will develop a standing for being solid and dependable. If people see how trustworthy you are with the small projects, they will be much more likely to recommend you for the big projects. That said, you will need to exercise good judgment and think first before you promise to take on a task or a role. Sometimes you may just have to say no to an opportunity if there is any doubt that you will be able to fulfill the commitment.

Be True to Yourself

You know that this business is hard. You are going to doubt yourself and question your abilities, your looks, your talent, and your choices for years. That is not me being pessimistic; that is simply a fact of life in showbiz. But when those insecurities creep into your consciousness, remember the words of Polonius and "to thine own self be true." When you lose a part to another actor, do not try to figure out her formula and do whatever she does. Keep on track and "do you." Remember what I have said before: You cannot be all things to all people. All you can be is who you are. Trust in that and let your instincts and your training guide you and do not give up.

Be Bold

Nothing is more exciting to a director than when an actor comes into the room and makes big, bold choices in an audition. There is an obvious risk involved with being bold, and there will no doubt be times

when you will fall on your face. But as long as you are being professional and not making a mockery of the process, you will likely be
respected for your audacity. This notion of boldness is very much tied
to the earlier dictum of being specific. Sometimes, the easy choice
is to be general and generic (translation: boring). But if you come in
and allow yourself to be bold and distinct, it could have a remarkable
payoff. You will be remembered beyond that audition, even if you do
not get that part. If you establish a reputation for always coming in
making big strong choices (consistency!), casting directors will keep
you in the forefront of their minds and you will find yourself being
called in for roles you may not have even auditioned for in the first
place. Never be afraid to be fearless in an audition.

BE AUTHENTIC

All of the above "rules" that I have laid out for you, plus the entire
section on maintaining a stellar reputation, must be secondary to
the notion of you being authentically *you*. It serves absolutely no
purpose for you to put on an act for people and to pretend to be
nice to them or to pretend to be one thing when you are actually
another. While a façade may get you through certain doors, it will
be short lived and people will catch on to your guise before long. Always be who you are and let your honest personality shine through.
I had a student a few years ago who had greater success with every
single agent and casting director we put him in front of than any
of his classmates—even those who possessed more innate talent.
He was impressive to them because he knew how to be absolutely
comfortable with himself. He stood up there, chose material that
clearly radiated from his heart and soul, and he conversed with our
industry guests with great comfort, ease, and humor. They were
charmed by his ability to be 100 percent genuine with them and not
let his nerves cause him to put on any sort of mask. He was signed
by one of the agents the moment he moved to New York.

   The work I have laid out for you on creating your own personal
brand and developing a marketing strategy for it is not something
that will be achieved overnight or likely even over the course of

several days or weeks. It is a long, arduous, focused project that will keep you busy for quite some time to come. You cannot read this book once through, close it, and have all of this business "stuff" fall into place. You need to create a game plan for yourself. Start setting goals and work toward them over a period of time. Once you conquer one goal or set of objectives, step back, reevaluate, and set new ones. Always be looking to improve yourself, your image, your brand, your network of contacts and advisors. And above all, do not settle for a life in which you place your entire career, fate, what have you, in the hands of others. Take control and create a path to success for yourself by learning how you want to market your wonderful product to the industry and to the world. Once you empower yourself to do that, you will find that success will follow.

ENTR'ACTE

CHECK IN ON YOUR BUDGET LOG

I AM NOT SURE how long ago you began reading this book, but I thought this point between our branding and marketing setup and our further exploration of the business of theatre would be a good time to check in on your budget log that I assigned you back in the "Overture" section. You will remember that I asked you to write down every penny you spend for an entire month. If you breezed through the first half of this book, you may not be finished with your log yet. Take this as a reminder and a pep talk to keep it up and get through your thirty- or thirty-one-day (or twenty-eight—although doing this in February could be construed as cheating!) tracking.

If you are still working on that, how about pausing for a little while and digesting what I put forth in the first half before moving on to "Act II"? You may even want to go back and review some of the earlier material and spend some more time deepening your understanding of branding and creating your own personal brand. Have you come up with a branding statement at this point? Have you been able to list dream roles and actors with whom you could be compared? How is your list of goals coming together? Perhaps you have even achieved one or two of the short-term goals since we started working together on page 3. And how is that repertoire looking? Have you tossed out any material because you realized it is not consistent with your exciting new brand and business plan? Have you added new pieces? Maybe a new unconventional comedy song or some pop/rock? It is really a lot to think about. So if these questions have addressed areas that still need attention, take some time to look to them now and meet me at the next paragraph when your monthlong budget log is completed.

Hello again.

So let us take a look at your budget log. If you really wrote down every single expense from the significant to the minute for the entirety of a month, the first thing I want you to do is reward yourself for a job well done. It is not easy! So congratulations on sticking it out and getting through a real challenge. Buy yourself a coffee or an ice cream, and celebrate by not logging it in your notebook!

If you have not done so already, I want you to add up all the expenditures and come up with a sum total for the month. What we are working on creating is your "bottom line"—what you need to net in earnings at a minimum to sustain an average month. Next, do a little analysis and reflection. Go through the list of items that you spent money on and answer a few questions: What was surprising to you? (I had a student who was in shock at the amount he spent on Starbucks coffee in a year. We are talking over $1,000!) What expenses, if any, could you have done without? What came up over the course of the month that was unexpected? Which expenses are variable (e.g., electric bill) versus fixed (e.g., rent)? Were you able to include anything recreational, such as movies or concerts in the month? How much did you eat out at restaurants as opposed to cooking at home? Are there expenses that *did not* happen this month that might be likely to creep up next month? Really take some time to create a full analysis of your data, because the more specific you get, the more it will help you understand your finances and keep them under control.

All the above questions should be taken into consideration to determine a course of action moving forward—for that is what we ultimately want to create for you, an action plan. But the most important factor is that bottom-line number. Remember that I told you to write down even those freak expenses that are only likely to happen once every third harvest moon. I do not want you to get stuck being short of funds when those occur, and I want to help you not rely on credit cards to solve short-term financial problems, because credit cards almost always become long-term financial problems themselves.

The sum that you come up with should be the basis for you to create a budget. When you are deliberating over whether to take or to turn down work, that number needs to be met or exceeded in order for the job to be a feasible option for you. You must not allow yourself to accept work that will put you into debt. You cannot live on credit every time you want to build your resume—it will absolutely come back to bite you soon and it will keep you from possibly following other bigger, more exciting opportunities later. Aaron Galligan-Stierle's advice to you earlier to get your finances in order could not have been more urgent and spot on. This is why you must learn to save money *now*, when you do not need it.

As you read this book, you may be in college with a year or two ahead of you before you head out into the "real world." You are the lucky ones, because at this point, you are likely in a safe environment with little financial responsibility. (I know I am generalizing here and many of you are paying your way through school, so do not feel left out.) It only gets harder when you leave school and have to pay down student loans, rent, electric and heating bills, cable bills, metro fares, insurance, and so forth. So if you are in a position to be able to start creating a nest egg for yourself, *do it!* Do not wait. I know so many students who graduate with dreams of moving to New York or Los Angeles, but upon finishing school they decide they have to go home and live with their parents in suburbia for a while to make money. Many of these young aspiring actors get stuck in the rut of being home. They are not paying rent, and they are making decent money, so it gets harder and harder to leave that comfort. In addition, as they stay out of the city, they are also staying out of the game. They are not auditioning; they are not networking; they are not taking classes; they are not learning the ropes of living in NYC or LA or DC or Chicago or wherever.

I warn you, this is a dangerous option. I tell my students that they will never truly have "enough money" to live in NYC. I encourage them to go and couch hop or sublet for a short time if they need to, to make the initial transition. Jobs in New York will generally pay better wages than they will out in suburban USA because of the increased cost of living, so it all balances out in the end. But you just have to dive in with both feet and create a game plan for yourself. Certainly, saving money in advance will create a great deal of relief for you when you move, in addition to fostering good habits of money management. But now that you have got that bottom line established, you know what you need to live, and you can begin to craft a plan that helps you live within your means. There will be struggles, no doubt. It happens to everyone who takes on the big cities to make it as an artist. However, the clearer you are about your budget and your needs, the better off you will be in the long run. And just as we used your personal brand as a guiding factor in making decisions about wardrobe, repertoire, and so forth, we will use your budget log as a template to determine what work you can or must do in order to survive and to thrive as an adult in the city.

If you have not done so already, I think you should get and read Suze Orman's book, *The Money Book for the Young, Fabulous, and Broke*. Suze's book was invaluable to me when I was restoring my credit and my financial standing. Oh, perhaps I did not mention that to you. I will get personal for a moment and share a little story about poor money skills. But do not worry, this is a story of redemption and there is a happy ending.

When I was in college, I worked part-time for a credit card company doing telemarketing. I was very good at my job (although I personally hated sales and talking on the phone—two things that you really ought to like if you are going to make a career in telemarketing!), and I learned a lot about the wonderful features of my particular bank's various cards. I was on a fixed budget from my parents, and the money I made at work supplemented me for things like rent, food, and recreation. I was not actually a big drinker, nor did I smoke, so I was not dropping money on those vices. However, I loved to go out to eat, I always had a girlfriend whom I liked to treat, and I definitely spent way too much money on movies, theatre, and frequent road trips to see whomever I was dating or to visit New York.

All in all, I spent above my means and always found myself strapped for cash. But then I got the brilliant idea to apply for one of my company's credit cards—just to make living a little more comfortable. I somehow got a card, and before I knew it, I had maxed it out and gotten to the point where I was stuck in debt with no foreseeable solution in sight. I would not tell my parents because I was too proud and I did not want to burden them. So I just added a minimum payment to my monthly expenses and went on with life. When I moved to New York out of college, I found two part-time jobs right away, so I was making decent money. However, I also found the need to buy a bed for my new apartment, which I did on credit through the mattress store—more debt. So now I have two credit card payments that I can barely keep up with, I have rent and bills for a New York apartment, I have a cell phone bill (which was a new expense at the time), and of course there was a student loan. Not to mention the fact that I was a very social person, which meant that I was going out in New York all the time.

You can probably guess where this story is going without any more boring details. I got in debt way over my head and it got unmanageable. I finally had to resort to a credit-counseling agency, which consolidated my debt into one low-interest payment, but shattered my credit for some time to come. After finishing graduate school a few years later, during which time I was able to further defer my student loan, I finally had to face the music on that as well and start paying it back at a substantial monthly rate to make up for the time I had fallen behind on it.

Long story short, I learned an immense lesson about money management from all of my earlier mistakes. I consulted with Joe Abraham and Christine Negherbon (whom I told you about earlier) and got some advice from them. I picked up Suze Orman's book, and I determined to get my life in order. Within a couple of years, I had fixed my bad credit, paid off my cards, and made huge strides on my student loan. I was even able to buy a house and a car in the last few years simply because I had brought myself back from the credit graveyard. I still wish I were better with money—perhaps that will be my next project—but I must say, I do not worry anymore.

And I know now how I can live under virtually any circumstances, even if I did not have a full-time professor job with benefits.

It was a tough road, though, and I do not recommend it to any of you. Being behind on bills is not fun and worrying if you will have enough money to pay your rent and eat this month is a horrible feeling. When you have money worries, it makes you stressed out and you are unable to focus on the things that you came here to do. I found myself unable to take any theatre work for over a year, simply because I could not afford to work for low pay and give up hours at my full-time job. I started asking myself what I came to New York to do in the first place, and ultimately, I made the decision to leave for graduate school and start anew. Since I knew I wanted to be a director, that choice was pretty easy; however, if I were still trying to be a musical theatre performer at the time, I would feel cheated of the opportunity to "strike" while I was still young and in my prime.

So I cannot stress enough to you the importance of sound money management. Get it under control now, wherever you are in your life. Create a budget and stick to it. Allow yourself some room for recreation, drinks, and so forth, but keep it in check and make sure you are putting away money for when you will really need it. Trust me, you do not want to fall out of the loop and get discouraged about living in the city because you cannot afford to do what you came to do.

Now one other thing I want to recommend to you, in addition to creating your fantastic budget by which you live and manage and save, is establishing some credit in your name. You may have had a credit card under your parents' names throughout college, but unless you have had a credit card in your own name, you have not established your own line of credit. Suze Orman goes into great detail about credit in her book, so I am going to save you having to hear my less-impressive version of the lecture; however, I will hit on a couple of very important and basic points.

First, your credit is basically measured by a numerical score (FICO score), which is determined by three credit-reporting agencies (Equifax, Experian, and TransUnion). These agencies track how often you apply for credit, when you are granted credit, how much debt you carry, what your credit limits are, your pay-back habits, any late or missed payments, and so forth. Essentially, these agencies are the "Big Brother" watching over any and all credit and loans in the United States (including student loans, car loans, home loans, bank loans, credit cards, department store financing), and they are the companies to whom inquiries are sent whenever you apply for anything requiring a credit check, including cable TV services, some apartment leases, and any utilities that are going into your name.

These agencies are in charge of determining if you are eligible for any sort of loan, credit, or trust, and their decision is based solely on your previous record. Therefore, if you have no established credit history, you have no previous record on which to base a decision; thus, you will likely not be granted much (if any) credit when you decide to apply for a card or a loan of some sort later in life. This is why I recommend establishing credit fairly early on—not to put you in debt, but rather to create a record of your flawless payment habits for that day when you want to make a big purchase.

You can begin by seeking out a credit card offer that has (a) no annual fee, (b) low or 0 percent introductory interest rate (which you will not worry about anyway, since you are going to pay it off every month), and (c) some sort of air miles or rewards program. If those criteria are not met, you probably should not apply for that card. If you are not sure what kind of card to go with, consider meeting with a financial consultant at your bank. They may even be able to help you get an offer through your bank based on how you have managed your checking and/or savings accounts.[1]

Either way, contrary to what your parents might tell you, I think it is important for you to start establishing credit in your name. However, there are some hard-and-fast rules I want you to live by once you get this card. First of all, do not use it to spend anything above what you would have put on your debit card or paid with cash. This will ensure that you are not spending more money than you have—

---

1. In fact, if you have absolutely no credit background, you may have to get what is called a "secured credit card" through your bank. This is a card that limits you to what is in your bank account, thus you cannot get into trouble with a limit that is above your means. I had to start with a secured card since I had no history.

we do *not* want you to go into debt. This will take a lot of willpower and discipline on your part, but I know you can do it. Secondly, I want you to charge anything you can on your new credit card rather than using your debit card. Since you will not be spending above your means, doing so will only demonstrate your ability to manage a credit card well. You will also get rewards along the way for every dollar that you spend (I have one card that gives me points toward airfare and other nice gifts, and I have a second card that offers a percentage of cash back). Third, and most importantly, you *must, must, must* pay off your credit card in full with each billing cycle. I do not want you to carry a balance from month to month. We are going to beat the system, you and me, and we are going to do it by not giving those banks any of your hard-earned money for nothing.

Each month, when your bill comes in, it will tell you how much you owe in total, and it will tell you what your minimum payment is. The bank hopes you will pay only the minimum, because after a certain date (called the "grace period," which will be listed in your credit card agreement), any additional money that you owe will be compounded with interest, and the bank starts to make extra money off of you. As long as you pay off your bill in full each month before the grace period is up, you will never owe the bank a penny of interest.

Again, I cannot stress enough to you the importance of paying your bills in full and on time. Ideally, you will never falter on this directive. However, in the event that something big comes up—you need to fly home for a family emergency or pay a major doctor's bill, for example—and you are unable to pay off the bill in full, you absolutely must pay at least the minimum by the due date. If you do not, you will be charged an exorbitant late fee in addition to your interest, plus any introductory no-interest or low-interest deal you had will be removed and your rate will hike up into the twenties.

I am purposely trying to scare you a bit and I am being repetitive and nitpicky because I want to emphasize the importance of establishing great credit while staying out of great debt. So just to recap: get a card; use it in place of cash, check, or debit when possible; pay off the full amount each billing cycle; if you cannot pay it in full because of an emergency, at least make the minimum payment by the due date. If you can follow those simple guidelines, you will build a terrific credit history for yourself and open the door to receiving loans easily when you need them later.

And just to clarify for you what determines your FICO score, I want to share with you the factors that the credit reporting agencies use in their process—this way there is no mystery and you know exactly what is within your control. The numbers are a combination of (a) record of paying your bills on time (35 percent), (b) balance on your credit cards versus your total limit (30 percent), (c) length of credit history (15 percent), (d) new accounts and applications for credit (10 percent), and (e) mix of credit cards and loans (10 percent).

So what does this mean to you? In a nutshell, if you always pay your bills on time, 35 percent of your score will be flawless. If you pay off all balances and allow the bank to raise your limit whenever they offer to do so, your debt to limit ratio will be wider, increasing 30 percent of your score. If you establish credit and then keep your accounts open, even if you cut up a card and do not use it anymore, your history will be longer, increasing that 15 percent of your score. If you avoid applying for new accounts with much frequency, it will keep them from becoming alarmed and 10 percent of your score will reflect favorably upon you. And finally, if you have a healthy mix of credit cards and loans, such as student loans or car payments, it will account for the final 10 percent.

As I said, Suze Orman goes into much greater detail in her incredible book. It is so simple to read and to understand, and you must have it on your bookshelf. However, this gives you some information for starters. Establishing great credit will make it possible for you to buy a car or a home later in life. It will make it possible for you to get low interest loans when you need them, and it will keep you from ever being denied service by a bank, a utility, or a leasing agency based on inability to pay. But in addition to all of that, I think one should have a credit card available for emergencies. If you keep a card and never run up debt on it, you will always be able to pay for car repairs, plane tickets, medical and dental crises, and any other such necessities that come up and require money in a pinch.

SUPPORTING YOURSELF IN THE CITY:
DAY JOBS VERSUS SELF-EMPLOYMENT

Now that we have discussed in great detail coming up with a budget that suits your spending needs, let's talk about how you are going to bring money in when you are not working on a theatre gig.

As I mentioned earlier, the cost of living in major cities is generally higher than it is in the suburban or rural parts of the country, but the wages tend to be higher to reflect that differential. Depending on what kind of skill set you possess and what particular interests you have, you may be able to find a terrific "survival job" that fulfills you personally as well as financially—that is the ultimate goal (short of making your total living as an actor!). You have probably heard of the common actor jobs: waiting tables, bartending, catering, and temping. The reason these appeal to actors is because they tend to be flexible in hours and they are also inclined to suit actors' outgoing personalities. That said, these are not the only employment options for you, nor are they without downsides.

Let's start by looking at waiting tables, bartending, and catering. These are the most common actor side jobs, obviously for the hours. Actors need their weekdays free to audition. When you move to the city (any city) your primary job is auditioning. You must be getting yourself in front of casting and creative teams immediately and regularly. Repetition and consistency is how you market your brand, so it will not do to take a full-time day job that keeps you from getting to multiple auditions every week. The restaurant industry welcomes actors for their personalities and their ability to "schmooze" guests. Additionally, because actors need to be free during the days, they tend to be looking for night and weekend work, which is when restaurants, bars, and caterers are the busiest. It is really a perfect marriage—on the surface, that is.

Sure, you might get great hours and make a ton of cash each time you leave a shift, but we also must examine the cons to the food-service industries. For starters, you will likely be looking at excessively late hours. Bars in New York and other major metro cities will stay open as late as three or four a.m., and guess who has to clean up after the customers are gone? How well do you think you will sing at a ten a.m. open call when you got home to bed at five a.m.? I also know of a lot of actors who get restaurant or bar jobs and they wind up spending half their money and free time drinking at their own bar after hours. That is just a matter of willpower, but the temptation is certainly there. Also realize that the food industry takes a lot out of a person. You are on your feet running around for hours each shift. Depending on the restaurant, you may have a great team of helpers running food and busing tables, or you may be a one-man show, running yourself ragged each time you clock in. I cannot tell you how many actors I know who wind up passing up audition opportunities out of sheer exhaustion from their waiting gig. Finally, there is no bottom-line guarantee when you tend bar or wait tables. You make next to nothing in salary from the company, and you rely almost completely on tips. Depending on where you are located, how expensive the menu is, what kind of traffic you serve, and where the customers tend to be from, you may find that the waiting job does not provide a steady enough income to pay all your bills and keep you comfortable.

The worst thing that could happen is that you find that you are falling behind financially from waiting tables at night and so you decide to add an additional daytime job to your schedule, further barring you from getting to auditions with regularity. So just be careful when choosing to join the restaurant industry. You have to really enjoy that kind of work to thrive at it and not lose your soul in it.

The other popular day job for actors is temping. Temping basically means you register with an agency and they send you out on jobs that can last from a day to several months, filling in for someone in an office setting. I even know of many instances when a temp job turns into a full-time opportunity. The pros to temping are that you can call in each day and decide whether or not to take work when it is available. They work with actors regularly, and they understand that sometimes you will be tied up in auditions, so the great benefit is the flexibility to take work only when you want it. Of course, you only get paid when you work, and you must remember that until you go full-time with a company, the temp agency always takes a cut of your pay (and the wages are not particularly high to begin with). Another advantage to temping is the fact that you could potentially be doing different work in a different environment from day to day, so if you get bored easily, it gives you an opportunity to explore different industries and to meet different people. If you would like to find out more about what temping has to offer, many of my alumni recommend contacting Forrest Solutions Temp Agency (www.fss-staffing.com) in New York City. They apparently love to hire actors, and I know many friends who have been particularly successful with them transitioning from temporary to lucrative full-time permanent work.

But now let us discuss the negatives to making a living through a temp service. As I already indicated, the wages are not exactly high, even before the agency takes their cut. Almost all of this work tends to be traditional nine to five, which means that in order to take it, you may well have to be free for the entire business day, thus no auditions. If you do not work, you do not make money, as I said earlier. And because you are frequently jumping around from company to company, on erratic schedules, there is little chance to get something steady that includes benefits such as health insurance.[2] The people I know who register with a staffing service have to look at the audition postings each morning, as well as their finances, to determine if they are going to try to work or hit some auditions that day. After a while, it becomes quite unpleasant to have to make that decision. Ideally, you would be able to go to any and every audition you wish without having to sacrifice something else.

So what do the food-service and temp industries have in common? Both are flexible and commonly hire actors in spite of their tendency toward irregular schedules and frequent leaves of absence for regional or touring theatre work. Both pay variable wages that range from the unlivable to the extremely lucrative, but both can also change from day to day. Both require little to no artistry or creativity and offer virtually nothing in the way of expressive outlet. And above all, both can keep you from doing what you came to do because you are working for someone else on their schedule under their rules.

---

2. I am not even going to get into a discussion on health insurance and its importance because I do not know where we will be in terms of universal health coverage by the time this book is published. But suffice it to say, having medical protection is a serious concern.

So what is the alternative? Well, besides retail and barista jobs, which basically offer more of the same problems, there is not much else out there in the way of entry-level work for people with theatre degrees. This is when I want you to put on your creative hat and do a little thinking. I want you to think about what you *love* to do and what you are *really* good at. Start with that—actually make a list. Obviously performing as an actor would be on that list (I would hope—otherwise you are just reading this book for pleasure and I am flattered that you made it this far!). But what other skills do you possess? What hobbies do you enjoy? Let me give you some examples of things that you might list if they pertain to you:

- Carpentry and construction
- Piano or other instruments (with great proficiency)
- Photography
- Babysitting
- Household animals, such as dogs and cats
- Web or graphic design
- Math, science, or other academic areas
- Sewing and/or fashion
- Cleaning (if you really love that)
- Yoga or Pilates (certified)
- Massage (certified)
- Foreign language proficiency

And that is just a start. I am sure you can think of other ideas that I have not included. Now look at whatever you listed and think about how those skills could be marketable and profitable for you. Consider how you might go into business for yourself and make a living utilizing skills you already possess and pastimes in which you already partake.

If you enjoy carpentry, you might offer up your services to help people create space solutions in their metropolitan apartments. Since living spaces are generally so tiny, people need to be creative about storage and often pay a fortune to create shelving that helps them get the maximum out of their minimal domiciles. If you play an instrument with great proficiency, you might offer lessons. If you play piano, you might even be able to accompany auditions, local productions, voice lessons, and coachings. If you are a skilled photographer, perhaps you can learn to do actors' headshots or work as an apprentice and get into the wedding and special event industry. If you babysit, there are tons of parents in every city looking for help—possibly even a full-time nanny. If you love animals, there is always house-sitting, pet sitting, and dog walking. If you do graphic or web design, you can offer your services to actors or other businesses to build their sites or to design flyers for their companies. If you are a great academic, you can offer tutoring to students (with wealthy parents!). If you are great at sewing and stitching, you could either work in a costume house or offer your tailoring services to the public. If you enjoy the Zen of cleaning, you could clean homes or offices for a living. If you have training in yoga, Pilates, massage therapy, or even personal fitness, you can get certified and run your own business. And if you are proficient in a foreign language, you can tutor or teach the language to others.

Those are just the ideas that came to me in about five minutes of brainstorming. But do you see how many possibilities there are if only you possess some abilities and experience beyond theatre? And what does every one of those options have in common? You get to be your own boss. You can create a flyer or run an ad in the local papers and advertise your business. You can use social media and word of mouth to spread the word about the service you are offering. You get to be in charge. You get to set your rates. You get to choose when you work. And above all, you would be doing something you know you love to do.

Spend some time pondering the possibilities. Make a running list of your competencies outside of performing and see if you can draw a line from any of them to something profitable. I know a terrific musician who loves musical theatre and plays piano with great dexterity. He created a business of online coaching for performers so that when they have sides to learn for an audition, they can have someone play through the music and send it to them in MP3 format no matter where in the world they are (check it out: www.geton mysides.com). I know someone who offers herself up for general odd jobs from babysitting to pet sitting to housecleaning to grocery shopping. She has a ton of busy parents on the Upper West Side who rely on her for a multitude of daily chores. One of my recent grads had such fun building his actor website that he did one for each of his roommates. Now word is spreading and he is becoming a brand manager and a web designer (you've seen his website—it's www.ehlersonline.com).

I think you get the point. There is a lot out there that you can do without putting yourself at the mercy of someone else's employment. Going into business for yourself is challenging but ever so rewarding. And since we have harped so much on you being a business yourself ("You, Inc.") for your acting career, creating a profitable side venture could go in lockstep with your primary line. To survive and also thrive in this industry, one must think outside of the box, and if you can find something that makes you truly happy while also paying the bills, you will be in great shape and you will view each day with enthusiasm and optimism. Don't you think that might affect your auditions, too?

WORKING FOR FREE

After spending pages and pages telling you how to save your money and budget your money and earn your money, I am now going to give you one of the soundest pieces of advice about your career, and it actually pertains to taking work that is completely unpaid. Just realize that the only way you can even consider following this particular path is if you have saved money in advance and built yourself a comfortable nest egg (or if you have an alternate source of income).

I firmly believe that one of the most valuable experiences an actor can possibly have is interning for an agent or a casting director.[3] Nothing at all—no amount of reading in a book or being taught in a class—can possibly give you the insight that you will get from sitting behind the table at professional auditions or from being in an agent's office and seeing the daily operations.

---

3. In a later chapter we will discuss in detail what casting directors and agents do and the differences between them.

When I have students who are consulting with me about summer theatre opportunities I generally tell them that if they can get an internship and they can afford to take it, they should do that above almost any performance opportunity, and here is why: First of all, when you are young it is much easier to afford such endeavors, especially if you are still in college, still under your parents' insurance, and perhaps not paying rent yet (or at least not likely paying big city–sized rent). Secondly, as a student or a recent graduate, you have much greater access to a wider variety of interning opportunities. Theatre industry insiders love to bring young, eager, energetic types into the fold by shepherding them through intern or apprentice opportunities. And then there are the obvious benefits to you: you will learn so much about what works and what does not work in an audition room if you sit with a casting director as she screens actors. You will be privy to conversations that will prove my assertion that being the best in the audition does not always equate to getting the job. You will start to understand both the politics and the hierarchy of the audition room, which you will find immensely useful as an actor. And you will get to know what appeals to the particular casting director whom you are observing and what turns him off.

Working for an agent is similar in many ways, except you will not be sitting and watching auditions. Rather, you will learn how contracts are offered and negotiated. You will learn how casting breakdowns are distributed and how agents in turn submit their clients. You may even learn how your particular agency determines whom they will represent and where they find their talent. Politics and office hierarchy do come into play, and you will certainly be a pair of ears around many conversations that will illuminate vital parts of this business to you, such as how the unions work.

I have had performer students and friends who have interned for agents and casting directors and come out of it wanting to change fields and continue on the path that they discovered behind the table. I have also known many actors who came out of one of these internships considering themselves incredibly lucky to have the "inside scoop" about casting and feeling new confidence and poise going forward with auditions based on their new insight. But one thing I have never heard from anyone is that taking an internship was a waste of his or her time or anything less than a brilliant learning experience. The bottom line is, if you can do it, do it.

There are several ways to find these opportunities. The first is by word of mouth. Social media has played a huge part in my connecting students and alums with internships. Because I have relationships with many agents and casting directors in New York, I find that I am often at the center of their searches for young labor. Another possibility is for you to use ArtSearch. ArtSearch is a membership website, run through the Theatre Communications Group (tcg.org/artsearch), and it lists tons of internships on a weekly basis and tells you how to apply. Occasionally you'll even find some internships posted on Playbill.com in their free job listings tab. The third approach is to reach out and contact offices with which you are interested in working. I told you earlier to be bold, and nothing is bolder than sending an unsolicited e-mail to an agent or casting director and offering up your services should they need an intern. If your school does a showcase of any sort or brings industry people down to campus for master classes, you might be able to meet and connect with them that way. You may also have a friend whom you can use as a reference point (it is always good to break the ice with a common bond, e.g., "My friend Joe, whom you represent, told me to contact you. . . ." or "It was great talking to you at our showcase. . . .").

Just be sure to do your research on the casting department or the agency you are trying to work with, as each office is different and you should be prepared to tell them why you want to work for their specific operation. In addition, be careful not to take an internship with a casting director as a backdoor approach to getting seen for auditions; likewise, do not work for an agent because you want to angle for them to represent you afterward. This is not a stepping-stone to either of those ends. Rather, it is a chance for you to learn a lot about your business and gain unique perspective on how the industry works.

A BRIEF WORD ABOUT TAXES

I am no expert on taxes by any means, nor will I be able to educate myself to be an authority on the subject in time to print this book;

however, there are a few very valuable tips that I can offer you as a small-business owner to help you maximize your deductions every year and save some money.

First of all, if you have cobbled together a living from various sources of income (theatre gigs, part-time work, independent contracting, etc.) in a given year, do not try to file your taxes on your own. The simplest solution is to consult an accountant who can help you file everything correctly and avoid being audited. I know that in New York and Los Angeles there are CPAs who specialize in actor taxes—you can find them listed in *Backstage* generally from January to April. If you cannot find a specialist, a general accountant should still be able to help you, so long as you are very clear about what you did to earn money and what expenses you had to accrue in order to do each job. But either way, it is worth paying someone else to do your filing for you so that there are no mistakes and you get the maximum refund.

The trick is to realize that any money you spend directly on your business (your acting career or your side business) can generally be "written off" in some way—meaning that the government will hold your business expenditures against the taxes you would normally be charged when working a regular job and thus provide income tax relief for you based on the fact that you had to spend money in order to make money. Here are some of the things that can usually be written off for actors: audition clothing (as long as you only wear it for auditions) and shoes, photocopying charges for sheet music and resumes, headshots, business cards and postcards, union dues, classes and lessons, professional makeup, scripts and CD cast recordings, trade publications, professional viewing of theatre, and business meals. And those are just a few examples. Depending on how you use them, you may even receive a deduction for your cell phone and your apartment—if it is used as office space. A tax expert can help you find every deduction available to you so that you do not lose an unnecessary cent to Uncle Sam.

My recommendation to you is that you get into the habit of saving, labeling, and filing receipts. If you go to lunch with a director to talk business and you pick up the tab, write "Business lunch with So-and-so" on the receipt and file it under business meals. If you go to Kinko's or Staples to photocopy resumes or business cards, get the receipt, label it, and file it. At the end of the year, you should have a slew of invoices related to your profession in some way. If everything is clearly labeled and organized, it will be easy for a tax expert to go through them with you and help you determine what is write off-able and what is not. I suggest you even save receipts from things you are not sure are related to your business, such as movie tickets and gym memberships. A good CPA can likely find a way to tie them to your work and thus grant you a greater deduction.

As I said, taxes are not necessarily my forte, but I do practice what I preach. Since I take a good deal of freelance work directing, in addition to my full-time teaching load, and since I receive royalties from a book, I save receipts from anything related to either side income. I write off lunches and dinners with artistic directors; I write off travel to and from my summer gigs as well as to and from the auditions for the stock companies; I write off copies of my book that I purchase through the publisher to give away as gifts. This is all possible because these sources of income are done as independent contract work (as opposed to a standard W-2 form that comes when you are being taxed by a company who is paying your salary).

It is all fairly confusing, especially when you get into the nitty-gritty of independent contract work versus self-employment and where things fall and get categorized. I think it is enough to make one's head spin. But again, this is why I recommend that you consult an accountant. I know I did not shed much light on the issue of taxes with you, but at least I pointed you in the right direction to get assistance.

Act II

PUTTING IT INTO PRACTICE

Scene 1

―――――――――○―――――――――

General Audition Technique

THIS IS NOT INTENDED to be a manual on how to audition. I wrote my last book about that topic and it goes into pretty specific detail about the ins and outs of audition preparation, performance, and conduct. Most of what I wrote back then I still agree with today, even as the business has changed slightly and I have grown a good deal wiser and more experienced. All that being said, I will offer a very brief set of guidelines and advice for you to apply as you pursue casting opportunities. Some of this information can be found in more detail in *Get the Callback* while other tidbits will be new.

The primary directives to you when you get ready to audition are to *be prepared* and to *be present*. Just as our work on branding drove all the decisions about managing your career, so do these two dictates drive all decisions about your audition work. There is so much that is beyond your control during the casting process—you will never know what they are looking for (oftentimes *they* do not even know what they are looking for!); you will never know what they are thinking as you perform for them; most of the time, unless you have an agent who gets feedback on your behalf, you will never know what they thought of you after you leave; you cannot control their moods; you cannot control the abilities of the pianist; and on and on.

But you can control how prepared you are. And your preparation, including all of that lovely branding work, will give you confidence. That confidence will help you to remain present in the room at all times. And that presence will greatly enhance your performance in the audition.

Just to be clear, let me explain what I mean by being present. When you walk into the room, your mind must be there at that exact moment, constantly. You cannot be thinking about the person who preceded you in the room and intimidated you with her big, loud belt or the guy who spent fifteen minutes in there before you, singing through what seemed like his entire book of repertoire for the casting team. Those were their auditions; this is yours. You cannot be trying to read the creative team as you perform your audition. You cannot be thinking about what else you have to do today or about how relieved you will be once this audition experience is over.

You must learn to focus on each individual moment as it unfolds and deal with that rather than what came just before or what might come just after. So what that means in a practical sense is that you walk in the room, and the first thing you do is take in the room. It happens in an instant, but you must gauge the size of the space, the location of the auditors and of the piano if it is a musical audition. *Boom*, that moment is gone. Next you say hello and your moment is that of a greeting exchange between you and the creative team. When you say "Hello," or "Good morning," or "How are you?" you must mean it. Do not just go through the motions—that is not staying present. *Boom*, that moment is gone. (Did you notice how your voice carried in the room as you spoke? That will be important when you begin your performance, since you will need to fill the space but not overwhelm it.) Do not make the mistake of running to the piano and hiding behind it the second you enter the room. Listen to the people behind the table after you greet them—they may very well return your salutation and even open the possibility of conversation. The actor who is not present will brush them off in order to get to the prepared audition performance, but the smart artist who knows how to remain in present tense will recognize the opportunity for a little "face time." That being said, you must not anticipate that they will want to converse with you, either. They may give you a brusque "hello" or a grunt or nothing at all, and being present means catching that and moving forward.

When you are doing a musical audition and your next move is to go to the piano and present your music to the accompanist, be in the moment with her. Do not just plop your book in front of her and treat her like the hired help. She is your scene partner in the room, and you want to establish a bit of a rapport and make sure she is on your side. I encourage you to find out his or her name from the monitor outside the audition room so that when you approach the piano you can say "Hello, Jane" or "Hello, Scott" and immediately establish a human connection with this person who could really make or break your audition. Do not just give her directives, either, as you have your mind one step ahead to the coming performance. Really be in that moment, engaged with the piano player. Listen to her and check in to be sure that she got all the information she needed from you to be able to play your music successfully. Then thank her. *Boom*, that moment is gone.

Get to the spot in the room from which you are going to begin your audition and take a millisecond to recalibrate and once again make sure that you are present. Are they looking at you and waiting for you to begin? Are they engaged in conversation with one another? Have they asked you what you will be performing for them today? It is absolutely vital that you are actively listening and paying full attention to what is happening in the room. In my previous book (in which I go into much greater detail about the process of walking through every step of the audition), I teach a process for slating, or introducing yourself and your material. However, it is increasingly rare that you will be expected to fully slate in a professional audition, particularly in New York. More often, they will have your headshot and resume, they will greet you by name, and they will ask you what you are about to perform. In some instances, they will not break the proverbial ice, and you should just launch in by saying "This is _____" (just the title of the piece, not the playwright or composer). *Boom*, that moment is gone. And now you are into the actual audition performance.

If you have done your work in preparing fully, as we will discuss shortly, then once the performance begins, you should have absolutely no need to think of your next lyric or of the high note that is coming up that always gives you fits. The words and the notes and rhythms will all be there, in you, in your gut. And you will be able to live fully in the moment, interacting with your imaginary scene partner and dealing with each moment as it happens. For those of you who have studied Sanford Meisner's approach to acting (which everyone should!), this level of presence may sound awfully familiar. Meisner taught actors to stay absolutely present and work off of impulses, never preplanning anything. Can you apply this method to your entire audition? Can you let the people in the room be your scene partners up until your performance begins; then switch over to your imaginary partner (or your reading partner if it is a cold-reading audition) and back to the creative team when your piece is finished? Can you prepare and prepare and prepare, but then let it all go when you walk in the room and allow your impulses to carry you through based on what is actually happening at any given second?

This all might sound very well and easy to accomplish on paper, but if you have ever tried it, believe me it is very challenging. It will take a long time, a lot of practice, and a great deal of confidence to really get yourself to the point where you can consistently remain 100 percent present in the audition room. I suggest that if you do not already practice yoga, you may wish to begin taking a class if possible. I find that yoga, in addition to making you feel incredible physically, gets you in touch with your breath and teaches you to live utterly in the present moment. If you can find a shortcut to that, you will increase your success by leaps and bounds. Your presence will be palpable in the room and people will respond to it favorably.

And as I stated, the other component to the puzzle is being prepared—fully. You cannot be completely present if you are un-derprepared, of course, because you will be up in your head about lines or notes or physicality. All of that preparation needs to happen long before you walk in the door for an audition. You need to know exactly what it is that you are auditioning for—the show, the role, and the demands. You need to know who will be in the room. You will always know who the casting director is prior to the audition from the advertisement, so you can do your research on them; but you should also ask the monitor who else is in the room before you walk in. All I can suggest you do is research, research, and more research. What else has this playwright written? Does he have a consistent style? Is there a type of actor who turns up in his pieces with regularity? (For a great example of what I'm talking about, just watch several films by director Wes Anderson and you will see his style ring out in production design, actor types, and dialogue.) If the show for which you are auditioning is a published piece, the expectation is that you will have read it, understood the character for whom you are auditioning, and made some strong choices about context and objectives. Do not go in being general and wait for direction—it may never come. Educate yourself on the history of the play or musical—was it written to make a statement about something, perhaps political? Is it a send-up or an homage to a certain era or genre of theatre?

This all may sound like a great deal of work to you, but I will tell you what my acting teacher always reminded us: "If this were easy, everyone would do it." True success in the business of show will require a full-time commitment to your craft. The research, the learning, the specificity of choices, and the honing of the physical instrument are ongoing processes without which an artist has little to no chance of thriving.

Take a moment right now to brainstorm and list for yourself all of the things that are within your control when you walk into an audition. In other words, what kinds of things can you make a part of your preparation so that you increase your likelihood of achieving positive results? Go ahead and write down as many factors as you can, and we will compare notes in the next section.

How did you do? Did you hit on some important elements of your preparation? Did you discover anything that you may not have thought of before now? Let me share with you the pieces of an actor's preparation that come to my mind when I think of what we can control.

Knowing the Piece and the Character for Which You Are Auditioning

I know I already mentioned that you should read the play or musical if it has been published, but often you may be auditioning for a new production, for which there is no available script, music, or video clips. In those cases, you can try to research online and see if there has been anything written about the piece or its development. If you have an agent, you can generally have them request a perusal script for you, but that may not be an option. Basically, use every possible resource you can exhaust to gain as much knowledge about the show as possible so that you can make educated choices going in. If you are going in for a replacement in a show that is currently running or if you are auditioning for the touring company of a current production, the expectation from the casting director is that you will have seen the show and you will know the story, the characters, and the production style. Also remember that the casting team wants you to succeed. They *need* to find the right actors for the roles, so they will usually describe what they are seeking in the casting call. You may also be able to ask them some specific character questions before you launch into your audition, but that will depend on their time frame.

KNOWING THE CREATIVE TEAM THAT IS WORKING ON THE PRODUCTION

Just like my Wes Anderson film example, knowing the writers' bodies of work can be of immense importance before you go in for their show. It will also give you an advantage to know who is directing, musical directing, and choreographing (when applicable). The more you know about the people involved in the writing and the casting, the more you can gear your choices toward what you know will appeal to them. We will talk later about journaling, but for now I can tell you that this is a perfect instance of when consulting a journal can give you some insight into the artistic team's likes and dislikes.

READING THE CASTING CALL FULLY AND PAYING ATTENTION TO MINUTE DETAILS

Nothing irritates casting directors more than actors who walk into a room (or submit their materials) having no idea what the audition is seeking; especially in those cases where the casting ad listed in great detail exactly what was needed. Don't assume you know what they want just because you know the show. Sometimes they may be looking to alter the original production and go in a different direction.[1] Read exactly how they describe the characters in the breakdown and trust that what they have published is what they want. If they say to prepare a certain style or genre of material, *do it!* If what they are asking for is not something you do, do not go to that audition. Simple as that. But if you choose to submit yourself or attend an open call, you will be expected to have read the casting ad and to have paid attention to exactly what was required.

KNOWING YOUR PRODUCT, YOUR ABILITIES, AND YOUR STRENGTHS BEFORE YOU DECIDE TO AUDITION

All that work we did on branding in part 1 of this book will go a very long way in helping you be prepared for individual auditions. If you know what it is that you are selling and you have confidence in your abilities (and you recognize and accept your deficiencies as well), you will be able to accurately identify those casting opportunities that are the right match for you and your talents. You will know when they ask for a man who can sing an A-sharp while turning a triple pirouette if that is within your skill set. And when you do walk into the room, you will be able to operate from a place of complete self-assurance, knowing exactly what you bring to the table and believing that you are the best *you* there is. Remember to always show off your strengths and not your weaknesses in the repertoire you choose.

KNOWING YOUR MATERIAL INSIDE AND OUT

When you walk into the audition room, anything can happen. You may simply perform your song or monologue exactly as written and then be thanked and dismissed. You may be asked to perform something else from your repertoire. You may be drilled with questions

---

1. I have seen casting ads for *Les Miserables* requiring pop/rock audition material, and I have also seen ads specifically asking for no pop/rock. It all depends on the individual director and his production concept.

about your piece ("To whom are you speaking? What happened just before this? What do you want from the other person? Why is this important? Why did you choose this material? What is this piece really about?"). You may be redirected ("Can you do that again, only this time, sit in the chair and speak to someone who is interrogating you and convince them that you are innocent?"). Being fully prepared means that you will not get hung up on any of that if and when it happens, because you will have memorized everything in your repertoire book so fully and made strong choices with clear reasons for any piece that you are offering. You should never be thinking of your next line or of the music or of your singing technique. All of that is part of your preparation, and allowing any of it into your consciousness while you audition will force you out of present tense. Instead, I want you to memorize so fully that you could recite the lines or sing the melody backward in your sleep while doing six other tasks. Nothing should be able to shake you from your words and music. This way, you can focus on more important things, such as using those words to change your scene partner—regardless of whether he is real or imaginary.

DRESSING FOR SUCCESS

We spoke in detail earlier about attire as it relates to brand. Just make sure that when you attend an audition you wear clothing in which you feel comfortable and powerful. You do not want needless distraction, such as clothes that do not fit properly, shoes that inhibit the way you walk, or any kinds of "wardrobe malfunctions." Look at yourself in the mirror before you leave and check for skin popping out where you do not want it showing, as well as other features being over- or underaccentuated. Make sure you rehearse your audition in the clothing you plan to wear so that you know what your range of movement is in the outfit you have chosen.

REVIEWING YOUR RESUME REGULARLY AND KNOWING WHAT YOU HAVE LISTED

Anything on your resume is fair game in an audition room. If you have special skills listed, be prepared to demonstrate them without hesitation. If you have musical roles listed, be prepared to sing from any of those shows. If you have directors or theatre companies or teachers on your resume, do not be surprised if someone asks you to talk about your experience working with them. Try not to let anything catch you off guard and throw you in the room.

I was holding auditions for a summer stock production of the musical *All Shook Up!* last year, when a young lady with a great deal of talent stepped onto the stage. As she did her audition piece, I knew instantly that she had the requisite skills to perform the heck out of the role of "Lorraine," so I mentally cut away from her song to glance down at her resume. As it turns out, she had worked with a former student of mine at a theatre the year before. When she finished the song, I asked her if she knew this student. I expected that she would light up at knowing we shared a mutual association; instead, she hesitated, and I could almost feel her stomach drop. She simply said, "Yes, I know him," and put an implied period on the end of the statement that could only mean she was not thrilled to hear me bring him up. Well, of course I contacted him and found out that this actress was major trouble at the previous theatre. She alienated herself from the entire company and left on pretty bad terms. Needless to say, she did not get the role in my show. However, I guarantee you that I would have hired her to play the part had she not listed on her resume a theatre with which she had burned her bridge. Think before you include something on your resume!

LOVING TO SAY YES

As I said above, you never really know what they might ask of you in the audition room. Some things might throw you. Some direction you might question. But if you get into the mind-set of "yes I can" as opposed to "let me think about that" or "no, I can't/won't," you will really amp up your likeability and earn major points with the creative team. You must always keep in mind that they are not only seeking the best talent for their project, but they are also looking for actors to be a part of their ensemble; their troupe, if you will. They want to find artists who make strong choices, but who are also malleable and willing to alter their approach in order to meet the director's vision of the show. So to that end, just always be ready and happy to say yes if an adjustment is presented to you in your audition. The only time you should say no is if they are really asking you to do something that is completely out of your skill set (or if they ask you to do something inappropriate that goes against your moral standards—which does not really happen so much anymore).

KNOWING EXACTLY WHO YOU ARE

This one is hard to teach and even harder to quantify, but believe me when I tell you that a sense of self really goes a long way in this industry. If you can walk into a room in which—let's face it—there is a scary panel of people there to "judge" you and your abilities (or at least, that is the common perception), and you can feel at ease and confident in exactly who you are as a person, your poise will be incredibly sexy. Talent aside, I know that casting directors and agents are drawn to actors who exhibit a consistent air of honesty, ease, and self-assurance without being cocky.

Are you beginning to see how all of the puzzle pieces fit together? You figure out who you are; you craft a brand that you can broadcast to the world; you make career choices based on that brand and the confidence you have in being able to sell it; you prepare as fully as possible for every opportunity; you learn to be fully present and absolutely, genuinely you in the audition room—and people will respond favorably. You will find more and more that you are at least moved on from the initial audition to a callback. And possibly even more important: people will remember you. You will become *sticky*!

Before I move away from the subject of auditions, it seems important to mention that not all auditions are created equal. You will encounter many different variations on the audition process in your career, so I think it would be useful to go through some of the different possibilities with you and discuss the adjustments and the specific approaches to each.

THE OPEN CALL

The open call is probably the most common audition you will attend. It is exactly what it sounds like—you show up at the start time; you sign up and wait your turn in the first-come, first-served system; and you get your couple of minutes in the room. For an open call, you will be asked to bring your headshot and resume with you to the audition. They will be collected by the monitor and brought into the room ahead of you, so the creative team will have your information when you walk in. The casting ad will tell you exactly what you need to prepare, so you simply wait your turn then go in and deliver something along the lines of what they are seeking.

Open calls might be run as Equity Chorus Calls (ECC) or Equity Principal Auditions (EPA) for union gigs, or they may be general cattle calls for nonunion work. The casting director may even break down the auditions into more specific categories, such as "dancers who sing" or "singers who dance." In those instances, you would be wise to attend the call that really plays to your greatest strength as a performer. Just know that the dance call at a "dancers who sing" audition will be quite a bit more challenging than the movement combination for singers.

You will be amazed at how many people come out of the woodwork for open calls, especially for big-title Broadway shows and national tours. If the audition begins at ten a.m., you would be wise to arrive at least an hour early. (When *Rent* was revived for an Off-Broadway run a few years ago, people lined up as early as five a.m. to get seen!) If you are a non-Equity performer, you may be interested in attending an Equity call—it is possible, and we will talk about it more in detail when we get to the chapter on unions. However, you need to realize that any card-carrying union members will be seen first, and they will only see nonunion talent if there is time at the end of the day. In these instances, you will need to get to the studio a couple of hours early, sign your name onto what is known as the "unofficial non-Equity list" and wait around all day, hoping that they will decide to see you. Sometimes they will let you know at the start of the day that they will or will not see non-Equity performers. They may even tell you to come back at a certain time.

But there is the possibility that you will just have to wait it out and take your chances.

The other possibility at an open call—particularly a very heavily attended open call—is that they may be typing out. This means that they will literally bring actors into the room in groups, line them up, and based solely on looks decide who they will hear audition and who can go home. It sounds terribly unfair, and it is an ugly part of this business, but it is a part of the business nonetheless. Typing out usually happens only on projects for which a very specific look is required. If you are auditioning to replace an original cast member or if you are going in for a Disney musical or a show based off a movie, they may need actors who look like the iconic original characters. If they do type out, you must not take it personally. Just thank them for their consideration, appreciate that they did not waste your time if they knew they were not going to cast you anyway, and find another audition to attend on the fly.

THE APPOINTMENT CALL

The opposite of the open call is the appointment audition. In these cases, you will be given a specific time to come in for the team, based either on materials you submitted or that your agent submitted on your behalf. When you look through casting ads on Playbill .com or *Backstage*, they may say that if you are interested in auditioning, you will need to send them (via e-mail or "snail mail") your photo and resume and request an appointment. As I advised you back in the chapter on cover letters, always include a short, specific cover letter with any submission you send.

An appointment call may ultimately run just like the open call, where you are expected to come in with your own repertoire material prepared and geared toward the specific show being cast. However, the casting director is just as likely to give you material to prepare from the actual show. This is more common in plays and TV/film, where they will want you to read "sides," or pieces of the script, for them. But occasionally you will receive sides for a musical audition, too. (One of my students just received sides from the casting director of the nonunion *Mamma Mia!* tour. She sent in her picture and resume, and was contacted with an appointment time and specific pieces to prepare.)

When you are given sides, you should always do your best to memorize them in advance, time permitting. If you have had them for more than a day or two, the expectation is that you will have them memorized; however, I suggest that you always hold the sides in your hand when you go in—this way, if you start to falter on your lines you do not stop the audition cold, but rather find your place and continue. Be sure to make strong choices when you read from the script. Do not wait for them to direct you—they may not take the time if they do not see something exciting about you on your first pass. If you have read the script or at least researched it in advance, you should be able to have a strong handle on who this character is and how to approach him. However, in the case of a new work, when information is limited, you may want to prepare a couple of questions for the casting director, which you would ask before you read. Do not ask big, open, in-depth questions such as "So, what is this play about?" or "What can you tell me about this character?" Rather, demonstrate that you have drawn some conclusions based on your limited reading of the sides, and ask them to fill in the blanks for you. For instance:

"Am I trying to seduce him in this scene so that he'll leave his wife for me?"
"It seems like Nicki and Lorraine are sisters but their relationship is strained. Is that correct?"
"Do I have a romantic history with Charlie or are we strictly platonic?"

Do you see how these questions already imply that I have made some educated choices but that I need just a little guidance as far as context? These types of leading questions will establish for the casting director that you have read and analyzed the sides and that you have put some real thought into your acting choices. They will generally appreciate the conversation and the opportunity to guide you toward making the strongest choices. But once again, I strongly advise you not to come in asking plot and character questions on a play that is already published. You will be expected to have read the piece if it is available to the public.

When you attend a callback or an audition that involves reading rather than prepared repertoire, you will likely have a partner with whom to read your scenes. In first auditions, the partner is a hired reader who sits behind the table and reads the other character's lines with you. In callbacks, there may be a hired reader or you may be partnered with another actor who is called back for the opposite role.

In either case, you must use the partner you are given. Do not pretend that you are talking to someone who is not there while an off-stage voice recites the other lines. The reader is usually an actor,[2] and although he will not engage in a full-out performance of the scene with you (it is your audition, so they generally try to feed you the lines in a subtle, low-key way so as not to upstage your performance), it is still wise to work *with* him rather than ignoring him. To that end, unless you are directed otherwise, you should deliver your lines to the reader—you may even ask him to stand if you want to have him at eye level. This will give the casting team the opportunity to see you engaging with another and playing off him (hello Meisner!).

Allow me to digress for a moment to share a funny story with you. When I was finishing college, a directing mentor of mine let me come with him to New York for a day to sit in on auditions for the murder mystery play, *Accomplice*. I was to be the reader at this Equity appointment audition, and we were seeing some pretty accomplished actors for the leading roles. It was quite the day of learning for me as a young, up-and-coming director, getting to spend six or seven hours behind the table watching these professionals work—and most of them were quite good.

But the audition I remember most happened to be from a film actress whose claim to fame was a pretty major movie from the 1970s. I was so excited for her to come in, since I was still young

---

2. If you ever get the chance to work for a casting director as a reader, it is a great way to experience a day of auditions from behind the table while also reading script in front of a casting team all day—that cannot be bad for your career. Reach out to a casting office and offer up your services. I bet someone will take you up on the offer.

and fairly starstruck and this would be my opportunity to read a scene with someone whom I had seen in one of my favorite films.

The scene we were reading involved a woman and her male partner in crime just after having created a hoax of him being dead. I do not remember the specific lines, but I know the scene cutting began with her telling him that the coast was clear and he could stop playing dead and get up now. The actress walked into the room and we all exchanged greetings and pleasantries. Then the director asked her to go ahead out into the space and begin when ready. I watched her take a brief second to ground and center herself as she moved into the room. Then she looked at me and waited. I held her eye contact for a long moment, figuring that she was getting into the *zone*, but then she raised an eyebrow as if to say, "Well? I'm waiting." So I said to her, "I'm ready. You have the first line, so you can go ahead and start whenever you like, and I'll follow."

Then this actress pointed to the floor beneath her feet and asked me, "Aren't you going to come and lie here? You're supposed to be on the floor dead." I looked at the director, wondering if I had been missing some sort of reader's protocol all day, since I had previously just sat in a chair behind the table and read from there. He seemed just as thrown as I was in that instant. The actress added, "Come on and do the scene with me. Lay on the floor and we can do this right." And with the director's nod of consent, I ventured out from behind the safety of our table and *performed* this scene with the actress. She was very physical in the reading, and she performed it full out as if there were a paying audience. I had no idea what to expect from moment to moment, which was both scary and interesting.

It was certainly an example of an actor being bold, taking risks, and fully owning the audition. However, it may have pushed the limit of taste and decorum just a bit. While she showed her ability to command a room and make specific choices, she also came off as a bit crazy and overbearing. Some directors might have responded favorably to that kind of audacity, but the three of us in the room (myself, director, and stage manager/monitor) breathed a sigh of relief when she left the audition. We were thrown by her forwardness and her inability to read the energy in the room. Although she delivered a *performance*, she never really bothered to pay attention to what we were giving back in response, either in the preaudition conversation or in the actual scene itself. I might as well have not been there at all, because she was definitely not playing off what I was giving as her scene partner. Rather, she was delivering her preconceived, over-the-top rendition of the scene.

I learned the biggest lesson of the day from that single audition: bold is wonderful, but good taste and presence trumps it. I have never forgotten that audition, nor my experience playing a scene with a celebrity. But I was not the least bit surprised when she did not get the role, in spite of her name. The director decided that she was simply too big a risk to bring into the process. He did not feel that she would be directable based on how she conducted herself for us.

The Video Submission

Sometimes you will be interested in auditioning for a theatre that is far from where you live, or you will be unable to attend their call because you are off performing on another contract—either a tour or a cruise ship, perhaps. That does not always eliminate you from being seen by that company. We have made such strides in technology that now virtually everyone has the ability to record their own high-quality video using their phones, their laptops, or their flip cameras.

If you find yourself in such a situation and you really want to be considered for a gig for which you are unable to make the live audition, I urge you to contact them and ask if they will accept a video. Some theatres simply will not, but most companies and casting directors I know will allow it. All you have to do is ask, and the worst thing they can say is no.

Write to the director, the artistic director, or the casting director—whoever is listed in the advertisement—and explain why you are unable to make the live audition. Ask him if he will consider video and if so, find out what he would like from you in your recorded audition, when he would need to receive it, and how he would prefer you deliver it. Some will ask you to mail a DVD, while others might tell you to send them a YouTube link or an e-mail with your video attached. They may even get as detailed as to tell you what kind of camera shot they would favor (close-up or full body).

When you record the video, you want to try to give them the closest approximation to the live audition experience, so do not use a microphone in the shot and do not get fancy with editing and cutting multiple angles into the audition. If they do not offer you specific direction as to the distance they want in the camera shot, think medium length. This way, they can see your body, but they can also see your face clearly. (Obviously, if it is a dance video, you will need to shoot from farther away so that your entire body is in the frame.) If at all possible, use an accompanist for musical auditions. Singing a cappella is never recommended unless you absolutely have to. And if they send you sides to read, ask a friend to be your reader and have her stand just to the left or right of the camera, out of the frame. This will allow you to play the scene looking at your partner and allowing the casting team to see your face directly without you looking into the camera lens.[3]

Finally, take the time to watch the video, and be sure it shows you off at your absolute best before sending it. I am always amazed when I receive taped auditions and the actor or actress stumbles over a line or sings off-key. It makes me ask, "Did you even watch this before you sent it?" The benefit to a prerecorded audition is that you can do multiple takes until you get a really solid representation of your talent, so do not rush it and send off the first take if it is less than terrific.

I encourage my students to maintain their own YouTube channels, to which they upload videos of themselves performing audition repertoire from time to time. I tell them only to post high-quality performances with high-quality audio and video. Then, when they encounter situations in which they would like to submit an audition via recording, they can very quickly and easily direct the casting person to their channel or to their website to see representations of their performing abilities. I cannot tell you how many times I have had students book work or at least earn callbacks based upon their archived videos.

---

3. In any on-camera audition that involves reading a scene, unless you are directed otherwise, deliver the reading just to the side of the lens rather than looking into the center of the frame.

THE COMBINED AUDITION

The final common audition scenario you will likely encounter is what is known as the combined audition. This is when a large collective of professional theatre companies (or undergraduate or graduate college programs) hold a singular audition together and see a gathering of actors en masse, cattle call–style. These auditions generally take place in a hotel ballroom (great acoustics, let me tell you!)[4] over the course of several days. Actors prepare a "package" that may consist of a song and a monologue or two monologues, depending on the specifics of the audition, and the audition is on a time limit, generally between sixty seconds and two minutes. After performing the initial package audition, actors then check the bulletin boards outside of the audition hall, where the individual companies will post lists of which actors they want to call back. Callbacks are then held in the hotel rooms of the companies or in designated conference spaces throughout the hotel. (These combined auditions are the only time I would ever recommend that you [a] pay to audition, and [b] allow a company to audition you in a hotel room!)

When attending a combined audition, it is incumbent upon you to solidify your brand before choosing your material. You only have about a minute to make an impression on forty to seventy companies and you cannot tailor your audition to a specific show, since their needs and their seasons will be so diverse.[5] You need to make an impact and really show off what you do best in a very short amount of time, so find pieces that really showcase your greatest skills. I want you to be sticky in the minds of the attending companies.

When crafting a package that consists of multiple pieces, there are two logical approaches: you can either deliver two completely contrasting selections, with a clear break and transition in between them, or you can put together a true package where your monologue leads directly into the song or vice versa.[6] Either method is fine and obviously, as subjective as theatre is, different directors

---

4. That was sarcasm.

5. Although, I do recommend that you check out the attending theatres' seasons in advance to get an idea of what kind of work is being produced that season. It may guide you to choosing material that targets specific gigs.

6. Be sure to read the regulations on the conference website. Some combined auditions require you to perform your song first so that the next actor can go through her music with the accompanist while you deliver your monologue.

will have different preferences. Again, you need to do what shows you off best and what you feel is a "home run."

The one thing you will want to keep in mind as you begin to search for the right audition material is that you may very well be the four hundredth person they are hearing in the day. Selecting a beautiful ballad or an emotional and subtle monologue may not be the best avenue for getting the auditors' heads up out of their notebooks. Think of up-tempo, upbeat, fun, and light material if possible and save the heavier stuff for the callbacks. Go into the open call and just try to catch their attention and make them interested in seeing more from you.

When you go to these combined auditions, be sure to bring your entire audition repertoire with you. If you receive callbacks, you may be asked to repeat your earlier audition package and they may coach you on the material, or you may be asked to dig deeper into your repertoire and show them more of what you can do. Sometimes the companies bring accompanists and keyboards, while other times they will have you sing a cappella at the callback.[7]

You should also be sure to bring plenty of extra copies of your headshot and resume with you. When you register for the conference, the headshot you submit will be photocopied in black and white and shrunk down to about 2" × 4" to fit on the corner of your application page that each company receives. It would be wise of you to hand a full-color, full-sized picture with resume attached to any director who calls you in for a follow-up.

I also suggest that you get smart business cards printed out before attending one of these conferences. Although some of them are just quick in-and-out auditions where you do your package, hit your callbacks, and leave, others are full-weekend conferences complete with social mixers and workshops. You will not only audition for jobs at these events, but you will also find many opportunities to expand your professional contacts. You should be prepared to get up and perform at any workshop you attend, and you should also be ready to offer your business card to someone whom you meet that would be good to add to your network.

---

7. Another great tip for musical theatre performers: download a metronome and a piano application for your phone so you can always find your first note and tempo at an a cappella callback.

The other big piece of advice I can offer you in order to maximize your chances for success at these combined auditions is to contact some of the theatres in advance. About two or three weeks before the event, you can explore the conference website, find out which theatre companies will be attending, and do your research on their individual seasons. If you find some places and some seasons you feel would be a good fit for you and for your talents, reach out to those companies with an e-mail, attaching headshot and resume. Introduce yourself, tell them you are attending the conference, and if you can, tell them what number you are (or what time your audition appointment is scheduled). Ask them to keep an eye out for you and tell them you hope to meet with them at the conference. Almost without fail, these companies will look for you at the auditions. They will be flattered to know that you are interested enough in their company to have taken the time to target them specifically (do not do this for every attending theatre!), and they will come in and give you consideration in advance. Sometimes, they will even offer you a callback automatically without even seeing your initial cattle-call audition.

One other thing you should be aware of with some of these combined audition conferences is that they may offer what is known as an "actor walk-through" on the day of or the evening before your audition. This is a time during which none of the member companies are in the room, and actors may take a walk around the space, test the acoustics, and generally get a sneak peek at where they will be performing. When this option is offered, *do it*! You will learn about how much you will need to project, where you will want to stand to be powerful, and so forth. And you will also be able to see what color curtain they have hung behind the platform stage, so that you can be sure to wear a color that does not fade you into the backdrop.

The most well-known combined audition conferences follow.

UPTA—Unified Professional Theatre Auditions (www.upta.org)

These take place in Memphis, Tennessee, at Playhouse on the Square every year in early February. They have Equity and non-Equity slots available, and the companies generally tend to be seeking year-round actor availability; thus, you must be a graduating senior in college or a professional (nonstudent) actor in order to attend. Registration is first come, first served, so if you are interested in attending, you will want to start checking for registration deadlines in September.

SETC—Southeastern Theatre Conference (www.setc.org)

SETC is a roving conference. It takes place each year in early March, but the host location varies each year. Recent conferences have occurred in Atlanta, Georgia; Louisville, Kentucky; Birmingham, Alabama; and Chattanooga, Tennessee. Both students and professional actors attend this conference, and the professional companies that attend are seeking summer-only as well as year-round availability. In order to participate in SETC, actors must pass a screening audition in their home state. The screenings occur in October, so you will need to think ahead if you are interested in attending the spring conference. The wonderful benefit of attending SETC, in addition to being seen by dozens and dozens of potential employers, is that the weekend is chock-full of exciting workshops and classes that are all free with your conference admission. My students and I have made some incredible contacts at SETC over the years. If you go, you should look for my name in the program, as I usually teach one or two workshops at the conference!

NETC—New England Theatre Conference (www.netconline.org)

NETC is held in Natick, Massachusetts (just outside of Boston), in mid-March. The companies that attend are generally summer stocks, theme parks, and cruise ships, and many of them are based in or near New England. However, the auditions are open to actors from any region and the registration is first come, first served with no screening requirement.

StrawHat Auditions (www.strawhat-auditions.com)

StrawHat is a non-Equity audition that is held in New York City each year in mid-February. Most of the attending companies are summer theatres, theme parks, and cruise ships. The auditions are open to anyone who registers, so there is no screening process.

IOD—The Institute of Outdoor Drama (www.outdoordrama.org)

IOD is the combined audition for actors who are interested in Shakespearean companies, Renaissance fairs, and other such open-air performance experiences. Companies from all over the country attend the auditions in Asheville, North Carolina, every January, and registration is open to anyone, provided you solicit a sponsor to vouch for you, beginning in December.

LOWT—The League of Washington Theatre (www.lowt.org)

The league runs professional auditions for the greater Washington, DC, region every year in February or March. At the time of writing this, forty-five theatres from DC, Maryland, and Virginia are registered as member companies.

MWTA—Midwest Theatre Auditions (www.webster.edu/fine-arts/midwest-theatre-auditions)

Midwest auditions are similar to NETC and SETC. Professional companies from all over the country attend the conference at Webster Conservatory in St. Louis in late February. Applications open in mid-October and registration is first come, first served.

U/RTA—University/Resident Theatre Association (www.urta.com)

If you are interested in attending graduate school for theatre, this conference enables you to audition for many programs at once. They hold a New York audition at the end of January, a Chicago audition in early February, and a San Francisco audition in early February. The application process runs from late October to mid-November, and all the information you need is listed on the website. Read it carefully to determine what material to prepare and how to target specific graduate programs.

National Unified Auditions (www.unifiedauditions.com)

Unifieds are auditions for undergraduate BFA programs in theatre. They are held in early February in New York, Chicago, Las Vegas, and Los Angeles. Here, a high school student may audition for multiple degree-offering theatre programs across the country in one fell swoop. There are currently (as of January 2013) twenty-five member schools in Unifieds, and you must apply for each one that interests you before you attend the audition.

Whatever the audition format, your general approach to preparation needs to follow the same guidelines. Know all of your repertoire pieces fully and be ready to have an immediate answer to "To whom are you speaking?" and "What do you want from them?" Also, do not be surprised if someone asks you, "What is the moment just before this that leads you to speak or sing?" Have multiple copies of your headshot and resume, and be sure to keep the resume up to date and polished. Choose from your audition wardrobe the attire that both fits the specific occasion and represents your brand. Be sure to bring proper dance attire if there is a dance call involved.

A smart actor will also keep a journal, in which he will log after every audition: (a) what was being cast, (b) who was in the room, (c) what he wore, (d) what he presented, (e) any feedback or adjustments that may have been offered by the creative team, (f) whether or not a callback was earned, and (g) whether or not he booked the job. In addition, you may wish to add comments about the experience. This way, whenever you go in for a casting director, you can refer to your notes about what happened in previous encounters with her and build on that experience. I know actors who also journal about the studio in which they auditioned. When you move to any city to do theatre, you are likely going to find yourself auditioning in five to eight different locations around the city. It is very good to keep track of basic information about each studio, such as (a) what color any drapes or curtains are (so you do not wear the same color and blend into the background), (b) what size the room is, (c) how the acoustics pop, (d) and so forth.

One other piece of advice I want to offer you involves knowing the answers to a couple of uncommon questions, which although rare, do come up on occasion in the casting room. One of them is, "Will you cut/dye your hair for this role?" The other is, "Are you willing to do nudity?" Sometimes answering no to either of these might keep you from getting the job, if the role requires one or the other. In other instances, it will not keep you from getting cast, but the director wants to know how much leeway he has with you in terms of boundaries. I think it is important for you to reflect on your personal values and have an answer ready to go when either of these questions is posed.

Most of all, you need to learn to have fun and to love auditioning. You must not view it simply as a means to an end—you will be auditioning far more than you will be performing in shows. If you fear or hate the process, you will never conquer the audition and thus you will be denied the opportunity to do what you truly love. You need to consider the audition your time to get up and perform and tell a story and transform people by letting them get a glimpse into your soul. If you can adjust your mind-set and actually look forward to auditioning, you will notice your confidence soar, and your results will be much more positive. Control what you can control and let the rest go.

Scene 2

━━━━━━━━━━━━━━━━━━━━◯━━━━━━━━━━━━━━━━━━━━

Agents and Casting Directors

TWO OF THE MOST IMPORTANT players in the industry of theatre and film are the agent and the casting director. While most people have at least a vague idea of what these people do, many are confused at the distinctions and unaware of the specifics. It is important that you know how these industry insiders function and how they can impact your career.

To begin broadly, understand that there is no such thing as a "casting agent." This term is thrown around with regularity and it may be the reason for the confusion. Think of a *casting director* as a buyer and a *talent agent* as a seller, if you like. The agent works for the actor whom he represents. His job is to go to bat for his client and essentially to make a pitch to the casting director to see his actor or to negotiate the best possible contract for the actor. The casting director, on the other hand, works for the producers of the show being cast. She is looking to find the best talent and the most affable actors possible to bring forward to the producers, the director, and often the writer(s) of the production on which she is working. Although both are seeking talented actors with whom to build relationships and both are successful when their actors succeed, the nature of the relationships between agent and actor and casting director and actor are quite different. And there also exists a third important relationship—that of agent to casting director.

We will start by focusing on casting directors, since you will have far more access to and far more relationships with a wide array of them. As I mentioned, when a show begins the process of heading into production, the creative team often hires a casting director to lead them through the search for actors. Some companies have in-house casting departments (e.g., Disney and Disney Parks Talent Casting; Roundabout Theatre Company and Jim Carnahan Casting), and others hire outside firms. In either case, the casting director is hired for her expertise of the talent pool and her ability to bring in the right people for the job.

The casting process begins with the casting director (we will call her the CD) reading the material and meeting with the creative team to get a sense of which direction they are looking to go with the production. Once the CD has a clear vision of what the director wants, she creates what is called a breakdown. The breakdown describes in detail the characters that are being sought as well as the specifics of the job (date, location, audition information, pay scale, etc.). She will send the breakdown out to agents to solicit actor submissions, and in many instances, she will also post the breakdown on Playbill.com as well as in *Backstage* for the general population of actors to see.

Once the casting call is made public, she will start receiving headshots and resumes from agents and from actors alike. At the same time, she will go through her own files of actors with whom she already has a previous relationship, whom she has auditioned in the past. (This is why bringing a confident sense of self along with a consistent reputation really pays off in this business.) With the help of interns, the field of actors is narrowed into groups that fit each of the characters being cast, and appointments will be set. The CD may also hold open calls, which we discussed in the previous chapter, in order to see new actors who may not have agent representation and who may not yet exist in her files.

In general, the CD's biggest job is to narrow down the slate of actors auditioning for each role and to present the selected groups to the creative team for them to audition and to choose which ones they want to offer jobs. The CD will often vouch for an actor's abilities or reliability, so developing long-standing relationships with casting directors, their associates, and their interns is essential to you as you build a career. In addition, a solid connection to a casting director may lead you to landing an agent. I know many instances in which a CD has recommended an unrepresented actor to an agent colleague based on that actor's regular, consistent audition work at open calls and appointments.

Sometimes, the CD will also serve as an audition coach. If her success is dependent on how much the creative team likes a certain actor, and she sees great potential in that actor but also recognizes that the actor needs some adjustments before going in front of the director, she will often have a private session with the actor and help prepare him for the final callbacks.

Ultimately, the casting director does not often have final say over who is chosen, but rather acts as the gatekeeper between the actor and the team of collaborators who are hiring performers. Her job is high stress and fast paced, particularly when it comes to casting television and commercials, where casting will quite often happen just days before the actual shoot. It is absolutely imperative that you get to know the CDs in your city and that you let them get to know you. Although they might not utilize the language of "branding" and "marketing," I assure you it is of immense and implicit importance to them. The more consistent and sticky you can be, the quicker you will come to mind for them when they have a role to cast, and the more you will be called in by the same casting offices with regularity.

I interviewed some casting directors in New York to get the answers to some valuable questions for actors. These are CDs who you will likely encounter at some point if you choose to make New York your home, but their answers will provide insight to you no matter where you land. If you keep an acting journal, these might be points of information to log away for future reference.

JOY DEWING, JOY DEWING CASTING, WWW.JOYDEWINGCASTING.COM

JF: *What do you like most about being a casting director?*
JD: When I introduce an actor I love to a creative team and they fall in love with the actor. Also, when I get to make the phone call telling the actor they booked the job.

JF: *What excites you most when watching a young actor audition for you?*
JD: When they are lit from within.

JF: *What might a young actor do in an audition that drives you crazy?*
JD: Apologizing. Making excuses.

JF: *If there was one piece of solid advice you could offer to young actors coming to the city to try and make a career, what would it be?*
JD: Have a life beyond your job. Which is auditioning. Have other interests, hobbies, a side business, friends outside of the industry. Travel. Go to museums.

PAT McCORKLE, CASTING DIRECTOR, PAT McCORKLE CASTING

JF: *What do you like most about being a casting director?*
PM: I love actors, and I really enjoy putting the pieces of the puzzle together—the play, the director's vision, and the actors who can most fulfill that vision.

JF: *What excites you most when watching a young actor audition for you?*
PM: Their talent and how they can tie into the material and understand the material. I love when they are prepared for the audition and they can create moments in terms of combining the text and their individual talent.

JF: *What might a young actor do in an audition that drives you crazy?*
PM: Not prepare enough. Sometimes they don't realize this is a job interview and *this is it* and they need to focus on the material. It's not about just showing up in the room and deciding what you are going to do in that moment. You need to show me and the artistic team that you are the best person to play the role. I don't like it when actors don't commit enough to the audition. Sometimes it's like they're watching themselves, rather than really focusing on the material.

JF: *If there was one piece of solid advice you could offer to young actors coming to the city to try and make a career, what would it be?*
PM: Just be prepared. Be prepared for the city. Be prepared to *live* in the city (any city, be it New York, LA, Chicago, etc.) in addition to the work and the artistry. You are a living, breathing human being as well as an actor, and you have no protection from your university anymore. Figure out day-to-day survival structures and find a way to blend that into your craft.

Now we turn our attention to the talent agent. The agent makes a living by seeking out and signing great talent, getting that talent seen by CDs and producers, and then helping to negotiate contracts and guide careers forward. Agencies can range from small, "boutique" offices that have between one and four agents and deal with fewer than fifty clients, to mega-operations with upward of ten agent associates that handle hundreds of actors. Different size and different focus agents will be better suited to you depending on where you live, where you are in your career, and what part of the industry (theatre, film, TV, commercials, voice-overs) you are pursuing. At the beginning of your career, you are not in a position to be very choosy, and so working with any type of agency that shows an interest in your potential is probably a wise idea. Many agents will work on a freelance basis with young actors rather than signing an exclusive contract. This means that neither you nor the agent is bound to each other. If he sees an audition on which to send you and you book the job, he gets paid. If you decide to find work elsewhere through other means, that is your prerogative. Either party may end the relationship at any time. Once you sign an exclusive contract, however, you must allow that agent to represent you for the duration of the agreement and you may not take auditions through any other agency unless it is agreed upon in your contract. (For example, some people will have one agent for theatre and another for voice-over work, but that would be understood in advance.)

The important thing to remember is that although you rely on your agent to help you get seen for certain auditions, he ultimately works for you. He will advise you along the way, no doubt—and certainly, some agents are more hands on and nurturing than others—but at the end of the day, you must be the CEO of your company, and you need to make the final decisions regarding your product. The standard in the industry is that your agent will get 10 percent commission on any work you book with him working for you.[1] Aaron Galligan-Stierle wisely tells young actors that if they are getting 90 percent of the money, they need to be doing 90 percent of the work, while the agent earns his percentage by doing 10 percent of the work. In other words, do not be one of those actors who sit around waiting for the agent to call and send them out on auditions and who complain when they are not auditioning. Even with representation, you need to be finding and attending auditions regularly. The agent will help you get into the auditions that require appointments, but open calls are still advisable even when you have an agent.

When offers come in for acting work, they will go through your agent. He will negotiate the pay and the perks for you, and he will read the contract on your behalf and make sure that the gig is in your best interest. Then he will advise you, and you will make the final decision as to whether or not you sign the contract. It is a rare situation that an agent recommends work to an actor and the actor turns it down, but it is possible. I tell you that just to remind you that the final say is still yours. This is *your* career, and you need to trust your instincts and pursue your goals. But a good agent will talk to you about where you want to be in the next five to ten years and he will work with you to follow the right path to get you there.

Very often, an actor with agent representation will find work completely on her own. The actor will attend an open call or set an appointment herself, and without any input or help from her agent, she will get an offer. In those instances, the agent can earn his money on the other end by doing the contract and bargaining work on the actor's behalf. However, sometimes that service is not even needed. In these instances when an actor is working with an agent but she books work completely independent of the agency, there is a moral and a political question to ask: Does the actor still

---

1. If an "agent" ever asks you for money up front or tells you he is going to take a larger commission than 10 percent, do not sign with him.

pay the agent a 10 percent commission? First of all, I would say that the easy answer might be in the actor's contract, if she is exclusive with the agency. There may be language that states whether or not commission is due in such a circumstance. However, it gets dicey when one is freelancing and there is no prior agreement about the actor booking her own work. My advice to you, especially when the relationship with the agency is new and you are trying to establish a reputation with them: always offer to pay them the 10 percent commission. In the grand scheme of things, 10 percent is not very much, and the gesture (I have known the occasional agent who will not accept the commission) will go a long way toward making you a very likeable and popular client. The agent will remember that you paid on your own gig and he will be that much more likely to work harder to get you other work in the future.

In addition, you never know when things might turn sour in the job you accepted or when you might get a better offer during the course of your contract. In either instance, you might need an agent to step in and deal with the producers on your behalf to help make things better or to rescue you from the commitment you made (we will discuss contracts and contract breaking in great detail later), and the agent will certainly be more likely to come to your aid if he is being paid a commission for that particular job. I also believe that there is such a thing as theatre karma, and paying your agent whether he connected you to a gig or not is just good karma!

The big mystery for young actors really tends to lie in the question of "How do I get an agent?" I wish there were a simple, straightforward answer, but unfortunately there is not. In a moment, we are going to look at some interviews with agents in New York and they will share with you how they tend to find their clients, but let me tell you the six most common ways actors wind up getting representation.

The first possibility is through the college showcase. Many undergraduate and graduate schools put together what is called a showcase, either in New York, Los Angeles, or Chicago. Basically, a showcase comprises about an hour of material, which is meant to highlight each graduating student at his or her very best in small snippets. Agents and casting directors are invited, and these events are more or less a coming-out party for the new class of students. The hope is that they will make an impression and the industry guests will want to see more. The best-case scenario is that after the performance, an agent will invite a young actor to come to the office and interview to see if the chemistry is right to create a working relationship. Showcases were once the most direct routes for an actor to find representation; however, now there are so many schools presenting these events that the agents are not able to attend most of them. They go to see the schools with great reputations and with which they have long-standing relationships; they send their assistants and interns to some of the up-and-coming schools; and they skip many of the new programs that seem to add themselves into the mix each year.

To combat the showcase overload, some schools (Shenandoah being one of them!) will bring agents and casting directors out of their home city and onto the actual college campus. They will pay the agents for an entire day's workshop, during which they can really take the time to get to know the graduating class. With the flooding of the showcase market, this approach may be the future of colleges connecting students to the business. But ultimately, the premise is the same—the school introduces its talent to the industry, and then it is up to the students to follow up and massage the relationships if they are seeking representation.[2]

The other type of showcase that exists to connect actors to agents is the professional showcase. It is very similar to the school showcase, except it is composed of actors who are already out of college, living in a city, and want to invite agents to see their work. Some talent showcases are "pay to play," meaning the organizer will charge each actor a fee to be involved. That fee may go toward renting a space, paying an accompanist, and advertising. Essentially, all the performers are expected to pitch in on the costs involved with getting seen by agents. Many of these events are quite legitimate, but I do warn you to be careful. Before you pay one cent to a producer to get involved in a "showcase," ask a lot of questions and do

---

2. Note that I put the responsibility to follow up in your hands. If your school does a showcase, and you wish to land an agent, you must be the one to reach out to the agents after the event and request a further meeting.

your research. Find out how many of these showcases he has pro-duced and how successful they have been. Ask which agencies are guaranteed to attend, and make sure that you do your homework to see if they are legitimate agencies by whom you would want to be seen. Ask how much performance time you will be given and how the material is chosen and shown. You may even want to consider how the other actors are being selected. (If there is no audition process and one only has to pay to be involved, that should be a major red flag to you.) I have known actors who have been burned on these types of showcases, but I also have known actors who have found success in doing them. Just be careful and try not to let someone take advantage of you.

The third way to connect with agents is by getting cast in shows in or around the city and inviting them to see your work. Before we discuss this in more detail, I want to start by advising you to invite industry people to see you only when you are in a show that is really good, of which you are quite proud. Bringing agents to see mediocre work can be detrimental to your process, so do not just invite everyone whenever you get cast in a project.

However, when you do find yourself in an exciting production, especially if it is in a reputable venue, such as Goodspeed Musicals, Paper Mill Playhouse, or in an Off-Broadway house, it would be wise to send out postcards (or e-mails with your photo attached) to agents with whom you are interested in working and invite them to see your work. Many theatres will offer complimentary tickets to industry people; however, if your gig will not, I suggest you buy the tickets for the people you invite. Do not ask an agent to pay to see you in a show if you have no prior relationship with him.

Sometimes you will be performing in a show with a castmate who has an agent. If you talk to that actor and you both believe it would be a good match for you to work with his agency, it is that much easier to get on their radar, as they will likely come see the show for their current client. You can reach out and contact the agent in the weeks leading up to your performances and say, "I am working with so-and-so, who tells me we would be a good fit. I look forward to you seeing the show, and I hope that we might be able to meet sometime afterward and discuss working together."

Which leads me to the fourth method of connecting with an agent: the referral. When someone has a great relationship with a talent agency, her recommendation can often go a long way to bringing an actor to that agent. Either the currently represented actor will talk to the agent about her friend, or the friend can write a cover letter mentioning the friend's referral, just like the example in the previous paragraph. Agents tend to respond quite favorably to referrals, and although they will not always sign the person who is being suggested, they will usually at least consider him and meet with him.

That inside advocate, by the way, can be an actor friend who is with the agency, or it can be a casting director who has seen your work and wants to connect you with representation. Sometimes it can even be a teacher or a mentor who has a connection to an agent. I have on several occasions connected a former student or an actor with whom I have worked professionally to some of the agents that I know in New York and gotten them meetings. This business is small and it should not surprise you to know that everyone knows virtually everyone. That also means that everyone can be an important relationship for you, and it is vital that you do not burn your bridges. We will discuss networking more in a later chapter.

Another increasingly common approach to actors seeking and finding representation is taking classes. Many agents and casting directors now supplement their incomes and connect with a wider array of talent by teaching at places such as Actors Connection, One-on-One, or the Network. There, actors can study a range of topics, from monologue coaching to on-camera testing and commercial work. The two formats in which these workshops are generally offered are one-night classes, which usually cost about $25 and end with each actor getting some face time with the agent or CD teacher; and extended courses, which may run over the length of several weeks and meet regularly during that period. These workshops can range in cost from $200 to $600 depending on the frequency of meeting and the renown of the teacher. I know many actors who have booked work with CDs and signed with agents simply from attending these types of classes. Visit the websites of the host locations and read the details of the classes being offered.

They will always publish the bios of the teaching artists, so you can really target which industry people you are interested in meeting.

And finally, there is the old-fashioned approach: targeted mailings. This was once the most common way for actors to access agents, but with the acceleration of social media, the advent of online performer search engines such as Actors Access (actorsaccess .com), and the outcropping of networking businesses such as Actors Connection, mailings have become less common (although no less relevant, our friends at The Savvy Actor would tell us!).

You may notice I said "targeted" mailings, rather than simply mailings. This is an important distinction because, just like I warned you about audition submissions, you do not want to send out blind, generic letters of interest to every agency for which you find an address. Rather, you want to do your research on as many agencies in your region as possible and find out what distinguishes them from one another. Ask yourself which type of office would be best for you at this stage of your career and which among them would have the highest likelihood of being interested in working with you at your current level of experience. Do not waste your time and postage on the big houses like William Morris or Creative Artists if you have no major credits to your name, and do not submit for agencies that deal in commercials and television if you have no reel footage to demonstrate your experience. Instead, seek out representation that befits where you are in your career right at this moment. If you are just starting out, target the smaller agencies whose focus is in developing new talent. If you are interested in film, commercials, and TV, but you have little to no experience in those media, look for a theatre agent that also has an on-camera arm so that you can ease your way into that sort of work.

As I said earlier, one of the best sources for finding the right agent is to turn to your network of friends and colleagues. Ask around among your actor contacts and see if you can get some advice as to where you would be a good fit. If you approach the mailings from that standpoint, you will have a mutual connection with which to break the ice when you write to that agent. Whether or not you have a contact working with an agency, it is advisable that you only write to

them and submit your materials when you have something to say[3]—
particularly when you have a professional success to tout.

Once you have narrowed down your target list and you have
positioned yourself so that you have something to say that will make
you appealing, go ahead and create your mailings. They should
include a cover letter, a headshot, and a resume. If you have a reel
of on-camera work, you should also include it on a DVD (or give
them the URL link if it is online). You may also include reviews of
your work if you have them. Ultimately, you are putting together a
little marketing kit for yourself—and I do recommend you use actual physical mail for these as opposed to e-mail. It puts something
tangible into the agents' hands.

Your cover letter should be concise and catchy. Give them a
reason why you have chosen them, and give them a reason why they
should choose to meet with you. For example:

Dear Mr. Jones:

My name is Jonny Doe. I'm currently working with your client
Alexander Reed in *The Stu Revue* and he suggested I reach out to
you, as I am seeking representation. Since moving to the city last
March, I have been in final callbacks for three Broadway shows
with Telsey and Co. as well as Binder Casting. I got my Equity
card last summer at the MUNY, and I've also worked at Barter
Theatre and The Roundhouse in DC.

I hope that you will take a look at my attached materials and
consider meeting with me to discuss the possibility of us working
together. I would also love to invite you to see *The Stu Revue* as
my guest. Let me know if and when you can come and I'll have
comps at the box office for you.

Sincerely,
Jonny Doe

Do you notice how I referenced a relationship connection and
then I bragged a bit about some success I have had? (This is a Savvy
Actor technique, which I absolutely advocate.) If an agent is going

---

3. Other than, "I'm new to the city and I'm looking for an agent." That is not enough to
get them interested in you.

to take you on as a client, they will essentially be "selling" you to the casting and creative teams out there. What I am doing is helping them know how to sell me. Here is one more example for the case when you do not have a friend to recommend you:

Dear Mr. Jones:

My name is Jonny Doe and I am contacting you in the hopes that we might be able to meet up and discuss working together. I am an actor with my BFA from Syracuse University, and I have worked recently at Syracuse Stage, Houston Theatre under the Stars, and Highlands Playhouse. Currently I am not performing in the city, but rather I am honing my on-camera skills by taking classes with Alexa Fogel and Allison Estrin.

I am developing a reel, which I hope to have finished in the coming weeks. Ms. Fogel has told me I remind her of a cross between a young Ben Stiller and Matthew Broderick. She has praised my comic timing as well as my vulnerability.

Attached you will find my resume and headshot along with my contact information. If it would be possible to set up a meeting time either in your office or over coffee, please let me know. I would love to be on your radar.

Best,
Jonny Doe

Again, in this example, I found successes to mention. I also was able to list relationships based on classes I was taking, rather than on friends I had. And you will notice that I helped the agent know a little about my brand and how to sell my product through the mention of the actor comparisons and the feedback on my comic timing and vulnerability. In both models, I have done much more than simply tell them I am an actor who wants an agent. I have given them reasons to want to consider me. Whether or not they are looking for someone like me for their rosters is out of my control. All I can do is send the best mailing that I can put together.

Beyond the initial mailing, I think it is okay to follow up with agencies from which you have not heard back if and when you have something new to report that might tantalize them a bit more. But I am not a big advocate of a steady stream of mail going to the same agency if they have not responded to you along the way.[4]

I interviewed a few talent agents from New York to get their input about what they look for in a client. Here is what they had to say:

ASHLEY LANDAY, AGENT, PROFESSIONAL ARTISTS

JF: *What do you like most about being an agent?*
AL: Finding people jobs. It's pretty simple and basic for me. The foundation of my work is to help people find work and develop careers. I like knowing that I can help people. It's not saving the world and it's not brain surgery, but hopefully I can make a difference in someone's life in a positive way. That is the foundation. When it comes to the everyday aspects of my job, I like my clients. I like the interaction I have in this community of artists. I'm surrounded by some of the most open, honest, funny, and genuine people in the city and I love it. In the madness of it all, it's refreshing to help people that you genuinely care about and believe in.

JF: *How do you tend to find your clients? Do you accept/respond to unsolicited mailings? How do you recommend actors get noticed by an agent?*
AL: I find my clients a bunch of different ways. The easiest and most common is from other clients of mine recommending them to me to meet. Talented people surround themselves with talented people, just one of those things. The office accepts unsolicited submissions, but it's very rare that you meet someone that you want to sign out of a mailing. Granted, it does happen, few and far between, but it is rare. Be picky with your submissions via mail, don't bombard an office with multiple mailings a month and send five headshots. It's a waste of time and money.

---

4. This is one area over which The Savvy Actor folks and I disagree. But it is all subjective. I was never much for the hard sell, so it is a personal preference for me; but I know that many Savvy clients have found success in utilizing their mailing system. You should look into it and decide if it is right for you.

JF: *What excites you most about a prospective new client? In other words, is there something that stands out for you when you see actors do it?*

AL: What excites me most is their personality and drive. It's contagious. When you meet a client and they are fun, talented, interesting, charismatic, you can't help but catch on to that energy. When I meet a client and I think they're crazy talented, I just want to talk about them all the time and I want casting directors to meet them, and I want to work 110 percent for them and I'm immediately invested. A sense of humor stands out for me. I represent you if I believe you're talented, so that is the foundation. The talent. Okay, after that it's a matter of personality and whether we get along. My office is small and I'm not interested in bringing toxic relationships into my life and my work world. I like representing actors that have a good sense of themselves, actors that love their job, know how to handle rejection. There will be a lot of rejection and a lot of people will make you feel *less than*—the actors that have an armor to that sort of negativity are my kind of clients.

JF: *What might a young actor do that drives you crazy?*

AL: Overthink things!!! Do your work, prepare, be professional, and you'll be fine. Calling me twelve times per audition because you need to know how to say a line out loud—ya gotta be kidding me—I don't have time for that. Also, you have to be more confident in your choices and who you are as an actor.

JF: *If there was one piece of solid advice you could offer to young actors coming to the city to try and make a career, what would it be?*

AL: Be forgiving. Be thankful. Be grateful. Honestly, a majority of the actors will never receive fame, or lots of money, but they will have respected, wonderful, beautiful careers, and there is something to be said for that. Most people aren't and never will be "a star." Are you in this for the fame? The money? The recognition? The art? All are acceptable, but know WHY you're in it—and be honest about that. I think actors need to be forgiving of each other and of themselves. Everyone is doing the best they can, and this is a hard business, but treating people well and with respect is not hard. And I don't think that's just for actors—that's for agents, casting directors, managers, producers, etc. . . . We all need to be better people to each other in this business.

DIANE RILEY, AGENT, VICE PRESIDENT, HARDEN CURTIS ASSOCIATES

JF: *What do you like most about being an agent?*
DR: Every day is different. You never know what can happen by the end of the day. You can help to change someone's life in a matter of a few moments.

JF: *How do you tend to find your clients? Do you accept/respond to unsolicited mailings? How do you recommend actors get noticed by an agent?*
DR: We find our clients in every way imaginable. Mailings, casting director recommendations, college showcases, attending shows that clients are in. We do accept mailings and I open every piece of mail that comes addressed to me at the office. If someone's mailing sparks my interest, I have a file I keep and we have people come in to audition for us from those files.

JF: *What excites you most about a prospective new client? In other words, is there something that stands out for you when you see actors do it?*
DR: When I am looking at prospective clients, talent is obviously the first thing I respond to. The "talent crush"! I'm looking for someone who has talent, personality, and drive. I want someone who wants it more than I want it for them.

JF: *What might a young actor do that drives you crazy?*
DR: Have unrealistic expectations of what an agent does/can do. You cannot sit back and wait for us to call. You need to be twice as busy as you were before you had an agent. You have to give us something to sell.

JF: *If there was one piece of solid advice you could offer to young actors coming to the city to try and make a career, what would it be?*
DR: Once you are here, focus on getting work. Run your own race. Everyone's career path is different, so you cannot compare yourself to other people's success. Don't fixate on getting an agent; focus on getting work, building your resume, and improving your skill set.

Gary Krasny, Agent, The Krasny Office, a Theatrical Agency

JF: *What do you like most about being an agent?*
GK: Discovering talent and developing that talent into an actor that works. To me, making someone have a career that establishes them getting jobs, rather than getting just auditions, is appealing. I also like it when I find an actor who contributes to the agency.

JF: *How do you tend to find your clients? Do you accept/respond to unsolicited mailings? How do you recommend actors get noticed by an agent?*
GK: We find actors at college and conservatory presentations that we attend throughout the year and schools that we visit and with whom we participate. The unsolicited picture and resume is not my favorite. I prefer seeing their work.

JF: *What excites you most about a prospective new client? In other words, is there something that stands out for you when you see actors do it?*
GK: It's hard to say. There is a clear, visceral response. Instinct—I know when someone is going to work. The other agent in our office can tell when I respond immediately; I get a certain look sometimes. Lately the most obvious for me is "ethnically ambiguous"— that's what the market is looking for. Russian and East German are big right now.

JF: *What might a young actor do that drives you crazy?*
GK: They will not get new pictures.

JF: *If there was one piece of solid advice you could offer to young actors coming to the city to try and make a career, what would it be?*
GK: Don't come unless you're prepared; unless you have a picture that is good. Don't come unless the picture is really workable. We can always tweak the resume, but with a picture that's just okay—don't come. It is really the most important calling card you have. If the headshot isn't really a good facsimile of you—if it's not clear—if it doesn't sell you well—if it's not like you, it's not gonna work.

No matter which method of contact you employ to set up a meeting with a prospective agent, you will need to be prepared for the actual interview that will ensue upon that appointment. This seems like a great time to refresh the work we did way back in the Overture chapter of this book, when I had you go through the self-knowledge questionnaire and respond to the prompt, "So tell me about yourself." This will almost assuredly be the first thing (or among the first things) the agent asks you to do when you sit down to interview. Other very common questions, for which you will absolutely want to be prepared include: "With which actors would you compare yourself?" "What roles are out there for you right now?" "What are your goals for your career?" "What do you enjoy doing outside of theatre/film?"

I am sure the list of questions goes on and on and varies by agency, but those are some of the fairly certain standard questions they will have for you at most of these meetings. Work to know the answers to these queries without having to spend a great deal of time pondering in the actual appointment, and do your best to avoid saying "like," "um," "uh," or "well" when answering. You do not want to sound like you are reciting a rehearsed monologue, but you do want to sound intelligent and articulate.

Some other little tidbits of advice for the interview include having your own *educated* questions to ask. You have to demonstrate some working knowledge of the agent with whom you are interviewing, but it is certainly fair to ask questions about how they prefer to interact with their clients and how the office handles the various casting accounts. You could ask them how they would market you if you were to sign with them and how they see your career likely unfolding under their tutelage. Just be careful about asking whom else they represent or how many actors are on their books—you do not want to get too personal into their business and irritate them.

You should also be prepared to perform some audition repertoire or demonstrate some special skills from your resume when you meet with an agent. It does not always happen, but it is certainly possible. Just keep in mind that if you are asked to sing, it may very well be without accompaniment, so that earlier advice about having an application on your smartphone that can give you pitch and tempo might really come in handy in this circumstance as well.

Finally, I want to really urge you to get skilled in the art of the handshake. You would be surprised at what a turnoff it is to offer a handshake to an actor or actress and get a cold, clammy, dead hand in return or to have all of your metacarpals crushed in a vice-like grip. You need to be able to meet the other hand square on and interlock with a firm but not deathly squeeze. If your looks are the first impression, the handshake is a close second, and it is hard to undo the damage you might cause if your shake is too weak or too strong. Learn how to make it just right.[5]

Hopefully now you have a better handle on what casting directors and agents do, how they function within the business, and how you as an actor can best come in contact with them. As you pursue your career, you will continue to build relationships and note the different preferences among various industry people—remember, it's all subjective. Just stay true to your brand and remember to keep striving for that sticky consistency.

The other industry player you may encounter, whom I want to mention just briefly, is the personal manager. The manager is similar to an agent in some ways, only he deals with a much smaller clientele base and gets far more personal and hands on with his actors. Although the manager does not tend to submit actors for auditions, he certainly helps guide an actor's career by advising which gigs to take and which to turn down. He may also create the actor's

---

5. An important rule of thumb in the theatre business is only shake hands when the person interviewing or auditioning you initiates it. Many people are either germaphobes or just do not want their personal space invaded; so do not assume that a handshake is desired. Let them lead the way on that when you enter.

publicity and marketing package and work with the actor on his image. For this level of individualized service, the manager generally gets a 15 percent commission (which might be in addition to your agent's 10 percent).

Most theatre actors that I know function just fine without a manager. It is when one reaches a point in her career that she finds herself fielding offers for film, television, and theatre at the highest levels—essentially, when she *has a career* to manage—that the notion of signing with a manager comes into play. Suffice it to say that if you are at the beginning stages of your professional life, signing with a manager seems to be a way to lose 15 percent of your income on every job you book. I do not personally advise it for young performers.

Scene 3

─────────○─────────

Equity versus Non-Equity

I HAVE GLOSSED OVER, skimmed, narrowly mentioned, and beat around the subject of the actors' unions throughout the chapters of this book, but now it is time to tackle the topic head-on and clarify some information about Equity for you. Actors' Equity Association, or AEA, is the stage actors' and stage managers' union in the United States, representing over forty-nine thousand individuals at the time this book is being published. The union was established in 1913 to protect actors and stage managers from producers who would not or could not pay out their contracts or who would leave a touring company stranded on the road. The union also has created benefits over the years, including health insurance and a pension program. And AEA has the task of creating and negotiating artists' contracts for theatres varying from small, professional to Broadway production.

The union has its obvious advantages, from minimum contracts to priority auditions and many perks in between, but it also has its disadvantages. We will explore both sides of the Equity coin in this chapter, and then you will have to decide when the time is right for you to join.

I will begin with the basic facts. In order to be an Equity member, you must join the union. There are three ways in which you can become eligible to join: you can get hired by an Equity theatre on an Equity contract and simply be granted your union status; you can join what is called the Equity Membership Candidate (EMC) Program by getting hired at one of the many participating theatres and then earning the requisite fifty points (one point per week of work under an EMC contract) over time; or you can first become a member of one of the sister unions, SAG-AFTRA (Screen Actors Guild/American Federation of Television and Radio Actors), AGMA (American Guild of Musical Artists), AGVA (American Guild of Variety Artists), or GIAA (Guild of Italian American Actors), and then buy your way into Equity through their mutual agreements.

At the time you decide to accept an offer to join AEA, you will be charged an initiation fee of $1,100 (current, 2013), which can be paid off over the course of two years. You will then be charged membership dues of $118 (again, current to 2013) per year as well as a 2.25 percent "working dues" fee that comes out of your paycheck whenever you are employed on a union contract. All of Equity's fees can be deducted from your pay, or you can decide to pay the membership fee and annual dues directly to the union.

As a member of Actors' Equity, you will have access to the Actors' Federal Credit Union, as well as tax-return-filing assistance and frequent free ticket offers to Broadway and Off-Broadway shows that are given out at the Equity Lounge (165 W. 46th St., NYC—in the Actors' Equity main office). When you work for twelve weeks over a twelve-month period, you qualify for six months of health insurance, and when you work for twenty weeks in a year, you earn a year of health coverage. The union also has pension and 401(k) plans. (Visit www.actorsequity.org for the specific details of the retirement plans.)

You can find more information about member perks on the AEA website in great detail, so I will not fill these pages with every little benefit. However, I will touch on the major virtues of being an Equity member. The first has to do with auditions. When a show is under a production contract with an open-ended run—that is, at the Broadway level or major national tour—the producers are required to hold auditions for Equity performers every six months, whether they need replacements or not. This is one of the ways the union sees to it that its actors are getting seen on a regular basis. Earlier in the book, I mentioned ECCs (Equity Chorus Calls) and EPAs (Equity Principal Auditions). I told you that as a non-Equity performer, you could line up early, sign up on an unofficial list, and hope that they will see nonunion actors. However, as a member of the union you are guaranteed to be seen at any open-call Equity audition for which you show up on time. In this way, the union really provides the maximum opportunities for its members to have the chance to get face time with CDs. In addition to mandating auditions, Equity also has certain rules about how those auditions are to be run. There are guidelines for how long an audition may take, how many times an actor can be called in before the producers need to start paying her for her time, and what may be asked of an actor in the audition.

The other major function of the Actors' Equity Association is the negotiation of contracts. If you look on the AEA website, you will find the list of contracts and codes and their specifics in the "About" section. There are currently forty-five different variations on Equity agreements listed in the drop-down menu on the website, each one representing a different aspect and level of the business (e.g., Guest Artist, League of Regional Theatres, Small Professional Theatre, Production, etc.). Each contract dictates a minimum salary, maximum rehearsal time, certain rules for rehearsal periods, rules regarding the total number of work hours allowable under the particular contract, and general procedural protocols for theatres that hire union actors. Although an actor's individual contract with a theatre may be negotiated with additional benefits and agreements, the Equity contracts basically ensure that the actor will not receive lesser treatment in any of the aspects enumerated.

When an actor arrives at an Equity gig, a member of that company is elected the "Equity deputy" of the cast, and it is this person's responsibility to see that the theatre follows all of Equity's guidelines, from amenities to breaks to paychecks. When a company violates union code, the deputy will contact the AEA representative and the union will intervene on the actors' behalves. The union takes these complaints and violations very seriously, and a theatre could lose its Equity status for continued violations. AEA is fiercely loyal to its members, and that is certainly an argument for joining.

However, there are some downsides to joining AEA, especially depending on where you are in your career and where you choose to make your home. For starters, realize that once you join Actors' Equity, you can only ever work under Equity contracts.[1] This means

---

1. In very rare exceptions, you can receive a special letter of permission through the union to undertake a non-Equity job, but it involves writing to the union, demonstrating why you should take the gig, etc. It is a difficult and time-consuming process that generally will not result in you being granted consent.

that you are no longer eligible to audition for or accept any non-union theatre work in the United States (overseas theatre work and film are different jurisdictions). Consider how many professional credits are on your resume. Do you think that you could compete with other actors in your age/type range at this point or will you run the risk of being overlooked because you have not built up professional experience? This presents a particular challenge to women, mainly because there are more of them and less roles for them, thus the competition is much stiffer. When young actresses jump at the opportunity to join Equity in or just out of college, they immediately bump up a "weight class" and find themselves competing for a slim number of roles against women who have been establishing themselves in the business for some time. It is not an impossible task, but it certainly makes the odds seem greater against your success. For men, the same challenge exists but to a lesser degree since there are so many more roles for men in the theatre (hopefully we will see that change, but for now it is and has always been a reality).

Over the last decade or two, more and more national tours are being sent out on nonunion contracts so that the producers can save money. For better or for worse, this is the trend, and so joining the union when you are young could keep you from touring possibilities, and national tours are a great way to build up experience as well as resume credits. Some tours will even start out union and then switch to nonunion after the first year.

You would be wise to do your research on any city outside of New York in which you may be considering living (more on that in a later chapter) before you join the union. Some cities have a plethora of union theatres while others tend to be more nonunion friendly. You would not want to join the union and then move to a city in which most of the work available is non-Equity and thus unavailable to you. Additionally, just because a theatre is an Equity house does not mean it only hires Equity actors. Many regional theatres have agreements with the union that they will hire a percentage of union and a percentage of nonunion performers (again, a cost-saving approach for the producers), meaning that you could be working professionally at an Equity theatre without being a member of the union and paying union dues. Of course, the downside is that you do not have the protection of AEA nor the contractual guarantees when you are not a member.

The bottom line is this: you need to make an informed, considered decision before you join Actors' Equity. It offers clear advantages, but joining before the time is right can damage your career and make it an uphill battle for you, while also costing you money each year in dues. I generally recommend that young actors stay non-Equity throughout college and for a while afterward in order to build their resumes and expand their networks. This way, when they join, they will be well positioned to compete in their new marketplace. Therefore, be wary of signing on to jobs that require you to go Equity before you are ready. The other factor to consider is whether or not you have an agent. Realize that once an agent signs you as a non-Equity actor, one of his primary goals is going to be to help you get that card. Trust your agent's advice in these circumstances and let him push your career forward.

Pittsburgh CLO and the MUNY in St. Louis are both very reputable regional theatres that tend to hire ensembles featuring young college-age performers. They both also require that their performers join the union if they are not already members. I have known many students who jumped at the chance to work at either of these venues, only to find it impossible to book summer work for many years thereafter. Think about it—if a theatre has two or three Equity contracts to award, they are going to use those contracts for older roles that are harder to cast. They can hire non-Equity younger actors for much cheaper! There are also some companies out of New York, such as Theatreworks/USA and the Jekyll and Hyde Club that hire actors and grant them Equity status. Again, the same dilemma applies.

Ask yourself a few questions before you commit to going union. First of all, do you have a resume worthy of getting you called in for an appointment against other seasoned actors on the Equity level? Secondly, are you booking work and making a living as a nonunion performer at this point or have you reached what feels like the apex of your non-Equity career? Third, do you have a particularly unique talent or skill set that would let you stand out even against other Equity-level actors (such as playing an unusual instrument like the zither, which is a needed in the Blue Man

Group, or having experience with high-flying aerial stunts)? And finally, are you being offered a job that makes all the other questions irrelevant, because taking it would be a huge career move in and of itself (Broadway, Off Broadway, first national tour)?

Most actors say that they joined Equity when they knew it was time. Some of them had agents to guide them, while others had their education, their experience, and their instincts. The eventual goal for most theatre actors is to be a member of Actors' Equity because, whether it is true or not, the vast perception is that membership validates one as a professional actor. I do not necessarily subscribe to that belief; rather, I advocate the notion of actor as small-business owner. The main part of our work together has been in crafting goals, honing your product, and marketing it. We are essentially creating a business plan for your career. If that path includes being a member of Equity, then you will work toward that as one of your goals. If, however, your blueprint leads you in a different way, then the union will not be necessary for you to be successful. I just want you to have the knowledge to make an informed decision and to do what is in the best long-term interest of your career.

PERFORMER PROFILE
Megan Arnoldy, Actor

Laura Rose Photography

Meet Megan Arnoldy!

Megan is currently playing Lorraine in the Las Vegas company of *Jersey Boys*. Her national touring credits include *Drowsy Chaperone* (Swing, u/s Janet, Kitty). And her regional credits include *Drowsy Chaperone* at Ogunquit Playhouse (Janet); the world premiere of *Minsky's* at the Ahmanson Theatre; *42nd Street* at Tuacahn Center for the Arts (Peggy) and at Walnut Street Theatre (u/s Peggy); *Grease* at Marriott Theatre and Carousel Dinner Theatre (Sandy); as well as Milwaukee Repertory Theatre, Sacramento Music Circus, and Pittsburgh Civic Light Opera. She received her BFA in musical theatre from Penn State.

JF: *How long have you lived in New York City?*
MA: Approximately ten years, off and on.

JF: *How long did you live in New York and audition before you booked your first professional work?*
MA: I worked professionally during the summer between my junior and senior year of college. I booked my first Equity gig my senior year of college.

JF: *How long did it take you to book your first production contract?*
MA: I booked the first national tour of *Drowsy Chaperone* in 2008, about six years after moving.

JF: *How long did you stay non-Equity before joining the union and what made you join it when you did?*
MA: I joined the union right away out of college. The opportunity presented itself and I had to take it. I knew that it would definitely be a "small fish in a big pond scenario," but I wanted to jump right in.

JF: *How did you get an agent? Did you book work without representation or has your success come since you've had an agent?*
MA: I got my agent through a recommendation. I was able to book work on my own by going to Equity Chorus Calls, but I have to say that within one month of having representation with influence, I booked my first production contract. It made all the difference to me to have the opportunity to have an appointment and be seen.

JF: *You are married. Anything you want to share about how you balance life in show business with that relationship?*
MA: I think the most important thing is just that: balance. Matt is currently on the road and I am planning lots of Monday trips just to have dinner with him. That seems crazy, but it is totally worth it! It's all about taking the leap and making the commitment to spend time together and making each other the priority.

JF: *What is the biggest lesson you've learned since being in the biz?*
MA: I think the most important thing that I've learned is that this business is a journey. It's not a destination by any means. You achieve one goal, but what's next? Shows close. Shows do not make it to Broadway. It can be heartbreaking because so much of you becomes invested. You have to keep moving forward. It's about growth, discovery, development, and constant learning.

Scene 4

———————◯———————

Contracts and Taking/ Turning Down Work

PERHAPS THE MOST DIFFICULT course to navigate for actors, particularly when they are young and lack agent representation,[1] is reading, understanding, and negotiating contracts, as well as knowing when to accept and when to turn down work. Young artists generally feel like they should be grateful for any offer that comes their way, and they do not frequently ask questions before signing on to a gig. I would start by pointing you back to the work you did on goals and finances earlier in this book, as those are two of the major factors to consider when a job offer is on the table. But before we get into that, let's back up even further to the moment when your cell phone rings after you have been auditioning for a production and you do not recognize the number.

I encourage actors never to answer their cell phones when the call might be coming in from a producer or a casting director. It seems counterintuitive, especially if you have been waiting on pins and needles for days to hear back after a callback that you feel you nailed, but trust me, there is method to my madness. I can give you a few reasons for letting that all-important call roll to voice mail, but first let me ease your mind and assure you that job offers will not be rescinded if you miss the phone call (unless they are shooting a

---

1. Much of what I say in the paragraphs ahead about not answering the call and asking all the questions is irrelevant if you have an agent. The agent will do the negotiating for you, and when your agent calls, you can certainly answer the phone, as you will not need to be in the "business mode" of the unrepresented actor.

commercial and they need someone *right now*—in which case, you would answer the phone knowing that might be the call). The first reason not to pick up is that you may not be in the right place to take such an important call. You may be running around the city or about to jump on the subway or out to lunch, and when someone calls with an offer, you will want to be seated in a quiet place with pen and paper, ready to write down all the details and ask all your questions. You certainly do not want to run the risk of your cell reception cutting out in the middle of the CD's pitch!

Secondly, letting the call roll to voice mail allows the caller to leave you a message, which will likely contain some or all of the details of the offer. Then you can listen to it at your leisure, as many times as you need to, in order to catch everything they said and to formulate your list of queries regarding the offer. Even if the producer's call simply says to call her back and she does not make the formal offer or leave the information on the recording, at least you will be able to get yourself geared up for the probable offer and call her back when you are ready to write down the specifics.

Finally, letting the call go past avoids the risk that you might be so enthusiastic about the offer that you will accept outright on the phone without thinking things through. And this leads me to my next directive to you: do not accept a job outright on the first phone conversation, even if you know you are absolutely going to take the role. The purpose of this chapter—this entire book, in fact—is to empower you as an actor. We give away so much of our power every day in this career. We let others "type" us. We worry about what "they" want when we audition. We thank them after we have performed for them.[2] We are validated only by the offer of a job, and we will often work under unacceptable conditions and consider ourselves lucky to be employed. I want you to break that chain and take some of that power back into your own hands.

In many ways you have already begun that process. You have created your personal brand, through which you can tell others what you want them to think of and know about you. You have begun to get your finances under control so that you can choose

---

2. Every once in a while in an audition, I will encounter an actor who replies to my directorial "Thank you" with "You're welcome," as opposed to the common "Thank *you*." I love that!

what type of work you wish to do. You have selected the repertoire that you feel reveals your soul and lifts your spirits. And you have set personal goals by which to guide your life's choices, so that you have a road map for where you are going. All these actions equal empowerment. Now comes the next piece of the puzzle. You must learn the art of negotiation. You must make it clear that you are running a business and you will not be taken advantage of. Now, I am certainly not saying that every producer will take advantage of actors; however, if you establish some firm rules and habits that guide your behavior through the bargaining process, you will avoid getting caught in those occasional less-than-savory situations. And habit number one is: always ask for time to think about the offer once you have all the details.

Let us digress for a moment, though, and brainstorm some of the information that you will want to have in front of you in order to make the best decision possible for your career. I highly recommend that you keep this list of questions and bullet points somewhere handy for any time you are receiving a job offer. This way, you will never get caught making an uninformed decision.

Salary

Generally, they will tell you what the salary is, either by the week or as a lump sum. Beyond the numerical dollar value, you will want to ask if they take out taxes (IRS W-2 form) or if they pay you as an independent contractor (IRS 1099 form), in which case you will have to pay taxes on that money when you file your return if the total is more than $599.

You may also ask if they offer a per diem in addition. Most national tours include a per diem, which is an untaxed stipend on top of your weekly salary that is meant for meals, incidentals, and sometimes hotel costs. Per diems may come in the form of a check or cash.

I also suggest you ask how and when they pay their actors. It may be important to your budgeting to know whether they write you a check or deposit directly into your bank account (especially if you are touring or performing in a remote part of the country); also, if you are being paid weekly, biweekly, or monthly.

Room and Board

If you have to travel away from your home to perform the job, you will want to know if housing is included. Some companies provide housing and/or meals at no cost to the actors; others take a small fee out of the weekly paychecks; some make no accommodations and leave it to the artists to rent their own residences and furnish their own meals. You will need to know what is provided and what is your responsibility in order to determine if you can afford to take the job.

Contract Dates and Specific Schedule

You need to make sure you understand exactly when you are required to begin rehearsals, when the production opens and when it closes. If you are doing out-of-town summer stock, you generally need just the start and end dates at this point; however, if you are doing a regional show, especially in your own home region, you may want to find out the specific rehearsal schedule so that you know whether you are committing to days, evenings, or both. Many actors will accept a performing gig for nominal pay with the understanding that they will have their days or their nights or their weekends free to supplement their income with other work. You should also know how many performances a week will be expected.

In addition, you should find out if there are other contractual responsibilities such as publicity events or costume fittings outside of the set rehearsal times. Some productions even come with the possibility of a contract extension at the end. If extension is conceivable, you will need to know how and when that would be discussed and negotiated.

One other common scheduling scenario, particularly on tours, is the hiatus. Many shows will run for a certain number of weeks or months, then give the company some downtime (often over the winter holidays), and resume after one to four weeks off. If there is a layoff period in your contract, you will need to know if it still includes pay and if the company will cover your travel to and from your home, or your housing costs should you decide to stay around and wait for the performances to resume.

Role(s) and Requirements of the Job

Obviously you will want to know what role or roles you are being offered in order to fully consider whether or not to take a gig. Some theatres—particularly summer stocks that hire a company for their entire season—may tell you that you will be in all of their shows, but that they cast the individual productions out of the ensemble as they progress through the season. We will discuss this more in detail when we get to the negotiation in a little while, but I mention it here so that you come to expect it as a possibility.

In addition to performing in shows, some theatres require other work of the actors they employ. This work may include building scenery or costumes, striking the set at the end of a run, working in the box office, doing community outreach, and so forth. It is vital that you know what will be expected of you if you sign the contract.

Travel and Transportation

If the job offer is somewhere away from your residence, you will want to know if the company covers your travel or offers a stipend to defray your cost. You should also find out if you will need transportation during the course of your contract. Some theatres will only hire actors who have cars if the job requires any sort of commute; others will have a company van or a fleet of company cars to transport the actors.

Equity or EMC

If the theatre for which you would be working is a union house, you will want to know if you will be required to join the union. If you are not being hired on one of their Equity contracts, you should at least find out if they offer EMC points as part of the deal.

Gym Membership

Your body is your instrument. It is your product. Keeping in shape is imperative to actors, and many theatres understand that, so they provide gym memberships, either for free or discounted, to their employees. Find out if this is included in your offer.

PARKING COSTS

If you are bringing your own car to the gig, you should know whether you would have to pay for parking either at your residence, the rehearsal space, or the theatre.

COMPLIMENTARY TICKET POLICY

Every theatre has its own rules regarding comp tickets for company members. You should find out how many (if any) comps you would receive for each show so that you know if you can invite friends, family, or industry guests to see your work without having to pay for tickets.

OTHER REQUIREMENTS OF THE JOB

It does not hurt to find out if you will be expected to cut or dye your hair, to provide your own shoes or other personal articles of clothing, to bring your own musical instrument if your character will be playing one onstage, or to learn any specific skills pertinent to the role (such as stunts, circus arts, or dialects).

Those are the major aspects of any job offer that you will want to be sure you understand before you can begin to weigh the merits of the gig. You have already formulated your budget log, so you know how much your bottom line must be in order to make the job even remotely possible for you. You have also crafted a set of personal goals, so you know the direction in which you hope to be guiding your career and whether this offer falls in line with those goals. Assuming the producer or CD has told you much of the above information upon calling to offer you the part, and you have asked questions to determine the rest, you can now begin to make a calculated, guided decision about whether or not the job is worth accepting.

In the further interest of actor empowerment, I urge you to proceed with the discussion by asking a simple question regarding the salary offer: "Is that negotiable?" Go ahead and practice saying that out loud. Get it on your lips, in your mind, and into the universe. Those three little words can be a great bargaining chip for you if you have the courage to use them. The great thing about "Is that negotiable?" is that it is a polite, nonthreatening, straightforward question that can be answered with a clear yes or no. Some producers will curtly reply, "No. That is what we offer. Take it or leave it." You must be prepared for that to be the answer. You must know if negotiability is a deal breaker for you or if you are just asking to try to sweeten the already sweet pot. (Realize that there is nothing wrong with politely asking for more. You are not being a "difficult actor." The worst that they will say is no, but they will not nullify the offer on the basis of you asking for more money.)

The other possibilities that may come as a retort to your request to negotiate are either "Yes, we can go as high as X dollars per week," or "Yes, what did you have in mind?" Again, if you have a firm understanding of your finances, you should be ready and willing to tell them how much you need in order to accept the job without going into debt. Now, realize that if they are offering $150/week but you could not possible live on less than $500, you should not waste their time or yours trying to negotiate.[3] However, if it is a matter of getting a slight bump up, it is totally valid to ask. For instance: "I know you offered $275 a week, but I really need $300 to be able to make my share of the rent each month." A small increase like that is far more feasible.

I also want to make you aware that there are other possible negotiable terms besides money. Some of these might be important to you to haggle, whether they are flexible on salary or not:

- Will they give you your own room?
- Will they guarantee you certain roles?
- Will they allow you to earn additional money by doing other work for them (e.g., dance captain, understudy, publicity, scene shop, etc.)?

3. Most of the time, the approximate salary will be listed in the casting call ad. If they are not offering compensation that approaches the ballpark of what you need, you should not even audition.

- Will they throw in any of the perks we discussed above (parking, travel, gym, etc.) that might not be part of the initial offer?

See if you can think of any other terms that might be of interest to you. Maybe you are a vegetarian or you are anemic, and you want to see if they will include special meals. Maybe it is important to you that your name is billed above the title or in large font if you are offered the leading role. If you are expected to play your own guitar in the show, maybe you want them to buy you new strings at the end of the run. You do not want to become difficult or gain a reputation as a diva, but you should consider what is important to you and how you wish to be treated when you agree to a role.

Once you have asked all your questions and you and the producer have settled on the final offer, your next move is to ask them how soon they need an answer. Remember I told you a few pages ago never to accept an offer on the initial phone conference.[4] Even if you are resigned that the job would be in your best interest, you show yourself a savvy businessperson by simply taking some time (which could be anywhere from a few hours to a couple of weeks) before giving them a verbal answer. Besides, you may have other offers (or potential offers) in the mix to consider. You may have registered for a conference such as UPTA and you want to consider any bids that might come from that audition. You might have had six callbacks this week and this is only one of the many possibilities that might be presented to you.

Be honest with the person on the other end; do not tell them you are fielding offers if that is not true (bad theatre karma!). It is perfectly acceptable to say, "I need a little time to think it over and review the information." At absolute minimum, you should be granted twenty-four hours, although most companies will be comfortable giving you at least a few days to consider. Any producer or director who would pressure you into an immediate answer should be a red flag to you—is that really the kind of person you want to work for?

Once you establish a deadline for offering them a commitment, you can thank them for the offer and for their time, hang

---

4. Reflexively, I also suggest that you avoid turning down an offer, no matter how bad it seems, on the preliminary call. It is good form to show a producer that you are at least willing to consider his offer. It may make him more likely to consider you for other jobs in the future even if you turn this one down.

up the phone, and breathe. I might even suggest you get yourself a glass of wine or an ice-cream treat or whatever you would consider a reward for a job well done. Regardless of whether you take the job or turn it down, you need to acknowledge that someone has expressed the desire to work with you. Someone has essentially determined that you would be the best person for the gig. I think you also deserve a little bounty for the work you did on negotiating your contract offer. That is not easy, and many people are absolutely fearful of that conversation.

Once you have properly recognized yourself for a job well done, it is time to get down to brass tacks and really weigh the pros and cons of the offer. By this point, you will know what kind of compensation (including pay, accommodations, and perks) is available to you. Now you have to hold that information up alongside some career considerations:

1. *Is this a role that you really should have on your resume?* Review your branding statement and your goals. Will adding this part to your list of experience be consistent with the product you are developing and selling?
2. *Is this a theatre company you should have on your resume?* Sometimes it is totally worth playing the second spear-carrier on the left if you are doing it at a major venue that will attract attention on your resume. You may even take a small role at a great theatre just to break in with them and establish a relationship for possible future collaborations.
3. *Is this a director or choreographer you should have on your resume?* Just as in question number two, it may be worth accepting a minor role in order to make contact with and add to your resume an important director or choreographer.
4. *Will you make a lot of money?* We have discussed minimum salary needs, but a tangential possibility to consider is the job that pays extraordinarily well but may or may not be artistically fulfilling. (For instance, theme park gigs tend to have very handsome salaries, but not everyone finds the work to their liking.)
5. *Will this job be fun and/or artistically satisfying?* Sometimes you cannot put a price tag on personal growth and enjoyment. You may wish to consider a gig based solely on the fact that it would be like a working vacation for you. (I have been known to do

this frequently over the summers, when I am still receiving paychecks from the university and I can afford to take a low-paying directing gig in a fun town.)

As long as the job meets your minimum bottom line for survival—as long as accepting the offer will not force you into debt—you should reflect on those five questions. If you can answer yes to four or five of them, then it is a no-brainer. If you can answer yes to three of them, the job is probably worth taking. If your answer is yes to only one or two (or none) of them, then you need to contemplate what you will be giving up in order to do the gig. You should not feel compelled to take work if it does not somehow fit into your goal-action plan on some level. Similarly, you should not do it if you know that you will be unhappy throughout the process—you cannot possibly do your best work nor preserve your pristine reputation if you are working under miserable conditions. You may wish to consult a teacher, a mentor, or a colleague before making your decision final.

Once you have reached a firm conclusion, you should go ahead and call the producer, director, or CD back. If you are turning him down, do so politely and try your best not to burn a bridge. It is certainly acceptable to say, "I'm sorry, but I just cannot make it work on the salary you are offering at this time in my life. But I do hope to have the chance to work with you again when my budget will allow it." Or "Thank you, but I received another offer that I just could not pass on for my career." You may find with either of these turndowns that the person on the other end comes back with a counteroffer or an increase in the compensation in order to demonstrate his desire for you. Or he may simply thank you and end the discussion.

Assuming that you are accepting the job, however, you will want to thank them and ask what the next step is. Find out when you should expect a contract. Be aware that anything the producer agrees to verbally must appear in writing in the actual contract, otherwise you cannot hold them to it. Generally speaking, if you have negotiated "extras" into your deal, those additional items will be listed on what is called a "rider," meaning that the standard artist contract does not change, but your special requests to which they have agreed are simply tacked on to the end like an addendum. If you receive a contract and it fails to include any of the amendments agreed upon verbally, you should call the producer and ask them to add those on in rider form before you sign.

When you do receive your contract, you will need to read it very carefully. Remember that it is legally binding, both for you and for the employer, so you will want to understand exactly what it entails before you commit in ink. Depending on how long and intricate the language is, you may wish to enlist someone's help in interpreting every item. Contracts can range from the uncomplicated one-page to a very extensive, detailed document rife with legal jargon. On the next page I am going to show you an example of an actual contract that sits somewhere in the middle as far as complexity. I have removed the specifics of the show, the actor, and the producer for privacy and confidentiality purposes, but you will be able to get all the information you need nonetheless. Read through it, and on a separate notepad see how many of our earlier bullet points you can find enumerated in the articles. See if there is anything missing that you would want to discuss with the producer before signing. Ask yourself if anything appears as a concern or a red flag to you.

Does anything awaken concern in you? Is there anything you do not understand or anything you would want to discuss or negotiate if this were your contract offer? If so, how would you go about approaching that sort of issue without appearing difficult?

Learning to navigate the fielding of offers and dealing with contracts is a tremendous step in the process of becoming a mature actor as well as a seasoned business owner. It will no doubt take time for you to get comfortable asking for more money or requesting certain benefits. It may even seem an impossible notion to you to pass on a job. But if you have followed all of the previous steps set forth in this book, then you will have positioned yourself perfectly to manage your career and you will be guided by your own intuition and savvy. You will come to feel valued and empowered, and as long as you are reasonable and respectful to others in the industry, they will come to hold you in high esteem.

THIS LETTER DATED **OCTOBER 25, 2012** WILL SERVE AS AN AGREE-
MENT BETWEEN _____ ("Producer"), HAVING
AN ADDRESS AT _____ AND _____
("PERFORMER") PERTAINING TO PERFORMER'S SERVICES IN CON-
NECTION WITH **PRODUCER'S PRODUCTION** ("PRODUCTION") OF
"_____" ("THE WORK").

1. ROLE: Producer agrees to engage you and you agree to act as a Performer Role. It is understood and agreed that Performer is engaged
hereunder to perform a full time role, to be determined by Producer,
in the work. Performer understands that the performer may be required
to be trained into or perform another role at any time during the term
of this contract. Producer shall not be hindered or otherwise burdened
from making any and all changes, alterations or updates necessary to
any of the existing roles in the work. Performer further agrees that the
work is under the control of the Producer and the Producer's staff. No
aspect of the engagement shall be altered in any casual, inadvertent or
verbal manner.

2. DATES: SEE ATTACHED SCHEDULE

3. TERM: The term of this contract shall be from October 29th–December
30th, 2012. Performer agrees to attend all rehearsals and perform all
scheduled performances in each one-week period and up to one additional performances in the same one-week period as might be scheduled
from time to time by Producer.

4. REHEARSALS: The rehearsal schedule shall be at the sole discretion of
the Producer and therefore; the schedule may be altered or changed at
any time, and the performer agrees to be available. Any and all Rehearsals are deemed "closed" rehearsals by the Producer unless otherwise
posted by the Producers Production Stage Manager. Closed Rehearsals
are limited to those Performers on the schedule as "called." Visitors,
guests of any kind are not allowed during closed rehearsals unless previously approved by Producer and arranged through producers production
stage manager.

5. COMPENSATION: In full compensation for all of Performer's services
hereunder, Producer agrees to pay, and Performer agrees to accept for
the three weeks of rehearsal Oct 29–Nov 18, a weekly rehearsal salary
of Four Hundred Dollars ($400) and for the six week period of tech and
performances, Nov 19–Dec 30 a weekly salary of Eight Hundred Dollars
($800). Payments shall be made every Friday, beginning Nov 2, 2012.
Performers services shall encompass all rehearsals, technical rehearsals, performances, artist "talk-backs"/educational activities, pre-set calls,
backstage tours, put-in or swing rehearsals, clean-up rehearsals, Load-Ins,
Load-Outs as called by Producer. Attendance per the schedule set forth by
Producer is mandatory.

6. TAXES AND WITHHOLDINGS: Performer agrees that all services to be furnished by Performer shall be on a freelance basis and that Producer deducted no with-holding or employer contribution tax whatever and that Performer shall be responsible for Performer's own taxes, and shall work for the Producer on a non-exclusive basis.

7. ADDITIONAL ASSIGNMENTS: In the event Producer requests Performer to perform additional assignments Performer agrees to perform any such additional assignments.

8. ABSENCES: With limited exception, less than 24 hours notice to producer before an absence, will constitute a breach of contract. Excused absences include: Events beyond performer's control, Medical or immediate family emergencies. Planned absences from the show will not be excepted under this contract

9. ADDITIONAL SERVICES AND USES: Performer hereby irrevocably consents to provide any and all additional services as may be requested by Producer to publicize, promote, market or merchandise the Work (including Performer's performance on B-Roll footage) for use in: television commercials, radio commercials, in-flight or theatrical exhibition commercials, music videos and infomercials, documentaries, original cast recording, "making of" documentaries and programs and books, "opening night" specials, award broadcast programs, news and current affairs programs, promotional videos (including tour bus, sales kiosk, in-store, lobby, group sales, corporate in-flight and in house hotel) for no additional compensation whatsoever.

10. BILLING: Performer will receive billing on the inside title page of the program. All principal Performers shall be billed in groups or so-called "tiers." Performer's billing shall be in the second tier of the Performer billing below title in Name Alphabetical Order. All Performers in this tier shall be in the same size (height, width, thickness) and type. Performers' billing shall appear whenever and wherever any other Performer in this tier is billed. Producer reserves the right to: 1) bill leading Performers above the title, 2) bill the balance of the company in additional tiers; 3) use so called "run-on" or "box billing" in print and advertising. The foregoing requirements shall not apply to the use of extracts from critical reviews or awards where the names of any such persons associated with the Work are used in the context of quotations from such reviews or reference to such awards, or in congratulatory ads, or ads welcoming new Performers to the show. No inadvertent or casual omission to accord billing as herein above provided shall deemed a violation of this Agreement, provided that Producer shall make reasonable efforts to rectify prospectively such omission after written notice has been given by Performer to Producer.

(continued)

11. BIOGRAPHY: Whenever and wherever Performer's biography appears, biography shall be limited to Performer's professional credits only and in a form determined by Producer, uniform with the other cast members. Biography will be limited to 5–6 lines (approximately 60–65 words). Performers' biography shall be listed following the Performers billing order. Producer reserves the right to edit Performers biography.

12. COSTUME AND COSTUME FITTING: Performer agrees to be available for one or more costume fitting(s) during the rehearsal period. Performer hereby understands and agrees that the Performers costuming will be at the sole discretion of the Producer.

13. DISPUTES: Performers sole and exclusive remedy for Producers breach of the Agreement or any terms hereof shall be in action of damages. Performer hereby irrevocably waives any right to equitable or injunctive relief.

14. HOLIDAYS: Performer agrees to perform on any and all holidays, as required by Producer. No travel outside of the tri-state will be allowed over the period of this contract. All travel within the tri-state area needs to be given in written form to the Producer and Stage Manager.

15. COMPS AND HOUSE SEATS: Performer shall have the right to purchase tickets to the Work from the pool of the house seats set aside for use by the Company, subject to availability, at regular box prices. Distribution of these tickets from the pool shall be at the sole discretion of the Producer. Performer shall receive ONE complimentary ticket for the Work to be used during the week of Previews and to be requested by email to _____ no later than 72 hours in advance and subject to availability.

16. CONFIDENTIALITY: Performer agrees and understands that all aspects of Performer's engagement by the Producer are deemed strictly confidential; this includes, but is not limited to, compensation, scheduling, training, rehearsals, artistic content, publicity, company business etc. Any breach of this policy whatsoever shall constitute a breach of this contract by Performer.

17. INFORMATION, W-9, AND CONTACT: Performer warrants that all W-9 and contact information submitted to Producer upon signing of this contract is correct and true. Producer shall use the name provided on Producers Employee information sheet to issue payroll checks. Performer agrees to provide Producer with a reliable and current telephone contact number and internet e-mail contact address and to perform due diligence in receiving and responding to Producer and Producer's Staff's company correspondence.

18. OTHER ENGAGEMENTS: Performer represents and warrants that he/she has not heretofore entered into any contract or undertaken any commitment in conflict with this Contract and that he/she shall not accept any engagement in the entertainment field or otherwise for the rendition of his/her services which may or shall interfere with the

proper and timely rendition and performance of Performer's services and obligations hereunder. Performer agrees that his/her primary obligation is to render his/her services in the Work, as required hereunder, to the best of his/her ability.

19. PHYSICAL FITNESS, READINESS AND APPEARANCE: Performer acknowledges that Performer has been cast for the work based in part upon certain aspects of Performers' outward physical appearance and physical fitness. Performer therefore agrees to make no apparent changes to Performer's appearance or current physical fitness or readiness, which would interfere with the artistic interpretation or physical execution of the role as directed or designed without the prior written approval of Producer. Performer further warrants that Performer knows of no pre-existing impediment, medical, emotional, psychological or otherwise (i.e. chronic back or knee pain, vertigo, acrophobia, etc.), which would prevent Performer from performing in the production as directed and choreographed

20. PRESS AND PERSONAL APPEARANCES: Performer hereby agrees that Performer shall, at Producers request, make himself/herself available at reasonable times for personal appearances including but not limited to interviews for newspapers, magazines, and other publications, and appearances at trade shows, conventions and publicity events and on radio and television, in connection with the promotion and publicizing of the Work (which shall include promotions for additional companies of the work Produced by Producer), without additional compensation payable to Performer, except for reimbursement of actual approved out-of-pocket expenses incurred by Performer in connection therewith. Performer hereby agrees that Producer or its designated representatives shall have the right to approve in advance any and all press appearances made by Performer during the term hereof, such approval not to be unreasonably withheld.

21. USE OF LIKENESS. Performer hereby grants to Producer the perpetual right to use, and to allow others to use Performer's name, picture, photograph, voice and likeness in connection with his/her role in the Work or in connection with merchandising of any kind connected with the Work and/or advertising and exploitation of any other products, commodities or services in so-called commercial tie-ups (as that term is commonly understood in the theatrical profession) relating to the Work, at the minimum rate, in accordance with the making of the Work. Performer hereby consents to such publications and grants Producer the right to use Performer's name, likeness, photographs, and biography in such publications and the promotion thereof,

22. RECORDINGS: Performer hereby consents to the use of his/her recorded voice during pre-set, performance and backstage tour, for publicity purposes.

(continued)

23. EFFECTS: Performer acknowledges that in performances of the Work, Performer may be called to manipulate special effects, which may be created utilizing Roscoe fog, standard strobe, theatrical lighting instruments and special effect contrivances.

24. STAGE BUSINESS: It is hereby agreed that any material whatsoever, including any form of "stage business" performed by the Performer in rehearsals or any performance of the Work shall, insofar as the Performer is concerned, be the property of the Author and/or Producer of the Work, as their respective interests may appear.

25. TALK SHOW INTERVIEWS/PANELS/WORKSHOPS: Performer agrees to permit the use of taped footage of the Work in which he/she may appear in conjunction with the bona fide entertainment talk show interviews. All performers seen and/or heard on a clip must have given written consent to the above-described promotional use. Performers signature below shall be deemed Performer's consent for said use. Taped footage may be used under the following terms and conditions. (a) The clips (not more than two on any one program) must be used as part of a bona fide interview/panel/workshop in which the production is being promoted. (b) The total amount of usage of Equity show clips on a program cannot exceed two minutes.

26. USE OF MATERIALS. While Performer is under contract to Production. Performer shall not render any services in connection with or perform in any way material written for and/or contained in the Work, on his/her own behalf or on behalf of anyone other than as part of the performance of his/her role in the Work hereunder, without written permission of the producer.

The above represents the complete Agreement between the parties hereto with respect to the subject matter thereof and may not be altered, amended or assigned without an express written instrument to such effect.

AGREED:

_____

Date

_____

ADDRESS

_____

SOCIAL SECURITY NUMBER
_____, Producer   _____, Performer

Scene 5

———————○———————

Networking

CHANCES ARE YOU HAVE HEARD the saying "It's not what you know; it's who you know." I think that notion is slightly exaggerated and that *what* you know is of great value, but the adage is certainly not without truth. You have probably also said on many occasions, "It's a small world." That statement could not be more accurate, especially in the world of theatre. In fact, many performing artists I know will often remark that "there are only fifty people in the theatre and they all know each other." Once you get started in the profession, you will certainly start to see from whence that chestnut comes!

I cannot overestimate the importance of the actor's network to you. You may have great talent and you may be a wonderful person, but theatre is a collaborative art form and, to quote Keith Ferrazzi, "No one does it alone." Unless you plan on a career of producing, directing, and starring in your own one-man shows and playing for an audience of your immediate family, you will need to have a system of friends and colleagues in place to support you throughout your life's endeavors.

Here is the good news: unless you are a hermit with absolutely no family, your network already exists, so you will not be starting from scratch. Here is some even better news: if you have played your cards right and gone to college or to a training program, or if you have been a performer in a theatrical production or two, you already have the makings of a network.

A network is essentially a web of acquaintances of various levels—they could be work associates, family members, close friends, mentors, or even people that you met at a party. Any contact with whom you share at least a *mutual* familiarity can be considered part of your network. How you go about utilizing that network will depend on the actual relationship you share with each individual in your web.

I could not begin to count on my fingers and toes the number of instances in which I either helped someone in my network by leading them to a job opportunity or I was helped by one of my contacts. I would not be in my current position as program coordinator at a major conservatory if it were not for my skill at maintaining positive relationships in my life. This is powerful stuff, I assure you. And there is certainly an art to networking. But the key to the entire thing is generosity. You must have a generous spirit, and you must be willing to accept others' generosity as well.

I highly recommend that you pick up Keith Ferrazzi's book, *Never Eat Alone*, for a really in-depth look at networking and how it can be used to your advantage. I also suggest you look up The Savvy Actor if you chose to live in New York or Los Angeles, as they are brilliant coaches when it comes to helping artists understand and utilize the resources they have in their lives.

We are going to explore the fundamental notion of networking in a nutshell here, just to get you started thinking in a new way about relationships. The first exercise I want you to do is to go through your list of "friends" on Facebook and take stock. You may be surprised at how many people about whom you either find yourself thinking, "Who *is* that person?" or "Wow, I haven't had any communication with her in forever!" Some people lambaste social media as being shallow and useless, but I could not disagree more, if it is used in a positive way. Next, look at the contacts you have saved on your phone and your e-mail address book and note the ones whose interactions with you have become distant memories.

Keith Ferrazzi in *Never Eat Alone* talks about the notion of "pinging." In short, pinging is simply reaching out and keeping in touch; reminding someone that you exist. I think the brilliance of Facebook is that it allows us to "ping" very easily through comments on people's statuses, birthday reminders, and even hitting the little "Like" button when someone posts something that catches our attention. As you know, whenever someone comments on your post, likes your status, or tags your name in his own post, you get a notification about it. And instantly, that person has been put on your mind. This sounds shallow, but for maintaining hundreds or thousands of relationships it can be invaluable. I am not suggesting by any means that we reduce our friendships solely to Facebook interactions; however, I am saying that you can perpetuate bonds with a great many people through social media. On the simplest of levels, these media (Facebook, LinkedIn, Twitter, Tumblr, etc.) allow us to be thought of by someone in our network, and sometimes just appearing in someone's mind from time to time is enough to sustain the acquaintance. In addition to social media, the occasional text message, e-mail, or phone call is also a great way to ping people.

You should choose your method of pinging according to the nature of your relationship. I will often randomly text an alumnus of my program or someone I have directed in a show just to tell them that they were on my mind. But with someone like Eric Schaeffer (artistic director of Signature Theatre, DC, and Broadway director), with whom I have shared a slightly more formal business partnership, texting him for social purposes seems a little less appropriate. However, we "like" and comment on each other's Facebook statuses with regularity, and when we have specific business to discuss, we will utilize text messages or e-mails. For each connection in your life, you should determine the proper medium of communication. But whichever approach(es) you use, the vital objective is to stay in touch.

Furthermore, you must make staying in touch a regular part of your weekly and/or monthly to-do lists. Do not only "ping" when you need a favor from somebody to whom you have not spoken in a long time. Some people have very cynical feelings when it comes to the notion of "networking," and one of the reasons for the negativity is the misuse and abuse of contacts. In other words, people who only reach out and get in touch when they need something from you give networking a bad rap. If you have ever known a person who would call, text, or e-mail you every once in a great

while when they wanted something from you, you have probably
felt that you were being taken advantage of. What is slightly worse
is when that person manages to make a seemingly innocent social
correspondence with you to reopen the lines of communication,
only to follow it up a day later with a request. Then you feel like
the social call is really cheapened!

Suffice it to say, you should strive to be the type of person who
keeps in touch with people regularly because you care about maintaining relationships with them, not just because you need their
help. That way, when you do need someone's assistance, they will
be less likely to feel like you are trying to use them. Ferrazzi has an
entire chapter in his book entitled "Build It before You Need It," in
which he extols the virtues of staying in contact as a regular habit
in great detail.

One thing that always pleasantly surprises me about this industry
is how benevolent people are. Earlier I mentioned that you need to
be willing to accept people's generosity, but I want to go one step
further and say that you need to be comfortable with asking people
when you need that generosity from them. Many actors are uneasy
about calling in favors, but as I said, I believe in theatre karma, and
so I am perfectly happy to ask for help when I need it, knowing that I
will find a way to return the favor at some point.[1] I am also confident
in my ability to call for assistance from anyone in my web because
I know that I have kept in touch with them and "pinged" them with
regularity. I do not just reach out when I need something. I also know
that they are aware that they can call on me for just about anything
and I will bend over backward to help my friends.

And that is the other side of the networking coin: your generosity
toward others. There are few things from which I derive more pleasure than helping a friend make inroads within this industry. I love
introducing and connecting people I feel would benefit from knowing each other. I love calling in a recommendation for someone I really respect. I love finding a song or a monologue that really reminds
me of an actor and then sending it to them via e-mail or Facebook

---

1. *Never Eat Alone* also has a chapter entitled "Don't Keep Score," which reminds us not
to do favors with the expectation that they will be repaid. Be kind because you are a kind-
hearted person, not because you expect something in return.

and saying, "You should really know this piece." I love recommending products, services, and restaurants that I enjoy to others so that they may benefit from them and spread the word further. In general, I love being someone on whom people feel they can rely.

We all have things to offer. I cannot play the piano. I am not terribly good with children. I cannot fix the plumbing in your bathroom. You certainly do not want me to do your tax return for you. But I have spent a great deal of time over the last few years stockpiling a list of things about which I know that I am an expert. I have considered what I can offer others, and I have found as many opportunities as possible to make people in my circle of friends aware of what I am willing and able to do for them. Spend some time thinking about what you have to offer others. Even when you are young and just starting out, you should be able to come up with at least a short list of skills or knowledge that might be of use to someone else. Be the kind of person that people think of as resourceful and reliable, and you will unleash the true power of the network.

So how does a network develop? What constitutes your professional network and how can you grow and expand that web? We have already discussed the social media aspect and how useful it can be, but let us talk about how you can build your nexus over the course of your training and into your professional adulthood.

First of all, the core of your network begins in college when you are training for your craft. The classmates you live with, fight with, make love with, grow with, struggle with, perform with, and achieve with will form the very heart of your web for life as long as you do not alienate yourself. I have said this already, but it bears repeating: Do not burn bridges. Treat everyone as though they are important people. You never know when the actor in your class who is not quite achieving success will surface later in life as a powerful agent or casting director. Or perhaps the stage manager who called your senior musical will become a Broadway director. It is not about kissing up or being disingenuous; rather, it is about developing a reputation for kindness and affability. Then when people are in a position to help you in some way, they will be glad to do so.

The other piece of network building that can begin as early as college and will continue well beyond your training is meeting professional artists in summer stock and internship situations. When I graduated college, I took an assistant directing gig at a small summer theatre in western Pennsylvania. Although it was only a three-month contract, I met people there who would become some of my closest friends; who would help me transition to living in New York; and whom I would later hire for shows that I was directing. Think of these kinds of experiences as doors opening for you. It is then up to you if you are going to walk through those doors and maintain those relationships or if you are going to let them fall away. I always hit myself when I hear of someone I once knew and let disappear from my life becoming a huge success. I have learned a great deal about preserving and valuing every connection, and I pride myself now on my ability to sustain multitudes of contacts.

One of the other great places to develop professional connections is an industry conference or convention. In the chapter on auditions, I talked to you about SETC and other such combined audition events. In addition to the opportunity to be seen by dozens of theatres, the value of those big conferences is the "captive audience" factor of several hundred or several thousand theatre practitioners all lodged in the same hotel, eating in the same restaurants, and drinking in the same bars. Many of these conventions also include workshops and master classes. I urge you to take as many of these as you have time to do, and furthermore, take any opportunity to mingle and mix and to meet new people. You can read the conference program, find out who is presenting, and target specific industry people you wish to meet. But you can also just be audacious and introduce yourself to other people you meet over the course of the weekend, in the holding room, in the coffee shop, or at the bar. This is when those nice, fancy business cards you printed will also come in handy. While you do not want to be the guy who presses your card into every single hand you can shake (that gets gross—Ferrazzi calls that guy the "networking jerk"), it sure looks polished and professional to be able to hand over a card after hitting it off with someone and leaving the conversation open to an eventual follow-up.

Of course, many connections are made through mutual friends at social events such as dinner parties, birthday celebrations, or holiday events. And many actors are simply outgoing enough to connect with total strangers at bars, cafes, and in the holding rooms for auditions. The more sociable you are by nature, the easier it will be for you to expand your network on a regular basis, as you will see every opportunity to meet new people as it presents itself.

Keep honing your skills at connecting. Continue to explore the assets that you bring to the table in a relationship. Work to have patience with others and embrace that spirit of generosity of which I spoke. If you make an effort to build and to maintain a solid network—if you plant and water and tend to those relationships like plants in a garden—you will see your efforts pay off over and over again throughout your career. You will be able to trace a tremendous percentage of your success to the links in your chain of colleagues. In short, you will find that who you know is at least as valuable as what you know.

PERFORMER PROFILE
Matthew DeLorenzo, Actor.
www.matthewdelorenzo.com

Meet Matthew DeLorenzo!

Matthew is a graduate of Shenandoah Conservatory's BFA Musical Theatre Program, and I specifically chose to include his profile in this book because he chose a different path than the typical New York musical theatre life. Matt instead found his home in DC, where he has already starred in several major regional productions, and he even won a Helen Hayes Award for his portrayal of "Candy Darling" in the musical *Pop!*

Robert Mannis Photography

JF: *How long have you lived in DC and what made you decide to move there?*

MD: I'm based out of the Virginia/DC area and have called this home for the past twelve years. It's an incredible place to be with the theatre scene absolutely growing and thriving. You wouldn't believe how much mind-blowing talent we have here.

JF: *How long did you live in DC and audition before you booked your first professional work?*

MD: I actually began booking concerts while I was a sophomore in college through the Washington City Choir and had the privilege of booking paid gigs at venues like the Kennedy Center with incredible people. Junior year, I began working in the DC theatre scene by submitting myself to a new musical at Studio Theatre. I submitted myself, got the call/date to audition, and was fortunate enough to be offered the job the next day. Landing that role and the incredible journey it took me on gave me such wonderful opportunities and rewards. It truly changed my life.

JF: *Have you joined Actors' Equity? If not, is there a reason you have not joined?*

MD: I have not taken the leap yet into Equity. The main hesitation toward switching is the fact that turning Equity asks more of theatres in both time management and cost. As a result, some theatres in DC have limited budgets as to how many Equity contracts they can give.

JF: *Do you have an agent? Do you feel it's necessary to have representation in the DC market?*

MD: Though I am currently considering working with representation, I do not feel it's necessary for the DC market. Once you've got your foot in the door, you'll find that you meet more and more people from theatres who will then extend invitations to audition. I think representation is a great bonus on many levels. Not only will they help secure those invitations to audition and handle your contracts, but they'll also help to broaden your intake of work. What's better than having that extra teammate helping you and rooting for your success?

JF: *Any "pearls of wisdom" that you'd like to offer to young actors planning to make a go at this industry? Maybe share the biggest lesson you've learned since being in the biz?*

MD: Embrace yourself. With that, know how to show it. My journey has only begun and yet the biggest thing I've found that helps me in the long haul is to know how to showcase myself. If you believe there is a role out there for you in this crazy theatre world, you will find it. Take it from the tall, lanky boy who can sing like a girl! We all have faced rejection and those everyday struggles, they happen. What's important is to not lose sight of the journey that everyone takes. Find that spark in you that makes you unique, desirable, and of course special. Once you find it and show it, surely others will see.

Scene 6

———○———

The Cities Project

FOR BETTER OR FOR WORSE, we theatre people—especially musical theatre performers—tend to view New York City as the be-all and the end-all location for a career in the arts. While it cannot be denied that New York holds the greatest concentration of professional live theatre in the world, and that Broadway is widely considered the pinnacle of a stage performer's success, I must point out to you that it is not the only city in which an actor can have a professional life. However, that idea of NYC as the supreme objective for young actors tends to be perpetuated, especially in colleges in the eastern time zone.

As we come to the conclusion of our journey through branding, marketing, and business strategies—we have discussed the hows and the whys and even the whos—but it seems fitting to spend some time exploring the wheres. Sure, New York is great. But it is perfectly okay to admit if it is not the place you see yourself settling. New York is among the most exciting cities in the world, but it is also among the fastest-paced, most expensive, and most stressful to inhabit. It is certainly not for everyone.

Many schools will funnel their students into New York, Los Angeles (if they are more film/television centric), or Chicago (if they are based in the Midwest), and the majority of graduates tend to follow the alumni who came before them to their postcollege destinations of greatest concentration. However, I think you owe it to yourself as an empowered actor to relocate to the city that you feel will serve you best, based on your individual goals and the product you have to sell. You need to do your research and explore all your options instead of just following the fold and doing what others expect of you.

To that end, I created an assignment for my students a few years back called "The Cities Project." For this task, they are divided into groups and each team is given a major metropolitan U.S. city, other than New York, to research. Their charge is to explore a multitude of facets of life in that region in great detail: cost of living, climate, transportation, average wages, industry, attractions, arts and entertainment, residential neighborhoods, and general lifestyle. They must also determine what kinds of opportunities exist for actors in that town—from theatre to film to industrial and commercial work. More specifically, they need to uncover whether the city is largely union or nonunion based and, generally speaking, whether an actor can make a living as an actor in that town.

Once they compile all the information, they prepare a presentation for the rest of the class. I tell them that they are not just required to educate or inform their classmates about the city they have researched; rather, their assignment is to *sell* the collective on why their city is a great place for an actor to live. This sales aspect of the exercise ups the ante a bit and usually leads to clever, creative, and entertaining exhibitions. It also forces the participants to really dig for the greatest virtues a city has to offer, as opposed to simply using Google and Wikipedia to regurgitate factual information.

At the end of each presentation, I collect a hard copy of the data and research that the group compiled and I save it in a binder appropriately called "The Cities Binder," which is available in my office for any student to come and peruse if they are seeking information on a possible home city. Many of my students have availed themselves of the binder over the years, and this project has led quite a few of my graduates to explore the possibilities of living somewhere besides New York.

If you are a teacher, I highly recommend you create your own cities project for your students and encourage them to explore all of their options. If you are an actor, I urge you to do this work for yourself—you may discover that there is a great location out there that will make you happy and nurture your artistry.

The cities that I have had my students research and explore include the following:

- Washington, DC
- Chicago
- Los Angeles
- San Francisco (Bay Area)
- Seattle
- Pittsburgh
- Philadelphia
- Orlando
- New Orleans
- Miami/Ft. Lauderdale
- Dallas
- Atlanta
- Boston
- St. Louis
- Minneapolis/St. Paul
- Wilmington, NC

Some clearly have a greater concentration of theatre or film gigs than others, but all of them offer work for actors. And the students find that lifestyle and cost of living can sometimes make a city more livable for their particular needs and personalities. As I write this very chapter, I have two students about to graduate who are visiting Orlando and auditioning for Disney after having done this project and come to the realization that they want a warm climate and a happy environment. I have another student who will be spending spring break checking out Seattle with her musician/producer boyfriend. He wants to break into the music engineering industry, and she wants to live in a city that has theatre as well as a vibrant indie music scene. Environment and sustainability issues are also of great import to both of these young artists, and they liked what they heard about the vibe in Seattle. I will also be leading a trip next month for a few of my seniors to Chicago to show them around that city—these students are particularly interested in avant-garde theatre and improvisation, two of Chicago's mainstays.

I am of the firm belief that happiness and self-contentment are absolutely essential to one's physical health and psychological/emotional preservation. Choosing to move to a town because you feel you must in order to do what you love—even if that town drains your bank account and sucks your soul—will not be a recipe for long-term success. You will burn out, and you will wind up resenting the city as well as your failed career. You need to take the time to deeply consider your values and your goals for life as an adult. If New York falls in line with those goals, then by all means, go forth and give it your best effort. However, if you see a different life for yourself, you need to allow for alternatives.

I can tell you without hesitation that New York is the lifestyle for me. As much as I love teaching in Winchester, I know that eventually I want to make my way back to the New York area. My long-range intention is to get to a point where I can afford to live in Connecticut and commute into Manhattan for directing gigs or teaching opportunities. That is me, and I have come to that conclusion on the basis of many factors. I have also had the benefit of living in New York, Chicago, rural Vermont, rural and suburban Pennsylvania, suburban Florida, and small-town Virginia. So I have a good deal of perspective on what I like and what does not work as well for me.

When you first embark on your career, you might not likely have the benefit of all that experiential perspective; however, with the Internet you have the resources at your fingertips to do research and to come to a very informed decision about what kind of life would be best for you.

To begin your own cities project (geared toward your own personal use, rather than toward a sales pitch presentation), you should start by considering your answers to some basic questions:

1. What aspect(s) of the performing arts industry interest you most (musical theatre, children's theatre, film, television, military simulation, etc.)? List any and all areas in which you aspire to endeavor.
2. Do you have any geographical or climate preferences? Do you want to be close to family? To beaches and sunshine? To moun-

tains and snow? To tall buildings and mass public transportation? List any of these elements that are important to you.

3. Is there a certain lifestyle (outside of the theatre) that appeals to you (e.g., the environmentally conscious example I used before; the slow pace and politeness of the South; the history and culture of an older U.S. city such as Philadelphia, DC, or Boston)?

4. Is there a city you have visited or lived previously in which you really see yourself living again?

5. Do you have any sort of network of friends in any of the cities on the list?

Once you have answered those initial questions, you should be able to start narrowing the field. In the interest of time, go ahead and cross off the cities that do not meet your criteria, and then see which ones remain. At this point, you should create a spreadsheet with each prospective city listed in the first column. In the second column, list the factors that helped that city make the "cut." For instance, next to Washington, DC, you might write, "Close to family; Love the history and free museums; Easy access to Baltimore, Philadelphia, and New York." In the New Orleans row, you may include, "Mardi Gras; Great live music scene; Warm all year round; Love the rich Creole heritage." You get the point.

Now your real research begins. Column three is where you compile information about housing costs. It is not hard to find apartment listings by doing a Google search, but in any city you will find a tremendous range of costs, and you will need to have a frame of reference for what you find, based on information about each neighborhood. In other words, you may find some seriously cheap rentals, but they may be in extremely sketchy areas or they may be on the far outskirts of town and require a great commute. Consider the location-to-price factor as you explore the city's real estate market. If you see that in Chicago you can rent a one bedroom in Rogers Park for $750/month, the next thing you must do is read everything you can about Rogers Park.[1] What you ultimately want to create is a column

---

1. As it turns out, I lived in Rogers Park. I highly recommend it for inexpensive Chicago neighborhoods. It is far north in the city, but it is right on the Red Line train, and my apartment was a mere two blocks from the beach!

that compares apples to apples. For instance, you may specifically target studio and one-bedroom apartments in reputably safe areas, in which you would not need a car to get around the city. Or you may be looking to find a sublet with a roommate in a two-bedroom situation. In any event, just be sure that you are inputting information that lets you get a pretty clear comparison of living costs as you scan down the column. Craigslist (www.craigslist.com) can also be a pretty good resource for this kind of analysis, since there are always abundant rental and sublet opportunities, most of which contain details of the property and of the neighborhood.

The fourth column is for transit and transportation. Find out all you can about getting around in your possible destination city. Is there a subway or metro? Do they use buses or perhaps streetcars as the common method for commuting? Is it a bike-friendly city? Or will you absolutely need a car to survive? Find out the common modes of transit and be sure to list any costs involved as well (e.g., metro fares, average daily parking rates).

Your next column is about survival jobs and wages. Assuming that every city has hotels, restaurants, and offices, you should explore industries specific to each individual town. For instance, you might look into the wages for docent (tour guide) work in a historical city like Philly. You might explore job opportunities in the tourism industry of Orlando, and so on. Again, Craigslist can be a good resource, as can local papers, for job postings. Get an idea of what kind of comparative pay is offered for the types of work for which you are qualified in each city, and enter that in the column.

The sixth column is where you list extra "perks" to living in each particular city, things that you find important to a happy lifestyle. You might list nightclubs for Miami; maybe Denver is on your list and you would include nearby skiing; if you are a big sports fan, maybe getting to cheer on the teams in a specific town is important to you; San Francisco certainly touts easy access to wine country; and so forth. Really, you should include anything you find in your research that makes each individual city appealing to you.

Finally, we move on to your chosen industry. The last column of your spreadsheet is where you get to list all the possible work that a city holds for you as an actor. It may seem counterintuitive for me to have you save your acting research for the last column, but I have a reason for that. I want you to really concentrate on lifestyle and cost of living first and possibly whet your interest in a city for reasons beyond performing. If you can see yourself living happily in a city, you will likely find a way to work as an actor. All these cities have performance opportunities—it is all about where you feel you fit and how important a certain way of life is to you.

List the theatres and the type of work they present. Include information about union jurisdiction and average actor salaries, if you can find it. Investigate whether each city has casting director offices that oversee the hiring of actors for any or all facets of the business. Does your city have a booming film or television scene (such as LA or Miami)? If so, do they hire local actors or do they bring them in from New York or LA? Is there work for actors in other areas such as industrials or simulation work (the DC area, for example, offers a great deal of military simulation work for actors!)? Really dig deep and try to leave no stone unturned in your search for acting jobs.

By the end of this exercise, you should really have a good idea of all the professional work possibilities that each town can offer actors. And if you have done all your goal and branding work, you should also have a pretty solid sense of who you are and what you see yourself doing. If you know that children's theatre is your passion, you do not need to be in New York to have a fulfilling career. Seattle is a much better option. If stand-up and sketch comedy and improvisation are your bag, move to Chicago. If you really want to work on camera, but Los Angeles is not your scene, consider smaller hub cities such as Miami or even New Orleans, where a slew of film work cropped up in the aftermath of the Katrina rebuild.

Whatever you decide, I will warn you about two things: First, if your ultimate destination is New York, do not get in the mind-set of "I'll start in town X and build up some credentials, which I will use to launch my career in New York when I'm ready." Unfortunately, when you arrive in New York, unless you have a nationally known name and reputation, you will be starting from scratch. They don't really care if you were a star in Minneapolis. If you want to be a Minneapolis actor, go to Minneapolis. If you dream of being a New York actor, you must go to New York. Period.

The second piece of advice I want to issue you in regard to choosing a city is that you commit and just go for it. I know so many students who finish school and have a goal in mind for their career destination, but they decide to first go live at home and work a day job and make some money. During that time, they get out of the regimen of taking acting and dance classes and voice lessons; they stop auditioning; and they get rusty. They also get lulled into a routine that can become all too comfortable. You have created a budget analysis and a plan for your finances. You have started saving money. You need to decide which city is right for you and *just go for it!*

Wrapping Up

All this work that we have done on branding, marketing, financial planning, goal setting, and understanding how the business of show business works is exhausting and time consuming. The exercises I have offered you and the work I have set before you will be ongoing and ever challenging. You must continue to explore your brand and hone your product, especially as you grow and change. The mature adult you are ten years from now will not be able to be marketed in the same way as the youthful you of today.

You must approach each new day with joy and optimism and a firm sense of self. You should only do this if you really love it—if it makes every day worth living. But you must also be ever mindful of the fact that it is a business, and you must treat it as such. How lucky we are that we have chosen a career endeavor that can fill our spirits with such ecstasy and bliss! How truly lucky we are that we can touch people's souls with our stories and our voices and our art! How lucky we are if we can wake up every single day and be excited to go to work! Break a leg.

Bows

THIS BOOK HAS BEEN a true labor of love for me. Any of my students will tell you that the Preparation for the Theatre Profession class is easily my favorite to teach. I just love actors, and I truly believe that when they are empowered, they can thrive as artists and find consistent happiness. Seeing them make that connection is a reward like no other. In the past few years, I have had the great fortune to learn about the notion of branding and how it applies to the actor's business from some of the best advisors and colleagues anyone could ask for in a network! I am so proud to mention them throughout this book, and I hope you will look them up and learn from them as I have.

I also consider myself immensely fortunate to work with such high-caliber teachers and some of the most amazing students in the country on a daily basis! (I told you I love my job.) As a member of the Executive Board of Musical Theatre Educators Alliance, International (MTEducators.org), my personal web also includes some of the world's premier theatre gurus, to whom I owe a debt of gratitude for mentoring me through the tenure process and for teaching me more about how to teach each time we convene.

And where would any of us be without family? I happen to have a small but mighty one. I am so grateful for the constant love and support I receive from my parents, my brother, my grandparents, my aunt and uncle, and my cousins.

I want to specifically thank the following people for their contributions to this book:

Jodie Bentley, Kevin Urban, and Doug Shapiro at The Savvy Actor; Joe Abraham and Christine Negherbon at The Thriving Artists; Dr. Miles Davis; VP Boyle; Megan Arnoldy; Matthew De-Lorenzo; Joy Dewing; Aaron Galligan-Stierle; Jessie Hooker; Gary Krasny; Ashley Landay; Cary Libkin; Pat McCorkle; Diane Riley; Jenna Pinchbeck; Laura Rose; and Robert Mannis.

Special thanks to my supportive colleagues at Shenandoah who put up with my stress through the process of getting this book finished on time: Jenn, Tom, Sally, Mac, Carolyn, Wade, Will, Bill, JJ, Kirsten, and Cheryl. Also to an encouraging dean, Michael Stepniak, and president, Tracy Fitzsimmons—how fortunate we are to have you in our corner. And to my partner in crime, the best pop/rock voice teacher anyone could work with, Matthew Edwards (with special thanks to his wife, Jackie, for putting up with our "bromance" and our harebrained schemes!).

I send love and gratitude to all my students and alumni, without whom there would be no book. But I particularly have to thank Jenny Ravitz, Nicholas Cirillo, Michael Ehlers, Vassiliki Ellwood, Tyler Humphrey, and Zachary Durand, who directly affected this project.

And finally, I want to dedicate this book to the memory of Ira Lindberg Harris, who left his indelible mark on everyone who knew him.

> *Do any human beings ever realize life while they live it— every, every minute?*
>
> —Thornton Wilder, *Our Town*

Recommended Reading

The Savvy Career Manual (Jodie Bentley and Kevin Urban)
Audition Freedom (VP Boyle)
Acting in Musical Theatre (Joe Deer and Rocco DalVera)
Never Eat Alone (Keith Ferrazzi)
Get the Callback: The Art of Auditioning for Musical Theatre (Jonathan Flom)
Blink (Malcolm Gladwell)
The Tipping Point (Malcolm Gladwell)
Purple Cow (Seth Godin)
The Money Book for the Young, Fabulous, and Broke (Suze Orman)
Rock the Audition (Shari Sanders)
Eats, Shoots and Leaves (Lynne Truss)

Index

About the Author

Jonathan Flom is an associate professor of theatre, as well as the Musical Theatre Program coordinator at Shenandoah Conservatory in Winchester, Virginia. He is also a professional director and author. His first book, *Get the Callback: The Art of Auditioning for Musical Theatre* (Scarecrow Press, 2009), has become one of the foremost sources of audition technique across the country.

As a director, Jonathan's favorite credits include *Sunday in the Park with George*, *A New Brain*, *SubUrbia*, *Bat Boy: The Musical*, *Ragtime*, *The Wild Party*, *The 25th Annual Putnam County Spelling Bee*, and whatever he is working on at the moment. He is also venturing into the realm of musical libretti, coauthoring the book of a new musical, *Dance Yrself Clean*, which utilizes the music of LCD Soundsystem and seeks to bring the world of the nightclub and the electronic dance music sound to the theatre.

Jonathan holds a BFA in musical theatre as well as an MFA in directing musical theatre from Penn State University.

For more information or to contact the author, please visit www.jonathanflom.com or e-mail Actorcoach@hotmail.com.